A Sip from the "Well of Grace"

Studies in Medieval and Early Modern Canon Law

Kenneth Pennington, General Editor

Editorial Advisory Board

Uta-Renate Blumenthal, The Catholic University of America

Giles Constable, Institute for Advanced Study

Richard Helmholz, University of Chicago

John E. Lynch, The Catholic University of America

Robert Somerville, Columbia University

Brian Tierney, Cornell University

Studies in Medieval and Early Modern Canon Law

VOLUME 7

A Sip from the "Well of Grace"

Medieval Texts from the Apostolic Penitentiary

Kirsi Salonen and Ludwig Schmugge

The Catholic University of America Press
Washington, D.C.

Copyright © 2009
The Catholic University of America Press
All rights reserved
The paper used in this publication meets the minimum requirements of American National Standards for Information Science—Permanence of Paper for Printed Library Materials, ANSI Z39.48-1984.
∞

Library of Congress Cataloging-in-Publication Data
Salonen, Kirsi.
A sip from the "well of grace" : medieval texts from the apostolic penitentiary / Kirsi Salonen and Ludwig Schmugge.
p. cm. — (Studies in medieval and early modern canon law ; 7) Includes bibliographical references and index.
ISBN 978-0-8132-1535-8 (pbk. : alk. paper) 1. Catholic Church. Poenitentiaria Apostolica—History—Sources.
I. Schmugge, Ludwig. II. Title. III. Series.
BX1862.S25 2009
262'.136—dc22 2008016483

Contents

Preface and Acknowledgments

The purpose of this book is to offer students and scholars interested in medieval ecclesiastical history a closer look into one of the most important medieval papal offices: the Apostolic Penitentiary, as it is called now. During the Middle Ages the Apostolic Penitentiary was the main office for the granting of graces, mostly in questions of offending against the legislation of the Catholic Church (canon law). The archives of the Apostolic Penitentiary were closed to scholars until 1983, and therefore the medieval documents related to the office are still relatively unknown to researchers.

The two parts of this book are intended to introduce the reader to the functioning and authorities of the Apostolic Penitentiary in the Late Middle Ages, and also to the sources produced for and by it. In Part I, we aim to explain the kind of institution the Apostolic Penitentiary was, its role in relation to other papal offices, and the circumstances under which Christians turned to it. We will briefly present its history and officials, and explain which kinds of cases belonged to its authority, the regulations of canon law behind these cases, as well as the procedure for getting a case handled there. The first part also presents an overview of the different documents that were produced during the handling of a case before the office—petitions, copies of petitions, letters of grace, and their copies. The still rarely discussed matter of the diplomatics of Penitentiary sources is also explained.

In Part II, the reader will find an introduction to the different case types handled by the Apostolic Penitentiary. Each case type is illustrated with original documents that are preserved in various archives—the central archives of the Catholic Church, the Vatican Secret Archives, as well as numerous local archives in Finland, Germany, Italy, Sweden, Switzerland, and the Czech Republic. We have not included all possible types of cases, but have chosen the most common, as well as some more specific examples of the authority of the office.

The documents presented in Part II are the fully edited texts, translated from their original Latin into English. According to the norms for publishing texts of this kind, we have transcribed the originals in full. The original texts do not contain commas or periods, which were not in use in the Middle Ages; in order to facilitate the reading and understanding of these texts, we have added modern punctuation. In order that the reader may more easily compare the transcriptions to the photos, we have indicated the end of each line in the manuscript or document by a double shill (/ /); the line number is always given between the two strokes. Even though medieval scribes did not always use capitals when writing the names of persons or places, we have capitalized both in the edited version to facilitate reading. We also have followed modern practice in the use of 'u' versus 'v' and also 'i' versus 'j,' even though the texts vary between the two—i.e., we always use *ut* instead of *vt,* and *diversis* instead of *diuersis.* Also, the Roman style of dates in calends, nones, and ides has been translated into the modern form.

This is the first time that a collection of documents related to the Apostolic Penitentiary has been published with both the full texts and photographs. The reader is thus able to learn what the documents and writing actually look like. Presenting both the edited text and the photo helps the reader to realize, for example, in what kind of handwriting the documents are written and what kinds of marks there are in the margins of the documents—both matters which are explained in the first part of this book. Inclusion of the photographs allows readers to exercise their skills in paleography and Latin.

We hope that this book will give the reader an idea of the kinds of sources available regarding the functioning of this office. The documents in the archives of the Apostolic Penitentiary offer historians many new possibilities for the interpretation of medieval life, both lay and ecclesiastical. They enable new approaches to such questions as illegitimate birth, ecclesiastical careers, marriage, criminality, and Christian piety. We hope that this book might give scholars some inspiration; these exciting documents offer some quite new perspectives on the social and religious history of the later Middle Ages.

Many persons have been of great help while writing this book. We wish to direct special thanks to His Eminence the Major Penitentiary James Cardinal Stafford for kindly allowing us to publish this book, as well as to the personnel of the Apostolic Penitentiary for allowing us to use the precious material. Both the archivist of the Penitentiary, Johan Ickx, and Padre Ubaldo Todeschini have given important suggestions about the manuscript of this book and deserve our gratitude. We wish to thank the prefect of the Vatican Secret Archives, His Excellency Sergio Pagano, for his help, and the skilled personnel in the Reading Room of the Vatican Secret Archives, who made working there very pleasant—*avete un cafè pagato.*

The results and documents published in this book required visiting several archives where we found the staff very helpful and kind. We wish to direct our special thanks to Joachim Deeters of the Stadtarchiv Köln; Birgitta Fritz and Claes Gejrot of the Swedish National Archives; Juha Hannikainen of the National Library of Finland; Barbara Stieldorf of the University Library of Bonn; Zdenka Hledikova, Prague/Rome; Lorenzen-Schmidt of the State Archives of Hamburg; and the personnel of the Town Archives of Mainz, as well as Paolo Ostinelli and Milena Svec-Götschi.

We are extremely grateful to Kenneth Pennington for kindly accepting this book for inclusion in the series Studies in Medieval and Early Modern Canon Law. Tuija Ainonen has translated the Latin texts into fluent English and has given important advice concerning the texts, for which she has earned our gratitude. Equally deserving of our gratitude is James Andean, who has corrected our English into a readable text. We also wish to thank the Academy of Finland which has financed the research project "The Papal Penitentiary and the Local Church," of which this book is a by-product. Similarly our thanks belong to the German Historical Institute in Rome.

Romae idibus julii anno secundo Benedicti pape XVI
Kirsi Salonen
Ludwig Schmugge

Abbreviations

ASV	Archivio Segreto Vaticano
BAV	Biblioteca Apostolica Vaticana
CIC I and II	*Corpus Iuris Canonici, pars prima et secunda, Decretalium collectiones,* ed. Emil Friedberg (Graz, 1959)
Clem.	Constitutiones Clementis quinti
COD	Decrees of the Ecumenical Councils, trans. N. Tanner, eds. G. Alberigo et al. (Washington, D.C., 1990)
Penitenziera Ap.	Penitenzieria Apostolica
Reg. Matrim. et Div.	Registra matrimonialium et diversorum
RPG	Repertorium Poenitentiariae Germanicum
VI	Liber Sextus Bonifacii octavi
X	Decretales Gregorii noni (Liber Extra)

Part I

The Penitentiary in the Service of Christians

1

History of the Study of Penitentiary Material

1.1. The Archives of the Apostolic Penitentiary

Like all other papal offices, the Penitentiary kept a register of its decisions. The medieval registers of the office, thought to have been lost after the Napoleonic invasion of Italy, were rediscovered around 1913[1] and in 1928 were deposited in the Vatican Secret Archives.[2]

The registers of the Penitentiary can be found in the Vatican Secret Archives under the archival signum *Penitenzieria Apostolica, Registra Matrimonialium et Diversorum.*[3] This series consists of 746 register volumes covering the period between 1409 and 1890. There are 160 volumes from the period before the reform of the Penitentiary (which completely changed the structure of the office) that took place in 1569, under Pope Pius V (1566–1572). The reform of the office can also be seen in the registration technique, because prior to the reform the office registered only incoming petitions, whereas

1. E. Göller, "Das alte Archiv der päpstlichen Pönitentiarie," *Römische Quartalschrift,* Supplementband 20 (Festschrift A. de Waal) (Rome–Freiburg i. Br., 1913), 1–19.

2. About the archives of the Apostolic Penitentiary, see F. Tamburini, "Per la storia dei Cardinali Penitenzieri Maggiori e dell'Archivio della Penitenzieria Apostolica. Il trattato «De antiquitate cardinalis Poenitentiarii Maioris» di G. B. Boccino (†1641)," *Rivista di Storia della Chiesa in Italia* 36 (1982), 349–356.

3. ASV, *Penitenzieria Ap., Reg. Matrim. et Div.*

after the reform the office kept two different series of registers: one register series for the incoming petitions and another series for outgoing letters. In 1585 the Penitentiary stopped registering incoming petitions and thus there is only the series of registers of outgoing letters. In 1890 the office for registration was closed and the register series end with that year. For the years up through 1564, the records of the Penitentiary are consultable, with a special permit granted by the same office. Documents from later than 1564 cannot be studied.[4]

In this book we will talk a lot about the register volumes of the Apostolic Penitentiary, but what do these register volumes look like? The medieval parts of the volumes contain abbreviated copies of those petitions that the office handled and approved. The copies of the incoming petitions, known as "entries," are divided in each volume into several different petition categories according to the kind of case in question. Each of these categories forms an independent section under its own title. The most common titles in the medieval registers are *de matrimonialibus, de diversis formis, de declaratoriis, de defectu natalium, de uberiori, de promotis et promovendis,* and *de confessionalibus.*[5] In some petition categories (such as *de confessionalibus* or *de defectu natalium*) the entries are very much abbreviated copies of the original petitions, containing only a few lines of text; by contrast, the entries in some other categories (such as *de declaratoriis*) are copied almost word for word from the original petitions and thus can be very long, in some cases even several pages.

The entries are copied into the registers one after another. The text of the petitions runs down the middle of the page. In the left margin is written the place and the day that the Penitentiary approved the petition, and in the right margin is given the name of the diocese from which the supplicant came. In the later registers, above each entry is also mentioned the name of the proctor who

4. About the register volumes of the Penitentiary kept in the Vatican Secret Archives (even about those that cannot be consulted), see the preliminary inventary made by Filippo Tamburini, ex-archivist of the Penitentiary. See also F. X. Blouin et al., eds., *Vatican Archives: An Inventory and Guide to Historical Documents of the Holy See* (New York–Oxford, 1998), 215–216.

5. For more information about the different categories, see Chapter 2 in Part I of this book.

took care of the case as well as the sum of the tax that the supplicant had to pay to the Penitentiary for the costs of preparing the letter of grace.

The register volumes themselves are made of small quires (for the most part so-called *quinterniones,* five leaves of paper) which are tied up into large volumes. During the seventeenth century the volumes were re-bound in boards covered with red velvet. The volumes from the middle of the fifteenth century are not very big and contain approximately 300 to 400 folios (600 to 800 pages), but from the beginning of the sixteenth century the volumes become more and more voluminous, containing sometimes as many as 1,500 folios (3,000 pages). The increasing size of the volumes is the result not only of an increasing number of incoming petitions but also of the size of the handwriting of the scribes, which tended to get larger as the years went by: the scribes of the late fifteenth century were paid according to the number of pages they produced.

From the year 1459 (volume number 7) until the year 1513 (volume number 58) each Penitentiary register contains petitions that were approved during the period of a year (calendar year or pontifical year). As the cases became more and more numerous, the registers consequently became thicker and thicker. In 1513, the Penitentiary authorities changed their registration system, so that two register volumes were produced each year. Then, from the pontificate of Paul III (1534–1549) onwards, there could be three or even four registers per year.

The medieval archives of the Penitentiary do not cover the whole period beginning from the year 1409; unfortunately, there are some lacunae in the series of registers. The first register volume contains petitions handled during the years 1409–1411, while the next two registers (numbers 2 and 2bis) cover the years 1438–1442. Thus there are no preserved registers for the years from 1412 through 1437. The series of nearly complete registration begins with register volume number 3 (1448) and goes on until the end of the fifteenth century. Only the register volume for the fifth pontifical year of Pope Alexander VI (1496) is missing. The volumes from the beginning of the sixteenth century are, unfortunately, not as well preserved; there are some years for which the registration is partly or totally missing. In any case, even with these gaps, the archives of the Penitentiary are very well preserved, and consequently the material is suitable even for statistical analysis. The situation of the other medieval papal register series is much worse; for some series their losses are close to 50 percent.[6]

But what has happened to the registers of the Penitentiary for the years prior to 1409? Nobody knows. Scholars have not been able to show with certainty whether, prior to 1409, the Penitentiary registered the cases it handled.[7] At any rate, there are no traces of Penitentiary registers before 1409. The first volume is very peculiar, for it contains petitions approved during the pontificates of the antipopes of the obedience of Pisa, Alexander V and John XXIII. Thus the cases registered in this volume do not belong to the ordinary business of the Penitentiary, since the decisions were made under special circumstances.[8] The next two volumes of the Penitentiary, in their turn, are from the years of the Council of Basle, and thus were also composed during quite extraordinary events. Since the three first volumes seem to contain only matters registered under special circumstances, we cannot deduce from the existence of these volumes that the Penitentiary had in fact already been registering its decisions systematically since 1409, and that all documentation between 1411 and 1438 as well as that for 1442 and 1448 has been lost.

It does seem that the regular and systematic registration of the

6. Concerning the losses of the Vatican medieval archival material, see for example K. A. Fink, *Das Vatikanische Archiv: Einführung in die Bestände und ihre Erforschung* (Rome, 1951), or L. E. Boyle, *A Survey of the Vatican Archives and of Its Medieval Holdings* (Toronto, 1972; 2d ed. 2001).

7. Emil Göller claims that the Penitentiary should have registered the cases it handled, because a constitution of Pope Benedict XII (1334–1342) orders that all papal offices should register the cases they were dealing with. Göller, "Das alte Archiv," 2. It is nevertheless possible that the Penitentiary did not register its cases before the fifteenth century.

8. A partial edition of this volume, containing the petitions from the four Belgian dioceses (Cambrai, Liège, Thérouanne and Tournai), was published by Monique Maillard-Luypaert, *Les suppliques de la Pénitencierie Apostolique pour les diocèses de Cambrai, Liège, Thérouanne et Tournai (1410–1411) (ASV, Penitenzieria Ap., Reg. Matrim. et Div., 1).* Analecta Vaticano-Belgica, Première Série 34 (Brussels-Rome, 2003).

decisions of the Penitentiary began somewhat later, when the popes had finally moved back to Rome to stay after the conciliar period. Thus it could be argued that the systematic registration of Penitentiary decisions did not begin until the mid-fifteenth century. If this is true, it is possible that the archives of the Penitentiary are actually preserved almost completely, and that the first three volumes only resulted from registration of extraordinary activity of the office, while ordinary activity in Rome remained unregistered.[9]

However, it is also possible that the earlier archives of the Penitentiary have simply disappeared during the intervening years. Some tumultuous historical moments might have affected the number of preserved medieval volumes. The most difficult post-medieval period for the papal archives was in spring and summer of 1527, during the so-called *Sacco di Roma,* when the *Lanzikanecchi,* troops of the German emperor, were plundering Rome after they had defeated the papal army. There are signs that some of the papal archives were destroyed at that time, but it cannot be said whether the Penitentiary registers were also destroyed on that occasion.

The *Sacco di Roma* was not the only plundering that might have caused damage to the archives of the Penitentiary; other military operations have also been guilty of causing problems for the archives. When Napoleon, during his wars, had conquered the Papal States and Rome in 1809, he ordered that the papal archives were to be transferred from Rome to Paris, where he planned to establish the world archives. His troops transported 3,239 trunks of archival material from the papal archives to Paris, among which was the archives

9. First considerations about the number of surviving and missing Penitentiary volumes can be found in L. Schmugge, P. Hersperger, B. Wiggenhauser, *Die Supplikenregister der päpstlichen Pönitentiarie aus der Zeit Pius' II. (1458–1464)* (Bibliothek des Deutschen Historischen Instituts in Rom 84; Tübingen, 1996), 5. For a list of the medieval register volumes and their contents, see K. Salonen, *The Penitentiary as a Well of Grace in the Late Middle Ages: The Example of the Province of Uppsala 1448–1527* (Suomalaisen Tiedeakatemian Toimituksia—Annales Academiae Scientiarum Fennicae 313; Saarijärvi, 2001), 24, 425–426. Concerning the preservation of the earlier volumes see also K. Salonen, "Long Path to Forgiveness," *Quellen und Forschungen aus italienischen Archiven und Bibliotheken* 79 (1999), 284 (especially footnote 2) with slight corrections to L. Schmugge, P. Hersperger, B. Wiggenhauser, *Supplikenregister,* 5.

of the Penitentiary—all together, 4,256 volumes, according to the inventory made before the material was sent to Paris. After the defeat of Napoleon, the collections of the papal archives were supposed to be transferred back to Rome in their entirety; unfortunately this did not happen—a considerable amount of archival material never returned.

For one thing, losses were incurred during the journey when some of the ships carrying the archival material sank. Another and even more destructive factor was that the Catholic Church could not afford to bring back all the material that had been transported to Paris, because the transportation was simply too expensive. Some prelates of the Catholic Church, sent to Paris to supervise the transport, had to decide which material was valuable enough to be transported back to Rome. Much of what remained in France was either burned, sold to French fishermen as wrapping paper, or sent to the paper factories as raw material. In total only two thirds (2,220 trunks) of the archival material that left for Paris was transported back to the papal archives.[10]

Even though the Penitentiary registers were counted before being sent to Paris, we do not know what might have been lost during the journey, for the volumes that came back from Paris were never catalogued or counted. Most of these material probably came back from Paris, but the fact that certain volumes that are clearly registers of the Penitentiary are nowadays kept in the other series in the Vatican Secret Archives indicates that some of the archival material of the Penitentiary must have gotten separated from the rest of the archives and ended up in the main collections of the Vatican Archives.[11]

After their return to Rome, the archives of the Penitentiary were kept in *Cortile delle Corazze* in the Vatican, and their existence seems to have been forgotten. Emil Göller, the pioneering scholar of Penitentiary studies, even wrote his *opus magnum* without knowing of the existence of the archives. He was told about it only a year after

10. For the transportation of the Vatican archival material see R. Rietzler, "Die Verschleppung der päpstlichen Archive nach Paris unter Napoleon I. und deren Rückführung nach Rom in den Jahren 1815–1817," *Römische Historische Mitteilungen* 6/7 (1962/1964), 144–190.

11. ASV, *Armadio XXXII*, vol. 60.

his four-volume study had been published. In 1928 the archives of the Penitentiary were transferred to the shelves of the Vatican Secret Archives.

After the 1928 transfer, the Catholic Church began to discuss whether the archives of the Penitentiary should be open for research. Scholars had not had access to the registers of the Penitentiary because the Church was afraid that the registers might contain matters protected by the seal of confession, and thus should not be studied by anyone, but should remain secret forever. The registers of the Penitentiary were studied carefully by competent persons, and the Penitentiary became aware that the medieval registers of the office contained only a very few documents that would fall under the seal of confession. Thus Pope John Paul II, in 1983, made the important decision that the registers of the Penitentiary could finally be opened to scholars. Due to the delicate content of the documents in the archives of the Penitentiary, the registers are not available for open consultation; the archives were opened partially so that studying the registers of the Penitentiary became possible with a special permit granted by the Penitentiary upon request.[12]

1.2. Historiography of Penitentiary Studies

The first person to write a study about the history of the Penitentiary was Vincentius de Petra, himself an official of the Penitentiary. He published his study *"De Sacra Poenitentiaria Apostolica"* in 1712, the first institutional study of the office written by an insider. In his book he dealt mainly with the history and the authorities of the office, but he also made some historical remarks concerning the archives of the Penitentiary. His observations about the archives are very important, for they are the only information we have about the state of the archives before the Napoleonic transportations.[13]

12. For more about the history of the Penitentiary sources and about the opening of the archives to researchers, see F. Tamburini, "Per la storia dei Cardinali Penitenzieri," 349–356, as well as L. Schmugge, P. Hersperger, B. Wiggenhauser, *Supplikenregister,* 4–8.

13. V. Petra, *De Sacra Poenitentiaria Apostolica* (Rome, 1712).

After a long break, some scholars in the late nineteenth century began to be interested in the Apostolic Penitentiary and its history. Because the archives of the office were not available to scholars at that time, they had to try to find other material for their studies. Heinrich Denifle was the first to publish documents related to the Penitentiary; his article on tax lists of the Penitentiary appeared as early as 1888.[14] In 1890 Conrad Eubel published an article about an early formulary of the Penitentiary.[15] Henry Charles Lea followed, publishing in 1892 a study of another old formulary of the Penitentiary, as well as an article concerning the fees of the office.[16] In 1905 Charles Homer Haskins, in turn, published some documents concerning the history of the Penitentiary.[17] Alois Lang and Pierre Chouët also both published articles on the history of the Penitentiary.[18]

The first person to begin to study more profoundly the history and competence of the Apostolic Penitentiary was a German scholar, Emil Göller, later a professor of canon law in Freiburg, Germany. Göller worked in Rome as an archivist at the beginning of the twentieth century; he studied the documents in the Vatican Secret Archives and wrote several studies of different papal offices. His very profound—and despite its age still very useful—four-volume presentation on the history, competence, personnel, sources, etc. of the Penitentiary was published in 1907 (the first two volumes) and 1911 (the last two volumes).[19]

14. H. Denifle, "Die älteste Taxrolle der apostolischen Pönitentiarie," *Archiv für Literatur- und Kirchengeschichte des Mittelalters* IV (1888), 201–238.

15. K. Eubel, "Der Registerband des Cardinalgrosspönitentiars Bentevenga," *Archiv für katholisches Kirchenrecht* 64 (1890), 3–96.

16. H. C. Lea, *A Formulary of the Papal Penitentiary in the Thirteenth Century* (Philadelphia, 1892); id., "The Taxes of the Papal Penitentiary," *English Historical Review* 8 (1893), 424–438.

17. C. H. Haskins, "The Sources for the History of the Papal Penitentiary," *American Journal of Theology* 9 (1905), 421–450.

18. A. Lang, "Beiträge zur Geschichte der apostolischen Pönitentiarie im 13. und 14. Jahrhundert," *Mitteilungen des Instituts für Österreichische Geschichtsforschung* 7 (1907), 20–43; P. Chouët, *La Sacrée Pénitencierie apostolique: étude de droit et d'histoire* (Lyon, 1908).

19. E. Göller, *Die päpstliche Pönitentiarie von ihrem Ursprung bis zu ihrer Umgestaltung unter Pius V.* (Bibliothek des Königl. Preußischen Historischen Instituts in Rom 3, 4, 7, 8 [i.e., I/1–2, II/1–2]; Rome 1907–1911).

Unfortunately, Göller did not know about the archives of the Penitentiary when he was writing his study. The register volumes of the Penitentiary were not yet deposited in the Vatican Secret Archives and everybody except the officials of the Penitentiary seemed to have forgotten about the existence of the material. The Penitentiary did not publicize the existence of their archives, since the archival material was thought to contain documents that should remain under the seal of confession, and thus no one was allowed to use the material. Göller learned of the existence of the Penitentiary records only after his book had been published.

After the publication of his *opus magnum*, however, the officials of the Penitentiary allowed Göller to visit the archives of the Penitentiary, but for only one day. This happened in the fall of 1913. Göller had thus only a few hours to try to understand what the volumes of the Penitentiary contained and how much material there was. On the basis of his visit to the Penitentiary archives, he wrote an article about the registers of the Penitentiary, but as he had so little time in the archives, this article contains many small mistakes and inaccuracies.[20]

The first scholar to publish studies concerning the Penitentiary on the basis of its archives was its late archivist, Don Filippo Tamburini. He published his doctoral thesis concerning the first register volume of the Penitentiary in 1969.[21] Tamburini subsequently produced many articles concerning different aspects of the office, as well as some more detailed books with edited documents around different interesting themes, such as saints and sinners, infidels and heretics.[22]

Since the opening of the archives to scholars in 1983, several studies concerning the office have been published. The first large

20. E. Göller, "Das alte Archiv."

21. F. Tamburini, *L'archivio della penitenzieria apostolica e il primo registro delle suppliche (1410–1411)* (unprinted thesis; Rome, 1969).

22. F. Tamburini, *Santi e peccatori: confessioni e suppliche dai Registri della Penitenzieria dell'Archivio Segreto Vaticano (1451–1586)* (Milan, 1995); id., *Ebrei, Saraceni, Cristiani: Vita sociale e vita religiosa dai registri della Penitenzieria Apostolica (secoli XIV–XVI)* (Milan, 1996); F. Tamburini and L. Schmugge, *Häresie und Luthertum: Quellen aus dem Archiv der Pönitentiarie in Rom (15. und 16. Jahrhundert)* (Quellen und Forschungen aus dem Gebiet der Geschichte. Neue Folge 19; Paderborn, 2000).

academic project concerning the documents preserved in the archives of the Penitentiary was initiated by the German Historical Institute in Rome in 1992, and Professor Ludwig Schmugge (University of Zürich) was asked to coordinate the work. Editing began on all petitions coming from the territory of the Holy Roman Empire, the material to be published in a series called Repertorium Poenitentiariae Germanicum (RPG). To date, six volumes (pontificates of Eugene IV, Calixtus III, Nicholas V, Pius II, Paul II, and Sixtus IV) have been printed. The example of the RPG has led other scholars to publish the documents concerning their own countries; documents concerning Belgium, Italy (Diocese of Como), Norway, and Poland have now been edited, and several other projects are in preparation.[23]

In addition to his work on the first RPG volume—that of Pius II—Schmugge, with Patrick Hersperger and Béatrice Wiggenhauser, in 1996 published a detailed study of the German Penitentiary material from that pontificate.[24] A year earlier, in 1995, Schmugge had already published a major study on illegitimacy in the later Middle Ages, a book in which he studied all the *De defectu natalium* and the *De uberiori* petitions in the Penitentiary registers between the years 1448 and 1533.[25] The first academic dissertation on the Penitentiary in the late Middle Ages and its relations with the Swedish church province of Uppsala was published in 2001 by Kirsi Salonen.[26] Since then, numerous studies have been written about different aspects of the authorities of the Penitentiary, as well as about the connections between different parts of christendom and the Penitentiary.[27]

23. A list of the editions that have now been published can be found in the literature list at the end of this book.

24. L. Schmugge, P. Hersperger, B. Wiggenhauser, *Supplikenregister.*

25. L. Schmugge, *Kirche, Kinder, Karrieren: Päpstliche Dispense von der unehelichen Geburt im Spätmittelalter* (Zürich, 1995).

26. K. Salonen, *Penitentiary.*

27. We will not list all publications here, but at the end of the book there is a list of publications concerning the Penitentiary.

2

The Penitentiary in the Late Middle Ages

2.1. What Was the Papal Penitentiary?

According to the doctrine of the Catholic Church, the pope possessed the plenitude of power *(plenitudo potestatis)* within the medieval church. As the successor of St. Peter he was in charge of distributing graces, privileges, and forgiveness (i.e., absolutions) throughout christendom. In the thirteenth century, the rapid development of the regulations of canon law had two consequences: the papal administration began to expand at a rapid pace, and the number of matters directed to the authority of the pope increased.[1]

The development of canon law, especially in the twelfth and thirteenth centuries, changed the practice of confession and forgiving. During those centuries it had been noticed that the earlier ecclesiastical regulations stipulated by several church councils were interpreted in very different ways in diverse parts of christendom, and also that the practices in the handling of cases in different ecclesiastical courts varied greatly. It was a common conviction in the High Middle Ages that something had to be done to unify the ecclesiastical jurisdiction and the interpretation of the norms of the church. The first attempt towards this unity was made when the popes be-

1. J. A. Brundage, *Medieval Canon Law* (London and New York, 1995), 53–59.

gan to reserve to their own authority the handling of certain more severe violations of the regulations of the church.

For the first time, a case—violence against persons in clerical orders—was reserved to the papal authority by canon 15 (the *Si quis suadente diabolo* canon, as per the first words of the regulation) of the Second Lateran Council, held in Rome in 1139.[2] After that, several other sins were added to the list of cases reserved to the apostolic authority. The notion of papal reservation radically increased the number of cases brought before the authority of the popes, and as the popes were not able to handle them by themselves, they were obliged to delegate their powers to handle various kinds of matters to the officials within the papal curia. Since the apostolic successor could not alone handle all requests for special absolutions from these reserved criminal matters, he began commissioning the right to grant those graces to a special cleric within the roman curia called the *penitentiarius pape*. The task of this person was to hear confessions and absolve sinners by special papal authority. This was the first step towards the founding of the office of the Penitentiary.[3]

From the time of Pope Innocent III (1198–1216), the office around the *penitentiarius* grew rather quickly, due to the increasing number of cases submitted from all over the Christian West to the Apostolic See and delegated to the Penitentiary. The head of this office, the *penitentiarius maior* as he was called, who soon had to have the status of cardinal, was entitled to dispense and absolve from a great number of ecclesiastical restrictions on the basis of authorities (*facultates*) given to him by different popes.[4]

The manifold tasks entrusted to the Cardinal Penitentiary soon

2. The canon is edited in COD, 200. L. C. Götz, "Studien zur Geschichte des Busssakraments," *Zeitschrift für Kirchengeschichte* 16 (1896), 596, especially footnote 1. For the history of confession see now J. Goering, "The Internal Forum and the Literature of Penance and Confession," *Traditio* 59 (2004), as well as M. Ohst, *Pflichtbeichte* (Beiträge zur historischen Theologie 89; Tübingen, 1995). See also Goering's essay "The Internal Forum and the Literature of Penance and Confession" in *The History of Medieval Canon Law in the Classical Period, 1140–1234* (forthcoming from CUA Press).

3. Regarding the birth of the Penitentiary, see K. Salonen, *Penitentiary*, 40–41.

4. The faculties granted by different popes to the Cardinals Penitentiary are edited in E. Göller, *Pönitentiarie* I/2, 1–47 and II/2, 1–30.

required the creation of a special section of the papal administration: the office of the Penitentiary. It grew very quickly, and by the fifteenth century it already employed circa two hundred persons. The Cardinal Penitentiary, a sort of "Chief Executive Officer," was the head of this office. Since the tasks of the office increased enormously during the fifteenth century, the Cardinal needed by his side other persons helping him in decision-making. These persons were called *regentes*; a *regens* could be a bishop or the abbot of a large monastery. It was common for the Cardinal Penitentiary to have by his side several regents at a time; one based in Rome, by the Apostolic See, and the other(s) based in various places, depending on where the popes were traveling and where the papal curia was situated at a given time. Due to the mobility of the popes in the Middle Ages, some of the itinerant regents were appointed for only short periods of time—a few weeks, for example. Since the Penitentiary operated on a very vast field of canon law regulations, the office often needed the services of a specialist in canon law, called the *auditor.* These were appointed to the Penitentiary to check whether the decisions made by the office were canonically correct. Their task was also to ensure that canon law was applied in a way that wasfaithful both to its general norms and to the particular circumstances of the cases before them.

Along with those officially responsible for the care of souls of Christians, the Penitentiary also employed scribes and agents *(procuratores).* The Penitentiary appointed numerous scribes and other members of the college of officials, whose task was to produce the letters, *littera,* issued in the name of the Cardinal Penitentiary, and to copy the decisions of the officials into the registers of the Penitentiary. The process of producing the letters of grace involved, besides the scribes who performed most of the visible work, several other persons in different roles: abbreviators, *taxators,* sealers, and correctors, for example. The task of the proctors, in their turn, was to help the petitioners arriving at the Apostolic See to write down their requests (the supplications), which had to be submitted to the pope, and to take care of the cases being processed by the office.

Moreover, the Cardinal Penitentiary was the head of those priests who were called minor penitentiaries *(penitentiarii minores)* and who worked at each of the great basilicas of Rome (St. Peter's, St. John Lateran, and St. Mary Major). The minor penitentiaries were mostly friars, and their task was to listen to the confessions of those Christians who came from all over the world to Rome.[5] The number of the official minor penitentiaries varied: earlier sources talk about eight minor penitentiaries, while their number arises at highest at eighteen and was finally stabilized at eleven. There were also numerous other penitentiaries who could substitute for the eleven. The minor penitentiaries were arranged according to the languages they could speak and understand. Since the popes were equally concerned with the cure of the soul of every Christian, no matter where they came from, they appointed one or two minor penitentiaries for each European language group: English, German, French, Italian, Spanish, and the Slavic languages. Sometimes one of the minor penitentiaries might understand one of the rarer languages, such as Swedish or Czech, for example. The minor penitentiaries could issue in their own name special letters testifying that the holder of the letter had confessed his or her sins; these letters were called *litterae ecclesiae.* As the sins that were confessed belonged under the seal of confession, these letters do not mention what kind of sins were confessed, but only that the sins confessed were absolved.[6]

In the late Middle Ages the office of the Penitentiary was very busy; it can be roughly estimated that the office handled 2,800 to 3,600 petitions each year, more or less ten cases per day. In the early sixteenth century, as Pope Leo X (1513–1521) put it in his bull *Pastoralis cura* (1513), the Penitentiary was the place "in which the correction of behavior and the salvation of souls were daily business."[7]

5. There were also priests called penitentiaries *(penitentiarii)* in the cathedral church of each diocese. Though in practice they were doing the same job as the papal penitentiaries, these diocesan penitentiaries had nothing to do with the office of the Penitentiary in the papal curia, and we have to keep them separate when studying the history of the Apostolic Penitentiary.

6. About the number and the tasks of the minor penitentiaries, see E. Göller, *Pönitentiarie* I/1, 129–159, and II/1, 38–57.

7. "*. . . in qua morum censura et animarum precipue salus vertitur . . .*' in ASV, *Reg. Vat.* 1200, fol. 428r. See also L. Schmugge, P. Hersperger, B. Wiggenhauser, *Supplikenregister,* 9, note 26.

2.2. What Types of Matters Did the Penitentiary Handle?

According to the laws of the Catholic Church, men and women, lay people and clerics who had incurred excommunication or other ecclesiastical sanctions by severe offenses against the rules of canon law, papal decrees, or conciliar prescriptions, had to turn to the pope for forgiveness and reconciliation in the form of absolution from their sins. In less severe violations the sinners could receive absolution from their local parish priests or bishop.[8] Furthermore, the papal curia was in the service of those Christians who wanted to act in some way contrary to the norms of the Catholic Church; the curia granted the necessary licenses and dispensations for their pious purposes; to ask for such graces was also the reason why numerous Christians had to turn to the different offices within the papal curia.

Legally speaking, the popes had delegated to the Penitentiary the powers to grant four types of grace. First of all, it could grant special absolutions to Christians who had violated the rules of canon law in an especially severe way (in the previously mentioned matters of papal reservation). Secondly, it could grant dispensations to those Christians who needed for some good reason to act against the norms of the church and where the Church could grant them the possibility to do so. Thirdly, the Penitentiary could give different licenses to Christians who wanted to deviate from some usual Christian practice—for instance, to choose their own confessor or to make a pilgrimage to the Holy Land, for example. Lastly, the office could grant Christians letters of declaration that, for example, freed the petitioner from unjust murder accusations. The office had the authority to grant these graces in several different matters: marriage, illegiti-

8. There are numerous early prints called "*Casus papales, episcopales et abbatiales*" in which it is defined more closely who had power to absolve the sinners from different types of transgressions. These texts have been printed several times, mostly in Rome in the 1480s (by Bartholomeus Guldinbeck 1477/1480, by Stephan Planck, 1480, 1487, 1488, 1492; by Eucharius Silber 1485, by Johannes Besicken 1494/1500) as well as by many other printers in Italy, Germany, and France.

macy, promotion, violence, apostasy, and confession, just to mention a few of them.

Due to the multitude of different matters the Penitentiary could deal with, the registers of the Penitentiary are internally divided into different sections. Each section has its own title and contains petitions concerning a certain type of matter. This division—which can be found only in the Penitentiary registers and is not used in the other medieval papal register series—made it easier to record and to find the decisions of the office if they were needed later. The seven most common titles in the registers are: *de matrimonialibus* (concerning marriages), *de diversis formis* (concerning different types of cases), *de declaratoriis* (concerning declarations), *de defectu natalium* (concerning illegitimate birth), *de uberiori* (concerning acquisition of more than one benefice: here, for illegitimate children), *de promotis et promovendis* (concerning ordinations to ecclesiastical orders), *de confessionalibus* (the right to have a private confessor or a special privilege in confession matters). The content of each petition category will be explained in detail a bit later.[9]

In the later Middle Ages there was an ever-increasing demand within each of these categories throughout Christendom; Christians turned every year more and more often to the papal curia with their petitions, and the Penitentiary received its share of these supplications. In order to give readers a more concrete idea of the large number of cases brought before the Penitentiary, Table 1 presents the number of cases which were registered in each petition category during four pontificates of the second half of the fifteenth century.

Let us now concentrate on the main figures. From the numbers it can be observed that the number of cases handled by the Penitentiary varies quite a lot from one pope to another. This variation

9. The division into different petition categories varies a bit in the course of the late Middle Ages. For example, the two categories concerning illegitimacy, *de defectu natalium* and *de uberiori*, are in the later volumes unified under only one title *de illegitimis*. Also the *de diversis formis* and *de declaratoriis* appear in the later volumes under the rubric *de diversis materiis*. The petitions concerning confession, on the other hand, are, in the earlier volumes, divided into different, smaller categories such as *de confessionalibus perpetuis, de sententiis generalibus, de confessionalibus in forma Cupientes,* and *de altari portatili.*

Table 1. Types of Cases Handled by the Penitentiary during the Second Half of the Fifteenth Century (1455–92)

Case type	*Calixtus III* *1455–58*	*Pius II* *1458–64*	*Paul II* *1464–71*	*Sixtus IV* *1471–84*	*Innocent VIII* *1484–92*	*Total*
De matrimonialibus	2,379	4,173	7,270	15,339	13,530	42,691
De diversis formis	2,734[a]	3,645	5,717	6,656	4,937	23,689
De declaratoriis	. . .	334	1,241	1,742	993	4,310
De defectu natalium	1,602	2,695	3,606	5,736	2,485	16,124
De uberiori	246	483	778	1,136	3,818	6,461
De promotis et promovendis	481	1,003	2,036	2,972	2,485	8,977
De confessionalibus	1,440	3,352	3,455	3,458	1,957	13,662
Total	8,882	15,685	24,103	37,039	30,205	115,914

Source: ASV, *Penitenzieria Ap., Reg. Matrim. et Div.*, Vols. 5–41.

a. This number includes the *de declaratoriis* cases, because they are both registered under the same rubric.

does not, however, mean that the Penitentiary worked less during the pontificate of Calixtus III (8,882 cases) than during the pontificate of Sixtus IV (37,039 petitions). The difference can simply be explained by the fact that the pontificate of Sixtus IV was much longer than that of Calixtus III. In fact, if we calculate the average number of cases handled monthly during the different pontificates, we notice that the Penitentiary handled approximately 235 cases per month during the pontificates of Calixtus III, Pius II, and Sixtus IV, while the monthly average during the pontificate of Paul II was almost 300, and during the pontificate of Innocent VIII it was nearly 320. Thus we can say that there was some kind of variation in the activity of the Penitentiary, but not that the number of petitions per month tended to grow from the 1450s to the 1490s—as one might easily think if looking only at the absolute numbers.

Another, more general thing that can be noticed from the data presented in Table 1 is that there is quite a big difference between different petition groups. Some of the categories, like *de matrimonialibus,* which contains marriage petitions, show very many cases (42,691), while some others, like *de declaratoriis,* which contains the declaratory letters, contain relatively few cases (4,310). This shows that there were ten marriage petitions to one supplication for a declaratory letter. According to Table 1, marriage cases are absolutely the most common type of petitions handled by the Penitentiary. In second place—but far behind the marriage supplications—come the various cases registered under the title *de diversis formis.* The illegitimacy cases *(de defectu natalium* and *de uberiori)* form the third largest category of petitions, while the supplications for having a letter of confession are in fourth place. The other petition groups, *de promotis et promovendis* as well as *de declaratoriis,* are the smallest ones.

These differences in the numbers of petitions in the different categories represent the importance of these kinds of graces for the Christians. Marriage was a matter that concerned the majority of Christians at some point in their lives. Couples who wanted to make sure that their marriages were valid even though the parties were related to each other by too close ties of kinship needed marriage dispensations. Christians who had incurred excommunication had to get absolution before they could continue their lives as members of their communities, giving rise to the petitions in the *de diversis formis* category. In the Middle Ages, the number of illegitimate sons striving for ecclesiastical careers was also quite impressive. On the other hand, some of the other petition groups were of a kind for which there was not so much need. The number of priests who needed a dispensation in order to be ordained was obviously not so high as the number of people who wanted to legitimize their marriages, and therefore the petitions in the *de promotis et promovendis* category remain much fewer.

An important fact that has to be kept in mind when studying these numbers is that the impressive figures in Table 1 represent only those supplications that were copied into the registers of the Penitentiary, not necessarily all the cases brought before the officials of the Penitentiary; we have to be aware that researchers have not yet been able to assess whether all petitions handled and accepted by the office were copied into the registers. Nor do we know whether the Penitentiary rejected some petitions carried to its authority, for only the approved petitions have been registered. At the same time, no information is available on the *litterae ecclesiae*—the letters of absolution conceded by the *penitentiarii minores* in the major Roman basilicas. Thus the numbers given here in Table 1 do not represent all Christians who had turned to the authority of the different officials of the Penitentiary; the numbers here might just be the tip of the iceberg.

In order to clarify what kinds of petitions are registered under each title, let us discuss in greater detail each category of supplication. In the following chapters we shall explain what kinds of graces were granted again and again by the Penitentiary during the second half of the fifteenth century.

2.2.1. *De matrimonialibus*—Illegal marriages

The first category in the Penitentiary registers contains petitions concerning the impediments to marriage, *de matrimonialibus*.[10] One of the fields of competence of the Penitentiary was to grant dispensations and absolutions to Christians in marriage matters. Laypersons had to seek dispensation at the papal Penitentiary if they wished to marry someone too closely related to them. Those couples who wanted to regularize an already-existent marriage that broke the norms of canon law had also to request absolution for themselves as well as a dispensation for their marriage. The Catholic Church considered marriage matters to be of great importance and the handling of these matters was reserved to the papal authority because, according to St. Paul, a Christian marriage between a man and a woman was the living image of the indissoluble union between Christ and the Catholic Church.[11]

10. See L. Schmugge, P. Hersperger, B. Wiggenhauser, *Supplikenregister*, 68–95, and L. Schmugge, "Deutsche Ehen vor römischem Gericht. Matrimonialdispense der Pönitentiarie aus deutschsprachigen Gegenden Europas (1455–1484)," in K. Salonen and C. Krötzl, eds., *The Roman Curia, the Apostolic Penitentiary and the Partes in the Later Middle Ages* (Acta Instituti Romani Finlandiae 28; Rome, 2003), 115–125.

11. Eph. 5.21–33.

Marital matters were discussed by numerous Church Fathers and several popes; Alexander III (1159–1181) and Innocent III (1198–1216), for example, promulgated several important regulations concerning marriages and, in particular, their validity. The most important church council with regards to marital matters was the Fourth Lateran Council, held in Rome in 1215.[12] Despite the importance of marriage, it was not until 1274, at the Second Council of Lyons, that marriage was officially recognized as one of the seven holy sacraments of the Catholic Church. After that very few changes were made to the canon law rules concerning matrimony.

The basic rule for a legal marriage was that both of the parties be entering the matrimony of their own free will; if not, the Church did not consider the union valid. Canon law regulated the validity of a marriage in numerous other ways, too. It declared several fundamental impediments *(impedimentum matrimonii)* which prevented a couple from being legally married. Some of these impediments could be overcome with a papal dispensation, some could not.

The first impediment stipulated in canon law was consanguinity *(consanguinitas)*: potential spouses who were too closely related to each other by the tie of blood were not permitted to marry. Canon law did not allow persons who were related to each other by the fourth degree of consanguinity or closer to be wed. In practice this regulation meant that marriages between siblings, cousins, second cousins, and third cousins—just to mention some examples within the same generation (in horizontal line)[13]—as well as, for example, between parents and children or grandparents and grandchildren (in vertical line) were illegal. The impediment of consanguinity was, however, dispensable only in the horizontal line of relationship.[14]

12. Canons 50 and 51, edited in COD, 257–258.

13. The concept of consanguinity within four degrees is very complex and contains dozens of different possibilities of consanguinity. In *Corpus Iuris Canonici I* (hereafter CIC I) there is an appendix entitled *Arbor consanguinitatis,* which gives all the possible combinations for the different degrees of consanguinity. See CIC I, 1425–1426.

14. Regarding the canon law regulations concerning consanguinity, see R. Helmholz, "Consanguinity," in *Dictionary of the Middle Ages,* vol. 3 (1983), 539–540. R. Weigand, "Ehe," in *Lexikon des Mittelalters,* Band III, 1986 col. 1623–

Affinity *(affinitas)* was the second impediment to marriage stipulated by canon law. Marriage was forbidden in cases where a person had too close a blood relationship to the previous husband or wife, or even lover or mistress, of his or her future spouse. In this case also, marriage was forbidden within the fourth degree of affinity, which was counted based on the degree of consanguinity between the new and the former partner, so that third degree of consanguinity between the new and former partner resulted as third degree of affinity, and so on. As with the impediment of consanguinity, affinity was dispensable.[15]

The impediment of lack of public honesty *(impedimentum publicae honestatis iustitiae)* was, in fact, a form of affinity: no person was allowed to marry someone who was closely related to his or her previous fiancé(e). This impediment was also dispensable, and dispensations were often requested by members of families that wanted to strengthen their alliance by a marriage. If one of the intended spouses died, another member of that family replaced the one who had passed away.[16]

The fourth impediment to marriage was that of spiritual relationship *(cognatio spiritualis)*, which involved several different possibilities of relationship. Spiritual relationship was caused by a holy sacrament, Baptism or Confirmation: marriage was forbidden between a child and his or her godparents or their close relatives, but this impediment could be overruled by a dispensation.[17]

The fifth category was legal relationship *(cognatio legalis)* or legal fraternity *(fraternitas legalis)*, i.e., adoptive relationship. Persons re-

---

1625, 1635–1640. One of the more important decretals is X 4.14.1, 8, edited in A. Friedberg, ed., *Corpus Iuris Canonici, pars secunda, Decretalium collectiones* (Graz, 1959) (hereafter CIC II), 700–701, 703–704. As to the discussion between canonists, see the translation of Raymond of Peñafort's *Summa on Marriage* (Toronto, 2005).

15. There are many canon law regulations concerning affinity, for example, X 4.14.1, edited in CIC II, 700–701.

16. There are many canon law regulations concerning *impedimentum publicae honestatis justitiae*, for example, X 4.1.4, edited in CIC II, 662.

17. Concerning the different forms of spiritual relationship, see E. De Leon, *La "cognatio spiritualis' según Graciano* (Pontificio Ateneo della santa Croce. Monografie giuridiche 11; Milano, 1996).

lated to each other by the tie of adoption could not marry each other. This impediment was dispensable, but the Penitentiary granted such dispensations very rarely.[18]

These five impediments were the types of cases most frequently handled by the Penitentiary. The Penitentiary could grant dispensations for couples who wanted to marry despite an impediment; asking for a dispensation before getting married was the most common and correct way to act. It was the task of the local parish priest to check that the persons who wanted to marry were not related to each other in an improper way. Canon 50 of the Fourth Lateran Council stipulated that before a couple could be legally married, the parish priest had to read aloud the banns in the church on three Sundays; if someone knew something against the marriage, they were supposed to tell what they knew. This was very important, and canon law declared persons who did not express their doubts or information about the spouses' relationship immediately excommunicated. In the end it was, however, the task of the parish priest to make sure that no impediments existed.

If a couple knowingly managed to be married despite an impediment, they had violated the rules of canon law and thus were automatically excommunicated. The priest who had been present at the marriage was at least suspended if he had been aware of the impediment. But in these cases too, the Catholic Church was merciful and offered reconciliation. A couple that had knowingly been married despite an impediment could turn to the Holy See and ask for absolution and a dispensation that allowed them to return to the community of Christians and to continue in their marriage.

Sometimes a couple was married not knowing that they were related to each other in some way; in these cases, the couple did not incur excommunication, for they did not violate canon law knowingly and intentionally. Consequently, these couples did not need absolution but if they wanted to continue legally in their marriage, they had to turn to the pope and request a dispensation.

When local ecclesiastical authorities learned that two persons had married despite an impediment, the two were automatically

18. X 4.12.1, edited in CIC II, 696.

summoned before the ecclesiastical court, their marriage was pronounced void, and they had to separate from each other. Normally the couple could avoid the obligatory separation (or divorce) only by receiving a dispensation, but in certain cases the local ecclesiastical courts gave a sentence tolerating their marriage.

Quite often, couples, wanting to ensure the position of their heirs, included with their request for absolution and/or dispensation a request for a special legitimization of their children. This was extremely important, as they were then assured that their children could inherit from them without problems. Otherwise in dubious cases there was always the possibility that some relatives might claim that their children were not born in legal wedlock and, as illegitimate children, were without right to inherit from their parents.

Apart from the Penitentiary, certain other papal offices (the Apostolic Chancery and the Apostolic Datary, for example) also had power to deal with similar kinds of cases. Bearing witness to this are the hundreds of such cases registered in the other medieval archival series kept in the Vatican Secret Archives.[19]

A marriage supplication presented to the Penitentiary always contained the most important details concerning the marriage. The first of these were the names of the supplicants and their home diocese. Next were given several other details that were important for the handling of the case. First of all, the supplicants had to tell whether they were planning to get married *(desiderantes)*, or had already gotten married *(contraxerunt)*; in the latter case, they had to state whether or not they had been aware of the impediment at the time of their wedding. This difference was important, for those couples not yet married needed only a dispensation from their impediment, while those couples that had already been married had to ask for a dispensation that would allow them to continue in their marriage or re-marry despite the impediment. Furthermore, if the couple had known about the impediment at the time of their marriage, they also had to request absolution, for they had knowingly acted against the rules of canon law.[20]

19. Especially in ASV, *Registra Supplicationum* and ASV, *Registra Lateranensia*.
20. Concerning the Penitentiary and marriage, see L. Schmugge, P. Her-

Next came the second important piece of information: the kind of impediment, and, if needed, its degree. In the case of consanguinity or affinity, it was important to know how close the relationship in question was; the closer the relationship (second degree was the closest dispensable, and fourth degree still needed dispensation), the more severe was the matter. In cases of spiritual relationship, the quality of relation was also given, i.e., whether the relationship was based on the sacrament of Baptism or Confirmation.

Those supplicants who were already married (and in certain cases also those who were not yet married but had been living together for a long time) also sometimes mentioned in their petitions whether they had consummated their marriage through sexual intercourse or not, and whether they had children. This, however, was not included in all entries. This kind of information did not affect the decision of the Penitentiary, and consequently some scribes did not copy these facts into the registers.

Normally the last information given in the entries is whether the couple wanted to legitimize their heirs. In certain entries this is simply mentioned with a general phrase referring to legitimization of children; in some other cases the supplicants specified that they wanted to legitimize their future children or both existing and future children. This fact also was quite often—depending on the copyist—left out of the Penitentiary records.

Marriage petitions, as we have already learned from Table 1, form the largest category of petitions approved by the Penitentiary in the late Middle Ages, with a total of 42,691 cases handled between 1455 and 1492. What is most striking in these numbers is the heavy preponderance of petitions from Italy; almost half of the couples asking for a dispensation and/or absolution in marriage matters were Italian. France, the German-speaking territory, as well as the Iberian Peninsula, seem to be on almost the same level, followed by the British Isles. Far fewer petitions came from eastern and northern Europe than from other regions.

---

sperger, B. Wiggenhauser, *Supplikenregister,* 68–88; K. Salonen, *Penitentiary,* 103–118. The classic study concerning medieval marriage is R. Helmholz, *Marriage Litigation in Medieval England* (Cambridge, 1974).

Table 2. Provenance of Marriage Petitions in the Second Half of the Fifteenth Century

Territory	*Cases*	*Percent of total*
British Isles	3,989	9
Eastern Europe	619	1
France	6,503	15
Germany	6,170	14
Spain and Portugal	5,001	12
Italy	20,163	47
Northern Europe	65	0
Not known	181	0
Total	42,691	100

Source: ASV, *Penitenzieria Ap., Reg. Matrim. et Div.*, Vols. 5–41.

The number of inhabitants is without doubt one important factor when comparing the numbers of petitions brought before the Penitentiary.[21] Table 2 shows that the four most populated European territories (Italy, France, Germany, and the Iberian Peninsula) are the best-represented areas, whereas from sparsely populated Scandinavia there are very few cases. The number of inhabitants does not, however, explain these numbers completely. The distance between the Apostolic See and the territories must also have played an important role when petitioners considered going to Rome with their petitions; traveling to Rome was much easier for Christians living in southern Germany or France than for those living in Norway or the Baltic countries.

The predominance of Italian petitions is not, however, only a re-

21. Ludwig Schmugge has used the following numbers of inhabitants in different territories of christendom: L. Schmugge, *Kirche, Kinder, Karrieren,* 166–167.

sult of the shorter distance from Rome, or of the greater population; another cause must have been the legal situation in the Italian Peninsula. Marriage regulations stipulated in canon law were born in many respects from the regulations of Roman civil law that had been in use in the Italian territory for centuries, and thus these regulations were well known and established among Italians; therefore, social control by means of canon law was, in the Middle Ages, much tighter on the Italian Peninsula than elsewhere. In the northern and eastern parts of christendom, on the other hand, the marriage regulations stipulated by the church played only a minor role, if any. This lesser importance is reflected in the minimal need to turn to the Penitentiary.

Speaking in terms of territories can, however, be somewhat misleading. Looking at the situation more closely, we can observe in Germany, for example, a declining tendency in the number of petitions from south to north; the southern dioceses of the Holy German Empire had much tighter connections to the Roman curia than the others.[22]

2.2.2. *De diversis formis*—Violations of canon law

The *de diversis formis* category contains, as one might guess from the title, several different types of graces, namely: absolutions, dispensations, and special licenses.

Absolutions and dispensations

Most of the petitions registered in this category concern absolutions. The Penitentiary had the power to absolve Christians, both laymen and ecclesiastics, from ecclesiastical sanctions (mostly excommunication), even from those that the pope had exclusively reserved to his own authority. In order to be freed of their status as

22. For more about German marriage petitions, see L. Schmugge, "Deutsche Ehen." Concerning the distribution of cases from different territories during the pontificate of Pius II, see K. Salonen, "The Penitentiary under Pope Pius II: The Supplications and Their Provenance," in G. Jaritz, T. Jørgensen, K. Salonen, eds., *The Long Arm of Papal Authority: Late Medieval Christian Peripheries and Their Communication with the Holy See* (Medium Aevum Quotidianum, Sonderband XIV; Bergen-Budapest-Krems, 2004), 19–28.

excommunicates, many people of both sexes flocked to the papal court for absolution, be it that they had been excluded from the community of the faithful automatically *(excommunicatio a iure* or *ipso facto)* or through a sentence that an ecclesiastical authority had explicitly pronounced against them *(excommunicatio ab homine)*.[23]

For laymen, being absolved from a crime committed was sufficient to regain all the rights of a good Christian; for a criminal cleric, however, this was not enough. If a cleric was accused of a crime the absolution of which was reserved to the Apostolic See, he had to turn to the papacy for a special dispensation that allowed him to continue his ecclesiastical vocation. Having violated the ecclesiastical canons, a cleric had incurred a so-called "irregularity" *(irregularitas)* and "disqualification or disability" *(inhabilitas)*. An irregularity implied the incapacity to be ordained, and barred the person affected from the reception of and functioning in ecclesiastical benefices, especially those that involved the cure of souls *(cura animarum)*. *Irregularitas* and *inhabilitas* thus formed a rather common obstacle to the exercise of ecclesiastical functions. If someone had been ordained without an impediment having been revealed—an illegitimate birth, for instance *(tacito defectu natalium)*—and then exercised his priestly functions, that person automatically became irregular and an excommunicate. Only the pope, in the plenitude of his power, could offer a fully secure and satisfying remedy in reserved cases, and the Penitentiary could restore the status of the offender in the name of the pope. Sometimes the petitioner confessed being guilty of excess *(excessus)*; this meant that he had performed sacramental functions even though he was excommunicated or considered irregular or disqualified. The situation in such a case was worse than it had been prior to the "excess," and he needed a special dispensation.

Several Christians incurred both excommunication and the other

23. Concerning different types of excommunication, see F. D. Logan, *Excommunication and the Secular arm in Medieval England: A Study in Legal Procedure from the Thirteenth to the Sixteenth Century* (Pontifical Institute of Medieval Studies; Toronto, 1968), 14–15, or more generally E. Vodola, *Excommunication in the Middle Ages* (Berkeley, 1986).

above-mentioned ecclesiastical punishments, of which they wanted to be free. In order to obtain the required absolution and dispensation, these persons turned to the Penitentiary. The petition category *de diversis formis* in the registers of the Penitentiary contains several different types of petition for absolution (and dispensation). In the following we will explain the most common types of crimes for which Christians needed absolution (and dispensation) from the Penitentiary.

Violence, murder, and participation in judging or warfare The use of force, or wounding or killing someone, were very common reasons for which petitioners turned to the competency of the Penitentiary. The norms of the Catholic Church strictly forbade priests to act violently and prohibited them from carrying weapons.[24] If a clergyman took part in a violent act—his mere presence was sufficient!—he was immediately *(ipso facto)* excommunicated. The major consequence of excommunication of a cleric consists in what canon law calls *"inhabilitas"* and *"irregularitas."* Thus an excommunicated cleric could no longer act in his office until he had received papal absolution (which freed him from excommunication) and dispensation (which abolished the irregularity and disqualification). Furthermore, if a clergyman took part in bloodshed, he was also suspended from altar service forever, as well as deposed from his office and incomes until he otained the necessary absolution and dispensation.[25]

In order to protect unarmed priests, constitution 15 of the Second Lateran Council (held in Rome in 1139) forbade the use of violence against priests; violation carried an immediate sanction of excommunication that could be absolved only by the papal authority.[26] Rehabilitation by a special absolution was thus also necessary for laypeople if they had killed or assaulted a cleric.

The regulations of canon law ordered that all Christians who had

24. See R. Metz, "Clergy," in *Dictionary of the Middle Ages*, vol. 3 (1983), 440–446. One of the central decretals is X 3.1.2, edited in CIC II, 449.

25. See the article by Metz cited just above, and X 5.12.24 and X 5.25.1, edited in CIC II, 803–804, 825.

26. Edited in COD, 200.

participated in violent acts where a cleric was involved (as violator or victim) had to be brought before the pope for absolution. Exceptions from the obligation of traveling to Rome for absolution were provided in the law; for example, women, children, the old and the sick, as well as the leaders of the local societies (whose presence in the community was necessary), could be absolved by the local bishop. Also, abbots had the faculty to absolve and dispense monks of their monastery who had acted violently towards another monk in the same monastic house. Persons who had hurt clerics only slightly were excluded from the obligation to travel to the Holy See; they could be absolved locally if their act was not scandalous.[27] The same also applied in cases of fights between two laymen. The Catholic Church was not interested in such cases and left them to be decided by the local authorities. This means that the records in the registers of the Penitentiary contain, with very few exceptions, cases of violence only where a cleric was involved.[28]

Canon law also held that clerics who had participated in violent warfare (very often only as military or personal chaplains of a knight or king, for example) or in sentencing someone to death (clerics were often employed as scribes of local authorities and, in this capacity, had to take part in court sessions) were guilty of violent acts, and thus needed absolution and dispensation in order to be able to continue in their clerical orders.[29] Thus several clerics who had been obliged to participate either in war or in sentencing had to turn to the Penitentiary in order to continue in their offices.[30]

27. The most important decretal here is X 5.39.2, 3, 17, 33, 50, edited in CIC II, 890, 895, 903, 910.

28. About the Penitentiary, violence, and murder, see L. Schmugge, P. Hersperger, B. Wiggenhauser, *Supplikenregister,* 98–116, as well as K. Salonen, *Penitentiary,* 128–138.

29. Canon 12 of the Third Lateran Council, edited in COD, 194; X 3.50.4, 5, 9, and X 5.37.5, edited in CIC II, 658–660, 881.

30. Concerning the Penitentiary and participation in warfare or judging, see K. Salonen, *Penitentiary,* 164–167. Quite often clerics accused of participation in violent acts requested, rather than absolution, a declaration that they were not guilty at all.

Monastic issues All members of the numerous different monastic orders were obliged to observe the monastic vows of obedience, chastity, and poverty they took at their profession. Taking the monastic vows meant that the person was supposed to wear the monastic habit, was bound to the house, to the order, and to the rule of the chosen order for the rest of his or her life, had to live chastely, and could not own anything. The nuns were even more bound to their monasteries, for as per the decretal *Periculoso* of Boniface VIII, the religious women were enclosed in nunneries. Men, especially members of mendicant orders, were freer to move from one place to another, but never to change monastery—or monastic order—without a permit.

If a monk or nun could not stand life in the monastery he or she had chosen, the regulations of canon law included the possibility of a special dispensation to change to another house. In some extreme cases a person was also allowed to change from one order to another. The constitution *Licet* of Innocent III (1206) made it possible to change monastic order, but only in cases where the receiving house or order was observing rules similar to or stricter than the house from which the person originally came. Another way to leave monastic life was to become a secular priest and to hold a benefice, but this option was obviously open only to men. In cases in which the person with the monastic vocation was very ill and could not endure monastic life for health reasons, it was also possible for the person to leave monastic life and live with his or her parents. In all of these cases, however, a papal dispensation was required. One of the competences of the Apostolic Penitentiary was to grant this kind of dispensations for monks, nuns, and friars who for some legitimate reason could not live in their monastic houses.[31]

Those monks, nuns, and friars who asked for dispensation to change to a different, better place were respecting the regulations of

31. Ecclesiastical legislation concerning monastic issues: X 3.31.1, 8, 11, 18, edited in CIC II, 569, 571–572, 575–576, as well as the bull *Pastoralis officii divina providentia* of Pope Leo X, edited in *Bullarium Romanum* V, 571–601, especially 580. See also J. A. Brundage and E. Makowski, "Enclosure of Nuns: The Decretal *Periculoso* and Its Commentators," *Journal of Medieval History* 20 (1994), 143–155.

the church; there were also, however, monastic persons who could not endure life in the place where they had taken vows, and decided to leave their monasteries without a dispensation or license. Such monks or nuns were considered, according to canon law, to be apostates, for they had committed the crime of apostasy—meaning that a professional religious has given up the religious life and returned to the secular life. After the year 1298, a person committing apostasy incurred immediate excommunication.[32] In the fourteenth century the regulations of canon law became so strict that even a very short absence from a monastic house was considered apostasy, and the person in question was excommunicated as a result. If a monk then continued carrying out his priestly functions, he made his situation even worse, for in addition to the excommunication and the consequent irregularity for priest monks due to apostasy, he also incurred suspension and excess. In order to free themselves from ecclesiastical sanctions, apostates had to turn to the papal curia and ask for absolution and a dispensation.[33]

Exercising clerical offices under excommunication Some priests were obliged to turn to the Penitentiary to ask for absolution (and dispensation so that they could continue in their office), for they had incurred excommunication through the illicit celebration of a Mass or the exercise of other priestly functions. This could occur when a priest celebrated a Mass in the presence of excommunicates or in a territory put under an interdict, which was strictly forbidden by the regulations of canon law. Excommunication and interdict were the most powerful means of punishing Christians who had not obeyed the Church. These punishments excluded guilty persons from ecclesiastical life, and a priest who did not observe these rules was excommunicated, as were the persons for whom he was illegally cel-

32. On the canon law regulations concerning apostasy, see X 3.31.24 and VI 4.24.2, edited in CIC II, 578, 1065–1066.

33. A good book about apostasy is D. F. Logan, *Runaway Religious in Medieval England c. 1240–1540* (Cambridge Studies in Medieval Life and Thought, 4th Series; Cambridge, 1996). For more details on the Penitentiary and monastic matters, see L. Schmugge, P. Hersperger, B. Wiggenhauser, *Supplikenregister*, 117–125, as well as K. Salonen, *Penitentiary*, 138–144.

ebrating the Holy Mass. The idea behind these punishments was to bring the offenders back into the fold.[34]

Incorrect celebration of Mass or sacraments was also cause for excommunication and suspension for priests. In some cases the Penitentiary dealt with questions of the second administration of a sacrament for one person—such as Baptism—that an individual could receive only once. Doing it twice was seen as a kind of insult to the sanctity of the sacrament in question and was considered a sacrilege. Such matters did not occur very frequently, but could sometimes happen, often in such a way that the priest guilty of the crime did not even know that he had acted illegally and thus incurred excommunication. Double Baptism could easily take place when a weak baby received an emergency baptism right after the birth and then later was solemnly baptized in church without the words of conditional baptism being used.[35]

Another type of incorrect celebration of sacraments could occur when a cleric performed a sacrament that was beyond his powers in holy orders—for example, if a cleric promoted only to the minor orders celebrated a Mass or heard confessions and distributed absolution. Similarly, a priest who was giving sacraments, celebrating Masses, or hearing confessions somewhere else than in his own parish without a permit from the local bishop or parish priest was guilty of abusing his priestly powers. In both cases the persons guilty of such abuses were punished by excommunication and removal from their offices, and they needed absolution before they could return to their offices.[36]

The cases related to sacraments and priestly functions in the Penitentiary archives were mostly petitions for absolution and dispensa-

34. Regarding the ecclesiastical legislation related to these questions, see D. F. Logan, "Excommunication," in *Dictionary of the Middle Ages,* vol. 4 (1984), 536–538. E. Vodola, "Interdict," in *Dictionary of the Middle Ages,* vol. 6 (1985), 493–497. One of the central decretals on this topic X 5.27.3–7, 9–10, X 5.39.18, 55, and VI 5.11.18, edited in CIC II, 827–832, 895–896, 1104.

35. Regarding conditional baptism, see S. A. Keefe, "Baptism," in *Dictionary of the Middle Ages,* vol. 2 (1983), 83–86. The main decretal X 3.42.2, edited in CIC II, 644.

36. According to the decretal X 5.28.1–2, edited in CIC II, 833.

tion for persons who had acted in an illegal way and who therefore had been excommunicated and suspended from their offices. The Penitentiary, however, also had the power to grant dispensation for persons who wished to act against these regulations. A priest might request a dispensation that would allow him to celebrate a Mass despite an interdict in his parish, and some mendicant priests turned to the Penitentiary for a license to celebrate a Mass or distribute other sacraments wherever they happened to be—even without the license of the local ecclesiastics.[37]

Simony Simony is the crime of buying or selling the property of the church, holy orders, ecclesiastical offices, or benefices, or taking money for performing ecclesiastical functions. The most frequent cases of simony appearing in our records occur when the holder of an ecclesiastical benefice who was about to leave his office asked for some money from the person who was supposed to be his successor. Similarly simony also occurred when a patron of an ecclesiastical office took money or goods from the candidate he was going to present to the office. Simony committed by selling or profiting from exercising ecclesiastical functions—for example, celebrating a nuptial Mass or hearing confession—was extremely rare according to the Penitentiary records, but this kind of abuse also existed.

Simony was considered a severe crime against the norms of the church, and both the seller and the buyer of ecclesiastical goods, orders, or offices were generally excommunicated; only the pope had the power to absolve the offenders. Furthermore, a person in clerical orders who was guilty of simony was also considered irregular and needed a papal dispensation before he could again practice his priestly functions. Persons who had profited economically from simony were obliged to compensate the church for the money they had received.[38]

37. Regarding the Penitentiary and excommunication, interdict, and overstepping priestly functions, see L. Schmugge, P. Hersperger, B. Wiggenhauser, *Supplikenregister*, 125–132, as well as K. Salonen, *Penitentiary*, 144–147, 169–170.

38. See J. H. Lynch, "Simony," in *Dictionary of the Middle Ages*, vol. 11 (1988), 300–302, and the decretal X 5.3.1–46. and Extrav. Comm. 5.1.2, edited in CIC II, 749–767, 1289.

The Penitentiary had the authority to absolve and dispense persons who were guilty of the crime of simony, mostly cases related to retiring from a benefice in favor of another person. The entries in the register of the Penitentiary also refer to the payments the guilty persons had to make to the church in order to compensate for the profits they had made committing a violation against the regulations of canon law. The compensations had to be paid to the Apostolic Datary, which was one of the offices within the papal curia.[39]

Sacrilege Those who committed a crime against the property or officials of the church were guilty of sacrilege. There were three different forms of sacrilege: violence against an ecclesiastic person; disturbing or polluting a church or another holy place, such as a cemetery, by unsuitable acts (bloodshed, robbery, or pollution by semen—i.e., having sexual intercourse); and disturbing or misusing the holy sacraments or the Mass. Anyone who committed such a violation against the church was excommunicated and considered irregular; for criminal priests, the punishments were even more severe.[40]

According to the Penitentiary documents, sacrilege was quite common during war, when military troops plundered valuable items from parishes or monasteries, or in some case murdered people who were hiding in the churches. However, simple stealing of church property was not rare either. Sex in a church, on the other hand, was not common, but did take place rarely—mostly between a father confessor and a woman who had come to confess herself. In its simplest and most common form, sacrilege could consist of an angry blow to a neighbor's nose, with bloodshed, taking place in a graveyard.

Those who had incurred excommunication and irregularity by committing some form of sacrilege could have their sin removed by

39. On the Penitentiary and simony, see L. Schmugge, P. Hersperger, B. Wiggenhauser, *Supplikenregister,* 134–137, as well as K. Salonen, *Penitentiary,* 147–148.

40. See the article by Lynch cited above and the decretals X 3.49.5, X 5.17.1–3, X 5.18.2, 5, and X 5.39.22, edited in CIC II, 655, 808–810, 896–897.

turning to the Penitentiary. The office could grant culpable Christians absolution from excommunication and dispensation from the irregularity. It could also remove from guilty priests their sins.[41]

Debt and special excommunication As we have already seen, a Christian could incur excommunication for any of a number of reasons. Those excommunications with which we have dealt up to now have been general excommunications—also referred to as major excommunications—which were stipulated by canon law for certain more severe violations against its regulations. There was also another type of excommunication, pronounced by local authorities, which very often resulted from disobedience towards the local ecclesiastical authorities, who then tried to discipline members of local society with this sort of punishment.

The excommunications pronounced by local ecclesiastical authorities were not reserved only for laymen who refused to obey their parish priest or bishop, but were also used against clerics who were not willing to act according to local rules. In most of the cases it was a question of priests who kept concubines even though this was strictly forbidden in canon law. If the men in ecclesiastical vocation did not want to give up their women, the local bishops could excommunicate them for it. In many cases, excommunication due to the keeping of concubines was not even a sentence pronounced against a specific person, but a general thing—for example, against all priests of the diocese.[42]

Another very common reason for being excommunicated by the local ecclesiastical authorities was debt: failure to settle one's debts or failure to pay one's annual payments to the church. In fact, excommunication because of debt was, according to Elisabeth Vodola, one of the most common reasons for local excommunications.[43] In

41. On the Penitentiary and sacrilege, see L. Schmugge, P. Hersperger, B. Wiggenhauser, *Supplikenregister,* 132–133, as well as K. Salonen, *Penitentiary,* 148–150.

42. Concerning excommunications, see E. Vodola, *Excommunication,* and the article by Lynch (note 38).

43. E. Vodola, *Excommunication,* 39–40.

order to be excommunicated because of a debt, the excommunicated person did not necessarily have to owe money to the church; money disputes between two laymen could lead to ecclesiastical punishment. Very often excommunication was used in cases where the creditor found that he could not get his money back via secular courts. If the debt was sealed with an oath on the Holy Bible, it was possible for the creditor to take the debtor to ecclesiastical court, since, by not paying back his debt, the debtor had broken his oath, which was a violation against the church. In these cases the ecclesiastical courts could sentence the debtor to excommunication for perjury. Obviously the debtor could not be rid of his status as perjurer before settling his debt.

The entries in the Penitentiary registers do not always give the reason for special excommunication; the copied text only says that an absolution and/or dispensation was needed because a person had been excommunicated locally by the authority of the local bishop, *ordinarius.* Thus in many cases the Penitentiary documents do not tell the reason for these special excommunications. The only way to know the reasons is to study the local sources, which often reveal the reasons behind special sentences of excommunication.

If a person who had been sentenced to special excommunication could not get the matter resolved with the local authorities—for example, perhaps a person might not have wanted to reconcile with the persons who had condemned him—he had the possibility of turning to the Penitentiary to ask for absolution from the local sentence of excommunication. In theory, the Penitentiary had nothing to do with these excommunications, and it would have been the task of the local ecclesiastical authorities to absolve those persons they had excommunicated; but as the officials of the Penitentiary had the same authority as any bishop, they also had the faculty to absolve Christians from these sentences. In these cases, Christians used the Penitentiary as a kind of court of appeal against the local ecclesiastics.[44]

44. Concerning the Penitentiary and special excommunications, see L. Schmugge, P. Hersperger, B. Wiggenhauser, *Supplikenregister,* 137–139, as well as K. Salonen, *Penitentiary,* 150–151, 171.

Breaking oaths or vows As we already learned above, canon law stipulated that a person who had sworn an oath *(iuramentum)* was bound by it and thus had to act according to what had been promised. In cases where a person was not able to abide by his oath, he was considered by canon law to be a perjurer, and was consequently subject to ecclesiastical punishment. The reason for the interest of the church in matters of oath was not the content of the oath; it arose from the fact that the oaths were generally sworn in the name of God or on the Holy Bible. Thus, if a person broke such an oath, it was considered perjury. Sometimes perjury was committed intentionally, whereas sometimes the persons were simply unable to do what they had promised, even though they might have fully intended to do so. Committing perjury resulted in an excommunication that only the pope could absolve. In addition, clerics who were guilty of perjury were punished by a lifetime suspension from their benefice.[45]

Christians had two possibilities when turning to the Penitentiary in matters of perjury. Firstly, the Penitentiary had papal authority to absolve perjured Christians from excommunication, but it did not use this faculty very often. Most often, Christians who could not fulfill their oaths turned to the Penitentiary for a declaration that attested that they had been obliged to swear the oath under duress, and thus that it should not be considered perjury to have broken it. Canon law does in fact stipulate that an oath made against one's free will or under pressure was not considered to have been made voluntarily, and so breaking it was not considered a criminal act. Thus, Christians who could show that they had made an oath under suspicious circumstances or duress could turn to the Penitentiary for a declaration saying that they had not committed any crime by breaking their oath and consequently were also not excommunicated. Those supplicants who could show that the oath they had made under duress caused them enormous economic or other damage could thus be freed from their obligations by the declaration granted by the Penitentiary. Cases where a petitioner asked for a declaration

45. For the canonical discussion of breaking oaths and vows, see J. Lynch, "Oath," in *Dictionary of the Middle Ages,* vol. 9 (1987), 207, and the decretals X 2.1.13, X 2.24.8, edited in CIC II, 242–244, 361–362.

that he did not have to respect an oath that would cause him financial damage are generally called *ad effectum agendi* cases.[46]

As with persons who had sworn an oath, persons who had taken a vow *(votum)* were also bound to observe and obey their vows. As a vow was not as solemn as an oath, the church did not consider the breaking of a vow to be perjury; Christians were, however, bound to what they had promised. If they felt that they could not do what they had promised, they were obliged to turn to the ecclesiastical authorities to commute their vows to other kinds of pious works.

Normally, commuting one's vows—for example, vows to fast for a certain period or to visit the tomb of a local saint—was a matter for the local ecclesiastic authorities; only the cases related to the so-called solemn vows were reserved to the papal authority. These solemn vows were always vows that were supposed to last for life. In practice, the solemn vows whose commuting required papal intervention were of three kinds: vows for observing chastity, vows for entering monastic life together with monastic vows, and vows for making pilgrimages to the three major sanctuaries of the Catholic Church (Rome, Jerusalem, and Santiago de Compostela). If a person had made such a vow and could not keep it, he was obliged to turn to the Apostolic See.

Petitioners who could not observe what they had promised and who turned to the Penitentiary had two possibilities. They could ask for a release from their vow, which meant that they were no longer bound to it; they could also—and this was the case for most of the petitions—ask the Penitentiary to commute their vows, in the pope's name, to another kind of pious work—usually alms-giving or the making of local pilgrimages, but occasionally also payment of money to the papal curia.

The commuting of one's vow by the Penitentiary was possible if the person could show that he was not capable of observing what he had promised because of an impediment such as sickness or for political or ecclesiastical reasons. In certain cases, the petitioner asked

46. Concerning the Penitentiary and false oath, see L. Schmugge, P. Hersperger, B. Wiggenhauser, *Supplikenregister,* 140–142, as well as K. Salonen, *Penitentiary,* 152–153.

for a commutation because he had taken the vow under pressure, in special circumstances such as during an earthquake or in distress, or in ignorance of the consequences of the vow (especially in cases in which a vow had been taken at an early age).

The most common reason to turn to the Penitentiary was the commutation of vows for making pilgrimages. The Penitentiary also had the authority to commute vows to enter a monastery, to observe chastity, or to remain unmarried. Women who had promised to their late husbands to observe chastity for the rest of their lives or not to remarry can quite often be found as petitioners; similarly there can be found men and women who, in a moment of danger, had promised to enter a monastery or make a pilgrimage—vows which they tended to reconsider when the danger was over. Not all petitioners asked to have their vows commuted simply because they did not feel like observing them; often they truly were sick, and thus, for example, could not leave for a long pilgrimage.[47]

Others Besides the above-listed cases, in which the Penitentiary often granted absolution and dispensation, the office also had vast authority to absolve and dispense in several other matters; these, however, are minor in the number of cases handled by the Penitentiary.

One of these cases was the violation of celibacy regulations or the breaking of the sexual norms of the church. According to constitutions 6 and 7 of the Second Lateran Council, all clerics ordained to the holy orders (sub-deacon, deacon, and priesthood), as well as all monastic persons, were bound to observe celibacy.[48] There were, however, priests, monks, and nuns who did not always pay attention to these regulations, and had sexual relationships. Not observing celibacy was not a matter for papal excommunication; instead, the local bishop or the abbot of a monastery could punish a priest, monk, or nun for breaking the celibacy rules. For a priest to have

47. On the Penitentiary and commuting vows, see L. Schmugge, P. Hersperger, B. Wiggenhauser, *Supplikenregister,* 157–160, as well as K. Salonen, *Penitentiary,* 153–156.

48. Constitutions 6 and 7 are edited in COD, 174.

sexual relations with a woman who came to confess to him was considered especially serious, since it was considered a matter of incest—sexual relations between father-confessor and spiritual daughter. Such cases were, however, brought very rarely to the Penitentiary, for normally these matters were handled at home by the local ecclesiastical authorities.

Most cases where priests were accused of violations of celibacy were cases in which a priest had a concubine; cases where a layman or a priest had carnally known a nun were also brought before the Penitentiary but very rarely. The Penitentiary handled not only violations against celibacy regulations; some petitions brought to its authority concerned other kinds of sexual crimes: sodomy, homosexuality, or bestiality. However, these cases were extremely rare, for normally the resolution of such matters belonged to the authority of local ecclesiastical authorities.[49]

Heresy was a matter of which the Church was especially afraid. In the late Middle Ages there were several heretical movements in Europe, such as the Hussites in Bohemia and the Lollards in England. Heresy was not one of the main matters handled in the Penitentiary, but some petitions related to heresy can be found, and the office had the authority to absolve persons who had previously committed heresy, but had then returned to Mother Church.[50]

The records of the Penitentiary also contain some cases in which a Christian needed absolution because he had been in contact with non-Christians, normally Muslims. As canon law forbade Christians to trade with infidels (especially trade in weapons or foodstuffs) under pain of excommunication, persons who had had dealings with Muslims needed a special absolution before they could rejoin the Christian community. Such persons who appear as petitioners in

49. Concerning the Penitentiary and sexual violations, see L. Schmugge, P. Hersperger, B. Wiggenhauser, *Supplikenregister,* 147–151, as well as K. Salonen, *Penitentiary,* 157–159.

50. Regarding the Penitentiary and heresy, see F. Tamburini and L. Schmugge, *Häresie und Luthertum.* Regarding the Penitentiary and the Hussites, see L. Doležalová, "'But if you marry me': Reflections on the Hussite Movement in the Penitentiary (1438–1483)," in G. Jaritz, T. Jørgensen and K. Salonen, eds., *Long Arm,* 113–125.

the Penitentiary are mostly merchants who had had commercial connections with Muslims and who had sold them weapons such as knives, iron (important for making weapons), or grain, for example. In order to get an absolution from the Penitentiary, they also had to pay a certain sum of money to the papal curia, because they had profited economically from breaking the norms of the church.[51]

Besides heretics and infidels, forgery was also a matter that worried the medieval Catholic Church. A person who had falsified papal documents was subject to excommunication. The Penitentiary had the authority to absolve Christians from this kind of excommunication. The number of this kind of petition directed to the office is not large.

In addition to these briefly mentioned matters, dozens of other types of violations against the regulations of canon law could be absolved (and dispensed) by the Penitentiary; they are, however, so minor in importance that it is not sensible to list them here.[52]

Licenses

Special permits or licenses constituted another type of grace that the Penitentiary could grant. The office had the authority to grant special licenses to Christians who wanted, for a valid reason, to act against the rules of the Catholic Church. The matters that were within the competencies of the Penitentiary were mostly those that had something to do with the religious behavior or needs of individuals. The most common type of such grace were licenses that allowed a Christian to choose his or her confessor instead of confessing to the local parish priest. In addition to these so-called confessional licenses, which constitute their own group of petitions and are handled below in their own section, there were several other licenses that Christians sometimes needed, the most important of which were licenses concerning fasting, making pilgrimages, and studying.

51. The Third Lateran Council (1179) ordered in its constitution number 24 that everyone who traded with Muslims in arms, iron, or warriors was excommunicated. For more about the Penitentiary and the infidels, see F. Tamburini, *Ebrei, Saraceni, Cristiani.*

52. For a short list of other possible cases, with short explanations, see K. Salonen, *Penitentiary,* 123–124, 174–175, 332–333.

Licenses for not fasting Canon law stipulated that all Christians between the age of seven and sixty were not to eat the meat or other products of warm-blooded animals (i.e., eggs, butter, milk, and cheese) during the season of Lent or on other fasting days. The observation of the fasting regulations was, however, not obligatory if a person was sick or poor, had to do hard physical work, or was living in a region where finding olive oil, fish, or other products that could be substitutes for the forbidden ones was difficult. In order to be excused from the fasting regulations, Christians needed a special license that is often called a "butter-letter."

"Butter-letters" were licenses granted by the papal curia—most often by the Penitentiary—which allowed the holder(s) to eat the forbidden products during the fasting periods. Most of the "butter-letters" were granted for one person or for one family or household, who for some reason were not able to observe the fasting regulations. The reasons behind the personal licenses were quite often alimentary problems caused by an illness requiring certain products for recovery, old age, or allergy—to fish, for example.

Relatively often the "butter-letters" were granted to a group of persons or even to an entire village or town. These joint petitions arose from the fact that in certain regions it was impossible, or simply too expensive, to get products that were allowed during Lent. For example, in northern Europe there were no olive trees, and importing olive oil to substitute for butter during Lent was not possible. Therefore the jointly made petitions always came from northern Europe, or from the mountainous regions of Central Europe, especially southern Germany.[53]

Licenses for making a pilgrimage Those Christians who had taken a vow to make a pilgrimage to the Holy Land and Jerusalem met with a difficult problem: on the one hand, the regulations of canon law obliged them to observe what they had promised, while on the other hand canon law punished—in theory, with excommunica-

53. Concerning the Penitentiary and fasting regulations, see L. Schmugge, P. Hersperger, B. Wiggenhauser, *Supplikenregister,* 151–157, as well as K. Salonen, *Penitentiary,* 160–161.

tion—those Christians who were in contact with Muslims. The Holy Land was situated in territory ruled by Muslims; thus, a pilgrimage without contact with Muslims was impossible. How was this problem to be resolved?

What a Christian could do in this situation was to procure a special papal license to be in contact with infidels during his pilgrimage. It was one of the authorities of the Penitentiary to grant such licenses. Furthermore, the office could also absolve from excommunication those Christians who had made their pilgrimage without a special license.[54]

Studying The Catholic Church presupposed that any priest with the duty of the cure of souls would be present in his parish. This was extremely important, for a priest could fulfill his responsibilities towards his parishioners only if he was living in his benefice. For those priests who did not obey the obligation of residence, the church reserved the punishment of being deposed from office, which at the same time meant the loss of their income.

The obligation of residence for parish priests was intended to protect Christians from priests who simply collected the payments from their parishes, but never bothered to fulfill their duties towards the parishioners. Being absent from their parishes was allowed only if priests had a good reason for it. One of the most important reasons for not residing in one's parish was to study at a (foreign) university far outside the parish boundaries.

If a young and competent priest who was appointed to a parish as a parish priest wished to study further, he was allowed to reside outside his parish, but for this he needed a special license. These licenses were called *Cum ex eo* licenses—as per the constitution of Pope Boniface VIII (1295–1303), which began with those three words—and offered young, prominent priests the possibility of broadening their knowledge of theology or canon law at a uni-

54. Concerning the regulations of canon law with respect to contacts between Christians and Muslims, X 5.6.6, 11, 12, edited in CIC II, 773, 775. For more about the Penitentiary and pilgrimage licenses, see K. Salonen, *Penitentiary*, 167–168.

versity. The purpose of the constitution was to increase the number of well-educated priests, for which there was a need in every diocese. The constitution allowed a young priest to be appointed to a benefice, and to receive its income, while he was away. These licenses were normally granted for seven or five years.

Normally it was the task of the local bishop to grant the *Cum ex eo* licenses to suitable young priests, but sometimes young men turned to the Penitentiary with this kind of request. Why they did not turn to their bishops in such matters is not stated in the petitions, but we can assume that either the petitioners were near the Apostolic See when they realized that they needed such a license, or they used the Penitentiary because their local bishops had refused to grant them such a grace.[55]

The Penitentiary had authority not only to grant the *Cum ex eo* licenses but also to give other kinds of graces in matters of study. For example, canon law forbade clerics to act as surgeons or secular judges, because both of these professions could lead to someone's death; therefore, it was also forbidden for clergymen to study medicine or civil law. Those who did not respect these regulations were supposed to be excommunicated. It was, however, possible for clergymen to study these prohibited subjects with a special license granted by their bishop, or in certain cases also by the Penitentiary. The Penitentiary could also absolve those who had been excommunicated for studying the prohibited subjects without license.[56]

Others The three types of licenses already explained were the most important and most frequently requested graces. Another type

55. Concerning the constitution *Cum ex eo* as well as other aspects of the education of parochial clergy, see numerous articles of Leonard E. Boyle, and especially L. E. Boyle, "The Constitution 'Cum ex eo' of Boniface VIII: Education of Parochial Clergy," *Mediaeval Studies* XXIV (1962), 263–302. About the Penitentiary and the *Cum ex eo* licenses, see also L. Schmugge, P. Hersperger, B. Wiggenhauser, *Supplikenregister,* 161–162, K. Salonen, *Penitentiary,* 161–163, as well as L. Schmugge, "Boyle and Boniface: Cum ex eo-Dispensations in the Fifteenth Century," in A. Duggan, J. Greatrex, and B. Bolton eds., *Omnia disce: Medieval Studies in Memory of Leonard Boyle, O.P.* (Aldershot, 2005), 61–69.

56. X 3.50.9, edited in CIC II, 659–660. Concerning the Penitentiary and other types of study licenses see also K. Salonen, *Penitentiary,* 162–163.

of license the Penitentiary granted was for carrying a portable altar: the person to whom the license was addressed could, if he were a layman, attend, or, if he were a priest, celebrate Mass anywhere he wanted at a portable altar he could carry with him. The Penitentiary could also grant permission for clerics to pray according to the Roman prayer book rather than according to the practice in their own diocese, as was usually required.

The Penitentiary could also grant licenses for laymen to hear and for priests to celebrate Mass in parishes which were pronounced to be under interdict. The office could also grant a license to ignore residence regulations for priests who did not want to take their residence in the parish to which they were appointed. Sometimes the officials of the Penitentiary also handled matters such as commutations of vows or changing from one monastery to another as matters of license instead of matters of dispensation. These briefly mentioned cases were, however, brought to the authority of the Penitentiary only very rarely.[57]

As the reader can see from the cases described above (which cover only the most significant of the numerous different case types that belonged to the authority of the Penitentiary), the petitions in this category are very heterogeneous in content. This variety can also be seen in the phraseology used in the petitions, for each different case type obviously required its own kind of wording. Consequently, it is impossible to describe briefly what kinds of wordings are common for the *de diversis formis* petitions. The only common element in the forms of the petitions is that the name and home diocese of the supplicant were always mentioned at the beginning of each entry, followed by the necessary details related to the matter about which the supplicants had turned to the Penitentiary. Also, the decisions of the Penitentiary differed greatly according to what kind of grace the office was granting, so again at this point we cannot give the reader an all-inclusive explanation.

57. For more about the different kinds of petitions in the *de diversis formis* category as well as about their canon law background, see L. Schmugge, P. Hersperger, B. Wiggenhauser, *Supplikenregister*, 96–162; K. Salonen, *Penitentiary*, 119–175.

Table 3. Provenance of *de diversis formis* Petitions in the Second Half of the Fifteenth Century

Territory	*Cases*	*Percent of total*
British Isles	710	3
Eastern Europe	1,074	5
France	5,921	25
Germany	4,700	20
Spain and Portugal	3,802	16
Italy	7,103	30
Northern Europe	145	1
Not known	234	1
Total	23,689	100

Source: ASV, *Penitenzieria Ap., Reg. Matrim. et Div.*, Vols. 5–41.

As we learned from Table 1, the *de diversis formis* category, encompassing as it does a large number of different case types, is one of the biggest petition groups. This abundance of cases comes from all over Europe, but some specific differences in the provenance of the petitions in this group compared with, for example, the marriage supplications, can be observed.

In Table 3 we have given the number of cases coming from each territory of christendom during the second half of the fifteenth century. Analyzing the data in this table, we can see that the provenance of cases in this category follows, generally speaking, more or less the same pattern found in the other petition groups. Petitioners from the north are practically absent; from eastern Europe also there are few petitions, but somewhat more than in the previously presented marriage cases (see Table 2). Relatively few petitioners are from the British Isles (and most of them come from Ireland, not from the British mainland), even though they are relatively numerous in other categories. Again, Italy is in first place, but not so strikingly as with the marriage petitions. Italy is followed by the three other big territories: France, Germany, and the Iberian Peninsula.

Very often, local circumstances and customary laws drove Christians to turn to the Penitentiary to ask for help against unfair jurisdiction back home. Thus, in this category we often find petitions that actually refer to the use of the Penitentiary as a court of appeal when the petitioners did not get proper justice and due process at home.

2.2.3. *De declaratoriis*—Papal declarations

The fourth competence of the Penitentiary was that of granting letters of declaration; petitions concerning such requests were copied into the category *de declaratoriis.* There were three main purposes for which these letters were normally granted. Most commonly, the declarations were granted for a person (typically a cleric or a person who wanted to become one) who needed an official certificate that he was not—at least according to the regulations of canon law—guilty of a murder, even though he had participated in events that had led to the death of someone. Similarly, letters of declaration were granted for persons who needed a testimony that they were not members of a monastic order even though they had spent some time in a monastery, often because their parents had obliged them to do so against their free will. The third common reason for asking for declaratory letters was to get a marriage nullified. These letters were requested mostly by couples who had been forced to marry against their will or as very young children. Annulment of a marriage was important for persons who wished to be remarried, as persons who were separated or divorced could not do so.

In contrast to the entries in the other petition categories, which are generally quite short, the entries in the *de declaratoriis* category are normally very long, and have almost always been copied into the register *in extenso*—word by word. Like all the other petitions handled in the Penitentiary, the *de declaratoriis* petitions also are very formulaic. The petitions can be divided into different sections according to the kind of information that may be found in different parts of the text of the petition.

The first part of the text is a long and very detailed description of the events, called, in terms of diplomatics, *narratio.* These long descriptions contain important information on events and details that have significance for the petition. Having them all correct was important, for the Penitentiary made its decision on the basis of these details. In addition to the significant details, the *narratio* often also contains many other details on daily life that have very little to do with the actual issue of the petition, but which can be very interesting. For example, the petition may contain a hint regarding a plague in a certain region, a plague about which we lack any other documentation or other source of information. Sometimes references can be found to local habits, or even laws which describe customs in each area; these are important counterparts to the normative law texts in studying whether the law was really respected as it was written in its official form.

After the *narratio* follows the part in which the supplicant expresses his request, i.e., the *petitio*. By contrast with the *narratio*, which up to a certain point could be a free description of the events, the *petitio* is always composed in a very standard and formulaic manner. The use of correct phraseology was very important, for it formed the basis of the righteousness of the request in terms of canon law. Even if the details mentioned in the *narratio* were favorable for the supplicant, unless the *petitio* was composed in a correct manner, the officials of the Penitentiary could not approve the petition; therefore the correct wordings were very important, and they were also repeated from one petition to another—as readers can see in the documents edited in the Part II of this book.

In addition to the two parts of the petition, the entries in the *de declaratoriis* category also contain the decision of the official of the Penitentiary, which is copied in at the end of the entry, after the petition itself. Normally in these cases, the decisions were made according to the general authority of the Penitentiary, and thus we find the formula of approval *Fiat in forma*. We also often find as the formula of approval, instead of *Fiat in forma*, the phrase of approval *Fiat ut infra* under the petition. This formula refers both to the general authority of the Penitentiary as well as to the fact that the decision of the Penitentiary was not valid in and of itself, but that the case had still to be checked by the ecclesiastical authorities mentioned below.

After the decision we find two different additions to the text of the petition. First we find a reference to the *commission.* The cases registered under the title *de declaratoriis* were normally sent to the local ecclesiastical authorities (or, in cases for which the petitioner was personally present in the papal curia, to some prelates within the curia) to verify the details presented in the petition. If everything was found to be correct, it was the task of the person to whom the case was committed to declare officially that the supplicant was not guilty of murder, that he or she was not a monk, nun, or friar, or that the marriage of the supplicant(s) was void. The need for a closer examination was important, for it was impossible for the officials of the Penitentiary to know whether the supplicant was telling everything correctly or not. Since the validity of the decision made by the Penitentiary depended upon the accuracy of the details, these matters had to be examined by someone who had access to the places and persons mentioned in the petition. The commission is expressed at the end of the entry in a murder case with the following or similar words: *Committatur ordinario et, si vocatis vocandis sibi constiterit quod exponens consilio, auxilio, favore, adhortatione aut aliter quam ut premittitur in morte dicti N.N. culpabilis non fuerit et de aliis expositis, declaret ut petitur* (Let this be sent to the ordinary and if, having convened all who are to be convened, he concludes that the petitioner was not guilty through counsel, aid, approval, adhortation, or otherwise than is mentioned above in the death of the mentioned N.N. and concerning the rest which is explained, let him declare as is sought).

Together with the commission, we find below the text of the petition another detail referring to the process of deciding in the *de declaratoriis* cases: there appears the name of the legal expert, the *auditor,* to whom the case was referred for checking the correctness of the petition with respect to the regulations of canon law. Papal auditors were jurists, often doctors in both canon and Roman law, who specialized in these matters.[58] The referral to the competence of an auditor in the *de declaratoriis* cases is expressed at the end of each entry with the following or similar wording: *Videat eam dominus Anthonius de Grassis* (to be seen by Anthonius de Grassis—or in the

58. See G. Dolezalek, "'Audientia sacri palatii' and 'Auditor,'" *Lexikon des Mittelalters* I (1980), 1192–1196.

place of Antonius de Grassis the name of any of the papal auditors). The auditor had also to check the outgoing letters in those cases on which he had been consulted; for this reason, we often find his signature in the letters of grace issued by the Penitentiary.[59]

The *de declaratoriis* petitions had to be very detailed, for the supplicants had to present any and all details and events that could provide testimony in favor of their petition, so that they could obtain what they were asking for. Let us look more closely at the kinds of canonical "excuses" or mitigating circumstances which can often (if not always) be found in the Penitentiary petitions in each of the three different types of declarations.

Let us start with murder cases in which the supplicant wanted to have a declaration of his innocence. Canon law stipulated that if a person had participated (mere presence at the scene was sufficient to constitute participation) in an incident in which someone had died, he was considered guilty of the death, if there were no attenuating circumstances. Since priests guilty of murder were to be suspended or deposed from office, it was important for a priest to be able to show his innocence with the help of these mitigating circumstances, all of which had to be written down in the *narratio* of his petition.

The most often used canonical excuse for innocence of murder was acting in self-defense, for the regulations of canon law allowed the use of violence to defend oneself.[60] Consequently, the majority of the petitioners who turned to the Penitentiary in these matters tell in the *narratio* how their adversaries (i.e., the ones who had died) had first attacked them, and how they had been obliged to defend themselves against certain death. With this explanation always comes another point: the petitioner had to be able to show that he did not use excessive violence in defending himself, but only what was necessary. Thus, in most of the petitions, the supplicant explains how he hit his adversary only once. Further, because canon law did not allow clerics to carry any weapons (except a small knife that they needed

59. More about the role and signature of the auditors in the letters of grace, see Chapter 3.1.

60. The most important decretal is *Si furiosus,* Clem. 5.4.1, edited in CIC II, 1184.

every day, for example, in cutting bread), in the *narratio* it also had to be explained with which weapon the adversary was killed. In general, these three principal rules lead to a phrase which can be found in almost all of the standard murder cases in which the petitioner needed a declaration of innocence: *vim vi repellendo et se defendendo unico ictu cum parvo cultello percussit* (responding with violence to violence and defending himself, [he] hit [him only] once with a small knife). Of course, this phrase had to be preceded by an explanation as to why the petitioner found himself in a situation in which he had no other choice than to begin fighting with his adversary.

Being able to show that one had acted only in self-defense, using a minimum of violence and allowable weapons, was not the only way of getting rid of an unjust murder accusation. Sometimes Christians had to turn to the Penitentiary because they were accused of someone's death in which they really had had no part. Now and then we come across petitioners who claim that they had come by accident to a place—for example, someone's home—in which a person was killed. If they could show that they had not participated in any way in the events which had led to the killing of the murdered person, they could be freed from accusation and get a letter of declaration from the Penitentiary. In these cases, the Penitentiary often advised the commissioner of the case to verify that the supplicant did not help, advise, or approve the murder *(vocatis vocandis quod exponens in morte predicti defuncti non prestiterit auxilium, consilium vel favorem).*

In certain other cases, a petitioner who wanted a letter of declaration of his innocence claimed that he was guilty of someone's death, but that he did not kill this person intentionally, that it was a question of pure accident. As canon law does not consider persons who had not acted intentionally to be guilty, being able to show that the killing was purely accidental was also a way of getting a letter of declaration. An example of such an accident is, for instance, when a man riding a mad horse had run someone over.

Let us now take a closer look at the cases in which petitioners request an annulment of their marriage. As we learned earlier, canon law stipulated as to the validity of marriages and the different impediments that caused the invalidity of a marriage or prevented spouses from marrying. First of all, the spouses contracting a marriage had to do so of their own free will, and not by force. The spouses could not be relatives or related to each other in any way that could cause an impediment. If a couple could show that their marriage had taken place contrary to some of these regulations, it was considered void, and consequently the Penitentiary could declare the nullity of that marriage.

In order to get a declaration of nullity of a marriage, petitioners had to be able to show that their marriage had taken place in an irregular manner. Most often supplicants who turned to the Penitentiary in these matters explained that their parents (or the parents of one of the spouses) had obliged them to get married against their free will, i.e., the marriage was an arranged one into which they had been forced. Here the most frequently used phrase is *propter metum qui potest cadere in constantem virum* (because of a dread that would make a constant man to fall), a citation from a decretal of Pope Innocent III.[61] Again in these cases, the supplicant(s) had to be able to show details bearing witness to their story.

Another possible reason for a letter of declaration of an annulled marriage was if the spouses could show that both of them were, at the moment of contracting the marriage, too young to understand what was happening, and that they had been acting only according to the will of their parents. Here the petitioners could claim that their marriage was invalid due to a lack of understanding of the consequences. In certain very rare cases, the supplicant could also show that he had been misled into marrying a person whom he had not intended to marry. For example, one man had been married to the ugly and hairy sister of the beautiful girl he was supposed to marry. In these cases, the Penitentiary had no problem annulling the marriage, because the marriage had not intentionally been contracted in the manner which resulted.

Petitions for a declaration testifying that a person was not a professed monk, nun, or friar, even though he or she had lived for some time in a monastery, convent, or friary, were often a question of forced profession, which, according to the regulations of canon law,

61. X 1.40.4, edited in CIC II, 220.

was not profession at all, for profession—as with marriage—had to be taken by free will. Petitioners asked for declarations confirming that they were not professed monks or nuns because they—often for juridical reasons—needed an official document that demonstrated that they were not bound to monastic life. For this, the supplicants only had to be capable of showing that they had been put into a monastery by force by their parents or relatives who had wanted them to become a cleric.

Putting children into a monastery was quite common in the Middle Ages, because it was a good way to reduce the number of persons among whom the patrimony of a family was supposed to be divided after the death of the head of the family; because they were vowed to poverty, monks, nuns, and friars could not inherit property from their parents. We quite often find supplicants who, as young children, had been put into a monastery even though they had not wanted to go, but who had been too young or too afraid to oppose their parents. Petitioners here used as an excuse the same quote from Innocent III's decretal as in the marriage petitions above: *propter metum qui potest cadere in constantem virum;* in this instance, this quote is intended to attest that the petitioner had been put into a monastery against their will. This phrase played an important role in declaring the petitioner to be a lay(wo)man, for the regulations of canon law stipulated that no one could be taken into a monastery against his/her will, and that, if this happened, the monastic vows they might possibly have been obliged to take were not valid. Consequently, they could ask the Penitentiary for a declaration that they were not ecclesiastical persons, but laymen.[62]

The *de declaratoriis* category is one of the smaller groups of petitions. This is understandable, for the possible declaratory matters were few in number and concerned only rather complicated situations. Explaining the differences in provenance of the *de declaratoriis* petitions is, however, no easier than explaining the differences in other categories.

We can see from Table 4 that all the territories of Europe are rep-

62. For the first information on the subject, see L. Schmugge, P. Hersperger, B. Wiggenhauser, *Supplikenregister,* 175–182.

resented, which means that there was need for such graces throughout all christendom. Also, in this category we find that the four big territories (France, Germany, the Iberian Peninsula, as well as Italy) account for a majority of the cases; however, the dominance of Italian supplications is no more striking than it was with the marriage petitions. According to the data in Table 4, more *de declaratoriis* petitions came from the eastern parts of Europe than from the British Isles, whence only a slightly greater number of petitions were brought to the Penitentiary than from Scandinavia. Since most of the petitions from northern and eastern Europe concern violence, we might interpret this to mean that the inhabitants of those parts committed violent crimes more often than other kinds of violation against the regulations of canon law; however, we have to keep in mind that violence was such a severe crime that it was more likely for those who were accused of it, but not actually guilty of it, to travel to Rome in order to clear their reputation, than for persons who needed some other kind of letter of grace from the Penitentiary.

2.2.4. *De defectu natalium* and *de uberiori*—Creating a career for illegitimate children

Canon law stipulated very clearly that an illegitimate child could not become a priest. The Middle Ages was, however, a period full of illegitimate children. One reason for the existence of numerous children born out of wedlock was the celibacy regulations of canon law. The Catholic Church, since the Second Lateran Council, held in Rome in 1139, stated that men in the upper ecclesiastical orders, i.e., sub-deacons, deacons, and priests, were to observe celibacy.[63] In many regions it was, however, quite common for priests to keep concubines and to have children with them. Consequently, the children born out of this kind of relationship were automatically illegitimate. Many lay couples also could not be legally married due to some marriage impediment, but continued living together as though they were a wedded couple. Similarly, their children were considered illegitimate in the eyes of the church.

Illegitimate young men sometimes wanted to become priests. This

63. Canons 6 and 7, edited in COD, 198.

Table 4. Provenance of *de declaratoriis* Petitions in the Second Half of the Fifteenth Century

Territory	*Cases*	*Percent of total*
British Isles	103	2
Eastern Europe	364	8
France	930	22
Germany	846	20
Spain and Portugal	713	17
Italy	1,239	29
Northern Europe	89	2
Not known	26	1
Total	4,310	100

Source: ASV, *Penitenzieria Ap., Reg. Matrim. et Div.*, Vols. 5–41.

was especially common among the sons of priests, who could easily follow in their fathers' footsteps in an ecclesiastical career. Sometimes, the illegitimate sons of priests had already received the basic clerical education at home by observing their fathers in their duties. When it became clear that many young men, otherwise suitable and sufficiently learned, and willing to take clerical orders, could not do so because of the restrictive regulations of canon law, the church found itself in trouble, and so there developed a system of dispensation that enabled illegitimate but otherwise suitable candidates to enter an ecclesiastical career and to hold ecclesiastical office.

Pope Gregory IX (1227–1241) reserved to the authority of the popes the granting of such dispensations. Thereafter it was possible for illegitimate young men to gain a dispensation that permitted them to be promoted to holy orders, to be appointed to the higher ecclesiastical offices or ranks, as well as to hold a benefice with the cure of souls.[64] Popes later delegated this authority to the Penitentiary.

64. The regulations of canon law stipulated that the local bishops had the authority to grant dispensations from illegitimacy to persons who wanted to

Entrance into a monastery automatically functioned as a dispensation from illegitimacy; thus illegitimate children did not need dispensation to become a monk, friar, or nun, but if they wanted to proceed in their monastic careers and, for example, be elected to the post of abbot, prior, or abbess, they needed a dispensation.

The Penitentiary was authorized to grant three different kinds of dispensation concerning matters of illegitimacy. In the Penitentiary records, these entries can be found under two different titles: *de defectu natalium* and *de uberiori.* Dispensations of the *de defectu natalium* type permitted an illegitimate son to be ordained to the holy orders and to hold one benefice with the cure of souls. These cases were so-called simple *(in prima forma)* illegitimacy dispensations. The *de uberiori* petitions differed from the simple ones in that an illegitimate child requested, in addition to a dispensation from illegitimacy, a further permit to hold two—or sometimes even three—benefices at the same time, instead of just one. The third category of illegitimacy supplications contains the *ubi pater* petitions. In these cases the supplicant was the son of a priest, who wanted, besides the normal dispensation from illegitimacy, a permit to hold a benefice in the same church where his priest-father had held a benefice. The regulations of canon law, however, forbade that a priest's son could hold the same ecclesiastical benefice as his father had earlier held.[65] *Ubi pater* petitions are very rare among the Penitentiary records.

During the years 1449–1533, the Penitentiary handled as many as 37,916 petitions from illegitimate children, of which 37,400 were from male and only 516 from female petitioners. All female suppli-

---

be promoted to the minor orders and to hold a benefice without the cure of souls. On the other hand, those illegitimate children who entered a monastery did not have to gain a dispensation from their illegitimacy, even though they would be acting as confessor. Canon law considered entering a monastic order to be a dispensation in itself; but if illegitimate friars or monks wanted to proceed in their careers within their order, they had to be dispensed from their illegitimacy. On the ecclesiastical legislation concerning illegitimacy, see also P. Landau, "Das Weihehindernis der Illegitimität in der Geschichte des kanonischen Rechts," in L. Schmugge, ed., *Illegitimität im Spätmittelalter* (Schriften des Historischen Kollegs. Kolloquien 29; Munich, 1994), 41–53.

65. See L. Schmugge, P. Hersperger, B. Wiggenhauser, *Supplikenregister,* 187, with footnote 9.

cants were nuns who wanted to progress in their monastic careers.[66] The most common—more than 90 percent—are the simple *de defectu natalium* petitions; the *de uberiori* supplications constitute only 5 percent; only 2 percent of the records concern *ubi pater* dispensations.[67]

The documents concerning dispensation from illegitimacy always mention the name and home diocese of the petitioner. In addition, the supplicant always explains the social background of his (or, on rare occasion, her) parents—in other words, the reason for his illegitimacy. This extremely interesting piece of information offers scholars very useful knowledge about the social history of the Middle Ages with respect to illegitimate children and their (as well as their parents') backgrounds.

Clergymen constituted about 60 percent of the fathers. Most of these fathers were ordained to the holy orders (sub-deacons, deacons, or priests), and these illegitimate children were in most cases born of a relationship between a priest and his housekeeper. These priest fathers were not, as one might assume, only parish priests from the middle of nowhere, where nobody paid attention to whether they had families or not; a certain number of bishops are also mentioned as fathers of illegitimate children. This means that the breaking of the celibacy regulations was not a violation committed only by ordinary priests, but was a phenomenon that also involved the top of the ecclesiastical hierarchy. The lay fathers were normally, but not always, unmarried men. Unfortunately, the short entries do not allow us to study more closely the backgrounds of the lay fathers.

The majority (97 percent) of the mothers of these illegitimate children were unmarried women, as one might expect. Most of these women were probably concubines of priests, or for some other reason could not marry their partners. Only occasionally do the illegitimate petitioners mention that their mothers were married women, widows, or nuns.[68]

66. Concerning the Penitentiary and the petitions for dispensation from illegitimacy, see L. Schmugge, *Kirche, Kinder, Karrieren,* regarding the numbers of illegitimacy petitions, especially 145.

67. L. Schmugge, *Kirche, Kinder, Karrieren,* 161–162.

68. L. Schmugge, *Kirche, Kinder, Karrieren,* 181–188.

As seen in Table 1, illegitimacy petitions form the third largest group of petitions presented to the Penitentiary in the late Middle Ages, all together 16,124 *de defectu natalium* petitions as well as 6,461 *de uberiori* petitions. The data in Table 5 presents a wider picture of the situation, revealing as it does the provenance of all illegitimacy petitions handled by the Penitentiary during the years 1449–1533. This material was previously studied by Ludwig Schmugge.[69] As Schmugge has explained the same numbers in greater detail in his profound study, we will not repeat the results here minutely, but will limit ourselves to explaining the numbers more generally. Looking at the numbers given in Table 5, we see that illegitimate birth was especially an issue in Germany. In Germany, bastards were quite familiar within the nobility, and concubinage, despite canon law rules, was widespread among the clergy. Again, the social situation in northern and eastern Europe was quite different, where such attitudes towards extramarital relations were not common.

The extremely numerous German petitioners were followed by petitions from Spain and Portugal and France. These territories are also well represented in other petition categories. In fourth place we suddenly find Ireland (most of the more than 4,000 supplications listed under "British Isles" come from Ireland). As the petitions from Ireland or Great Britain are not so numerous in other petition categories, we can interpret this as meaning that illegitimacy was widespread in Ireland.[70] The scarcity of Italian petitioners in comparison with the other categories seems to indicate that illegitimacy was not an issue in Italy. [71]

2.2.5. *De promotis et promovendis*—Overruling ordination and promotion regulations

The category *de promotis et promovendis* contains various types of petitions concerning ordinations and promotions in ecclesiastical or-

69. L. Schmugge, *Kirche, Kinder, Karrieren.*

70. See M. Haren, "Social Structures of the Irish Church: A New Source in Papal Penitentiary Dispensations for Illegitimacy," in L. Schmugge, ed., *Illegitimität im Spätmittelalter,* 207–226.

71. More precisely on the provenance of illegitimacy petitions, see L. Schmugge, *Kirche, Kinder, Karrieren,* 152–154, 165–170.

Table 5. Provenance of Illegitimacy Petitions, 1449–1533

Territory	*Cases*	*Percent of total*
British Isles	4,054	11
Eastern Europe	604	2
France	6,627	17
Germany	13,648	36
Spain and Portugal	8,987	24
Italy	3,590	9
Northern Europe	406	1
Total	37,916	100

Source: ASV, *Penitenzieria Ap., Reg. Matrim. et Div.*, Vols. 3–84.

ders. As we have already learned from the illegitimacy cases, the medieval church was very severe in its regulations concerning the suitability of young men for ecclesiastical careers. Canon law regulated very strictly who could become a priest and who could act in an ecclesial office; it further stipulated how, when, and by whom a person could be ordained.

Along with the regulations concerning illegitimacy, canon law stipulated in the fifteenth century that a person who wanted to be promoted in an ecclesiastical career had to be old enough. For each ecclesiastical office there existed a minimum age limit—25 years old for priesthood, for example. According to the Catholic Church, minors suffered from a defect of age (*defectus aetatis*) and were not allowed to be promoted.[72]

72. Other age limitations were: 18 years for subdeacons, 20 for deacons, and 30 for bishops. Boys over seven years were allowed to be tonsured; for the minor orders the age limit was 14. For the canon law regulations see X 1.14.3–4; Clem. 1.6.3, edited in CIC II, 126–127, 1140; Canon 3 of the Third Lateran Council is edited in COD, 188–189.

A candidate for an ecclesiastical career was also supposed to be bodily perfect. This did not mean that he had to be good-looking and very handsome, but that he should not have any bodily defect that would impede him in altar service and celebrating the Mass. Those candidates who suffered from certain kinds of physical defects *(defectus corporis)* were considered irregular and could not be ordained. Most candidates who were considered irregular because of a corporal defect were persons who, for example, could not see well, or suffered from a physical disability such as missing fingers (as a consequence of injury).

Candidates for priesthood also had to be capable of carrying out their priestly duties; therefore, they had to be competent to read and understand Latin. They also had to have sufficient ecclesiastical education and knowledge of canon law to be able to act as confessors. Having such knowledge was very important, and the priest candidates were always examined before ordination. Persons who did not meet these requirements could not be ordained, because of a defect of knowledge *(defectus scientiae)*.

Canon law also regulated how, when, how quickly, and by whom a person could be ordained. For example, a candidate could not be promoted to two orders at the same time; also, ordinations were supposed to take place on certain days of the ecclesiastical year. There were four general ordination days (Saturdays) in a year, the so-called *sabbatum quattuor temporum*.[73] Furthermore, a candidate could not be ordained by any bishop other than that of his home diocese. In addition, according to legal theory, nobody could be ordained to priesthood without a "title" *(titulus)*—that is, without sufficient material funds, i.e., a benefice.

All of these regulations could, however, be overruled by a papal dispensation. The Penitentiary was one of the papal offices with the authority to grant dispensations to future clerics who, in order to be ordained, had to overcome such impediments. It also could absolve

73. On ordination see R. E. Reynolds, "Ordination, clerical," in *Dictionary of the Middle Ages*, vol. 9 (1987), 263–269, for the times of ordination, decretal X 1.11.3, 8, 16, edited in CIC II, 118–120, 124.

and dispense persons who had been ordained despite the existence of one of the above-mentioned impediments.

In roughly half of the petitions concerning promotions that were handled by the Penitentiary, the petitioner was asking for a dispensation beforehand; the other half were cases in which the supplicant had already been promoted against the regulations of canon law, and thus needed both absolution and dispensation. The most common of the case types were graces concerning defect of age; petitions regarding bodily defects and those to be ordained by someone other than one's own bishop were also quite common. Dispensations because of defect of knowledge, on the other hand, were extremely rare and concern only cases in which someone had cheated on the examination before ordination.

The petitions directed to the Penitentiary in these matters always contain the basic information concerning the petitioner and his case: name and home diocese of the supplicant, followed by the details of his case. If the petitioner was asking for a dispensation in advance, he would explain what his defect was and ask for dispensation; if he had already been promoted, he would again explain his defect, but would also inform the Penitentiary that he had illegally been promoted, and that because of this he had been excommunicated. If he had continued acting in his office without dispensation, this also had to be mentioned. Quite often the Penitentiary granted dispensation and absolution as requested by the petitioners; sometimes, however, the officials of the Penitentiary were quite strict with those supplicants who had been promoted illegally, and suspended them from their offices for one or two months.

The category *de promotis et promovendis* is one of the smaller categories of petitions handled by the Penitentiary, for the dispensable/absolvable matters were relatively few and concerned only those persons who wanted to be promoted to clerical orders.

If we examine the numbers presented in Table 6, we notice that petitions from the Italian Peninsula form a large majority compared with the other territories—just as with the marriage petitions. It would seem, then, that it was impossible for a candidate to be ordained in Italy if he was affected by some impediment. The next

Table 6. Provenance of Promotion Petitions in the Second Half of the Fifteenth Century

Territory	*Cases*	*Percent of total*
British Isles	572	6
Eastern Europe	232	3
France	1,597	18
Germany	1,129	13
Spain and Portugal	1,517	17
Italy	3,843	43
Northern Europe	16	0
Not known	71	1
Total	8,977	100

Source: ASV, *Penitenzieria Ap., Reg. Matrim. et Div.*, Vols. 5–41.

three territories—France, Germany, and Spain and Portugal—come far behind; however, they still form quite large groups of petitions. These territories are followed only by the British Isles as well as by eastern and northern Europe, from which there are very few petitions in each category.

It is possible to interpret these results as suggesting that in the eastern and northern parts of Europe the canon law regulations concerning ordinations were not so well established as in the central areas of the Latin West. We should not, however, forget that the local bishops in these remote areas often had great authority to grant similar dispensations to their diocesan clergy, which obviously diminished the need to turn to the Penitentiary.

2.2.6. *De confessionalibus*—How to get a private confessor

Confession is one of the seven sacraments of the Catholic Church. Confessing was very important, for the Church did not allow Christians to attend the Eucharist if they had not confessed. The Fourth Lateran Council, held in Rome in 1215, ordered in its constitution 21 that all Christians—men and women, laypersons and clerics—were obliged to confess their sins at least once a year to their local parish priest (*sacerdos proprius,* as the canon says).[74] The yearly confession normally took place during Lent, because the most important Eucharist of the ecclesiastical year was celebrated during Easter.

If a Christian could not or did not want to confess to the local parish priest, the papal curia offered another possibility in the form of a so-called confession letter, which allowed the bearer of the letter to choose an *idoneus* confessor and to confess his/her sins to this priest rather than to the parish priest. It did not, however, allow the Christians to ignore their yearly obligation to confess their sins. Confession letters did not have anything to do with the act of confession as sacrament or with the sins confessed; they simply allowed the holders to choose a confessor other than their parish priest. Thus these letters do not contain anything that should remain under the seal of confession.

The reasons for which Christians wanted to confess to some other priest than their ordinary parish confessor do not appear in the Penitentiary documents; there are, however, several explanations why someone might consider it important to possess such a document. The first possible reason was the rise of the mendicant orders. The spreading of Dominicans and Franciscans all over christendom meant that Christians began to have possibilities other than to confess to their parish priest. In fact, the competition of the mendicants with the regular clergy within the field of the cure of souls became a problem for the secular clergy. At the same time many people, most often merchants and administrative officials, regularly had to travel between several different places; it may have happened that these persons found themselves needing to confess but far from their own parish priest.

For these reasons, and probably also for other, more personal motives, noblemen, town dwellers, and, increasingly, simple lay people as well, began to ask the pope for the privilege of having a private confessor of their own. The pope could grant the most general and

74. Canon *Omnis utriusque sexus,* edited in COD, 245.

authoritative grant, and thus could give dispensation from this prescription in the form of confession letter that allowed a Christian to confess to a private confessor—usually a Franciscan, Dominican, or Augustinian friar.

As petitions for confession letters became more and more frequent, the pope delegated his authority to grant them to the Cardinal Penitentiary and to the office of the Penitentiary, which had the faculty to grant some different kinds of confession letters. The simplest one, the *littera confessionalia in forma minori,* entitled its bearer to choose a suitable private confessor instead of turning to his parish priest. These letters were granted either for the lifetime of the holder or for a certain period, for example, for five years. Sometimes the grace was combined with an indulgence *in mortis articulo*—"in the moment of death."

Besides these simple confession letters, the Penitentiary could also grant confession letters which allowed the confessor to absolve the person from heavier sins than priests normally were authorized to do. These letters were called *littera confessionalia in forma maiori.*

In addition to these standard confession letters—typically registered under the title *de confessionalibus*—there was a third and still more powerful form of confession letter, known as a plenary indulgence *(absolutio plenaria).* The granting of these letters was not within the powers of the Penitentiary.

Instead, the Penitentiary could grant confessors special licenses to absolve their parishioners from more severe violations. With this kind of license (a so-called *sententia generalis* license), for example, an ordinary priest could release his parishioners from a special excommunication, normally reserved to the papal authority. In some register volumes there is a special category for these petitions with the title *de sententiis generalibus.* Similar kinds of special licenses were also granted in other forms, for example, *in forma "Cupientes," in forma "Fervens,"* and *in forma "Si inveneris."* All of the different names refer to papal regulations beginning with these words. With the authority granted in these letters, a confessor could, for example, absolve a priest who had violated canon law by having a concubine or by assaulting someone. As with the petitions for special licenses in general sentences, these special licenses also sometimes appear under a special title which is identical to the name of the papal letter, i.e., *de confessionalibus in forma "Cupientes."*

The entries concerning confessional letters in the Penitentiary records are extremely short, consisting of only one or two lines. The entries for the most part contain only the name and home diocese of the supplicant, the kind of letter of confession, when the Penitentiary had granted it, and who made the decision.

Because confession letters were of importance for the petitioner only, their chances of survival were rather low. After the death of the person in whose favor the document had been issued, these documents were simply thrown away, for they were of no further use.

Popes delegated similar authority in granting confessional letters to other papal offices as well, not to the Penitentiary alone. Among the mass of medieval registers kept in the Vatican Secret Archives are copies of numerous petitions to choose a private confessor, made to the Apostolic Chancery.[75] Such petitions were submitted from all over christendom, but with special intensity from France, as the following statistics for the pontificates of Calixtus III through Innocent VIII neatly show.

Confession letters were also quite commonly requested graces among the entries in the Penitentiary registers. In Table 7, which describes the field of sin and confession—that is, the request for a personal confessor, and privileges for secular as well as regular clerics with *cura animarum*—we see quite a different picture in the provenance of the petitions than we are used to seeing in the other supplication categories. Suddenly the French are the most eager to have a personal confessor rather than rely on their local parish priests. This kind of result must refer to the fact that religious individualism was much more deeply rooted in France than elsewhere, for

75. For the German-speaking regions, confession letters requested through the Penitentiary have been published in the RPG, and those requested through the Apostolic Chancery have been published in the Repertorium Germanicum. Concerning the comparison between the petitions made both to the Penitentiary and to the Apostolic Chancery during the pontificate of Pius II, see L. Schmugge, P. Hersperger, B. Wiggenhauser, *Supplikenregister,* 208–217.

Table 7. Provenance of Confession Letter Petitions in the Second Half of the Fifteenth Century

Territory	*Cases*	*Percent of total*
British Isles	665	5
Eastern Europe	678	5
France	7,137	52
Germany	2,866	21
Spain and Portugal	841	6
Italy	1,257	9
Northern Europe	111	1
Not known	107	1
Total	13,662	100

Source: ASV, *Penitenzieria Ap., Reg. Matrim. et Div.*, Vols. 5–41.

more than half of all petitions have French provenance. Only the German petitioners can compete with the French in number of supplications, but they remain far behind, with a share of 21 percent. In all other nations, confessional privileges do not play a dominant role. The fairytale of the "guilt-ridden society" of the later Middle Ages should be reconsidered in view of the above numbers.[76]

76. T. N. Tentler, *Sin and Confession on the Eve of the Reformation* (Princeton, N.J., 1977); J. Delumeau, *L'aveu et le pardon: Les difficultés de la confession (XIIIe–XVIIIe siècles)* (Paris, 1990). For a critic of this, see P. Biller, "Confession in the Middle Ages: Introduction," in P. Biller and A. J. Minnis, eds., *Handling Sin: Confession in the Middle Ages* (York Studies in Medieval Theology II; York, 1998), 23–31.

3

How the Decisions of the Penitentiary Were Made

3.1. The *iter* of the Petition

The process of petitioning the Penitentiary began back home when someone who had violated the regulations of canon law turned to his/her confessor and confessed his/her sins. If the violation committed was so severe that the confessor could not absolve the sinner, he would advise the person in question to turn to the local bishop over the issue. Bishops had greater authority than parish priests, and in many cases the local bishop could absolve the sinner. There were, however, also crimes so severe that they were outside even the powers of the bishops. If our sinner had violated ecclesiastical law in such a way that the handling of the case was reserved to the papal authority, the bishop had no choice but to send the sinner (not necessarily in person, but only his issue) to the papal curia.

The second stage of the petition process was the carrying of the case before the papal curia. There were several ways by which supplicants could get their petitions to the curia. The first of these was personal travel to Rome, where they would take care of their own cases. This possibility was not very often used—mainly for cases in which the petitioner, usually a cleric, had done violence to another cleric and needed to be absolved quickly.[1] The second possibility was to have one's petition sent to the curia by the representatives of the local bishop, who traveled between the episcopal seat and the papal curia. This practice was especially often used by petitioners from larger dioceses or dioceses situated quite near to the papal curia, for the official connections in these cases were frequent, and representatives traveled back and forth regularly. The third way to get one's petition to the papal curia was to use as carriers friends or relatives leaving for pilgrimage to Rome, who at the same time could take care of the presenting of the petition.

Quite often it can be seen that the local bishop was the prime mover in sending petitions to the papal curia. Sometimes, however, supplicants turned directly to the Penitentiary without consulting the local bishop. This happened especially when the petitioner was in a hurry to clear his conscience, or if he was afraid of the reaction of the bishop and wanted to have a document from the papal curia in his defense against the local ecclesiastical authorities.

When the issue arrived in the papal curia in one or another of these ways, it was normally entrusted to a special Penitentiary proctor, who specialized in the presentation of petitions to the office and was paid to take care of the supplication process. The proctors knew how to proceed with the petition process and also wrote the supplication according to the curial rules for the composition of petitions. This was actually one of the most important parts of the petition process, for the right wording in the supplication helped the petitioner to gain what he or she wanted. If the phraseology or details were not correct, the letter of grace was void; thus the result of the petition process largely depended on the proctor.[2]

Once the supplication was written down (on paper) the proctor took it to the officials of the Penitentiary, who began handling the

1. This happened because canon 15 of the Second Lateran Council *(Si quis suadente diabolo)* (mentioned earlier) ordered that all Christians who had assaulted a cleric were obliged to come before the pope and personally ask for pardon and absolution.

2. As the Penitentiary registers contain only approved petitions, we cannot know whether some of the supplicants were turned down with their petitions, or why that might have happened.

case. The two officials to whom the petition was handed over were called *auditores.* They were well-trained jurists whose task it was to examine the supplication from a formal point of view: whether it was composed in the correct manner, and whether the issue concerned was one with which the office of the Penitentiary had the power to deal. If the petition was correct, it was taken to the head of the office, the Cardinal Penitentiary *(poenitentiarius maior),* or—in the absence of the cardinal, or in more routine cases—to his deputy, called *regens,* for the approval of the petition with their signature.[3] Before taking the petition to the approver, the *auditores* made a short summary of the contents of the petition, which they wrote in the upper left-hand corner of the original supplication. This facilitated and sped up the approval, because the approver had to read only the summary instead of the text of the whole petition. In a certain way, the *auditores* thus had a great responsibility in the petition project, for they were the gatekeepers for getting a case approved.

After the petition had been approved and signed, the original supplication was brought back to the proctor, who handed it over to a person called the *distributor,* who in his turn brought it to the *corrector* of the office. The duty of the *corrector* was to compose a draft for the letter of grace on the basis of all the necessary details mentioned in the petition. When the draft was ready, the *distributor* took it to one of the scribes of the office, whose task was then to write the letter of grace granted by the Penitentiary on the basis of the draft. When the scribe had finished composing the letter of grace, it was taken to a person called the *datarius* for the dating of the letter. After that, the letter was handed back to the *distributor,* who, together with a man called the *computator,* put the tax mark of the office in the lower left corner of the letter.

After all this, the letter of grace was handed back to the proctor, who took it, together with the original supplication, back to the

3. This was the normal practice in the more common cases, such as marriage, illegitimacy, promotion, and confession letters; but in the more difficult declaratory cases, requiring the signature of the Cardinal Penitentiary or the regent, the process was a bit different. These cases (which were often quite ambiguous) were committed to trained jurists *(auditores)* who checked again that all details being approved were canonically correct.

person who had approved the petition with his signature (i.e., the Cardinal Penitentiary or the regent, and in some declaratory cases the *auditor* to whom the case had been referred for further checking). The approver then checked that the contents of the letter corresponded to the decision he had made, and that the letter had been composed in a correct manner. If the letter was well written and there was nothing to correct, the *corrector* wrote a note in the upper margin of the letter *(Videat eam N.N.*[4] */ dominus regens*[5] */ dominus auditor*[6]*)*,and the approver wrote in the left margin at the level of the fifth line of the letter of grace a note stating that he had checked the letter *(Visa per me . . .)*, and at the same level in the right margin he wrote his name and title. This practice guaranteed that the letter had been checked and found correct. The checking of the letter in this quite complicated way was not always necessary; in the most routine cases it was enough for the *corrector* to check the letter and write in the left margin, as a sign of the checking, *Bene* (well). In these cases the letters were not carried to the approver.

At this stage of the *iter* of the petition, the proctor had in his hands both the original petition and the letter of grace issued in the name of the Cardinal Penitentiary. Now he had to bring the letter to the *sigillator* who sealed it with the seal of the Penitentiary, thus guaranteeing the authenticity of the letter of grace. Before the whole process of making supplication was over, the proctor had to make sure that the case was recorded into the registers of the Penitentiary on the basis of the text in the original supplication. It is also possible that the original petitions were at this point left at the Penitentiary, but scholars have not been able to prove this, as there is not enough evidence left. Once the registration was done and the proctor had paid the taxes for the preparation of the letter, the supplication process was complete, and the proctor could leave the office with the letter of grace and hand it over or send it back to the petitioner or his representative.

4. This form was used when the approver was the Cardinal Penitentiary. In those cases, his name was written in the place of *N.N.*

5. This form was used when the approver was the regent.

6. This form was used when the approver was the *auditor.*

In certain rather rare cases, the composing of the letter of grace was not necessary, and thus the proctor did not have to take care of all of these different phases of the *iter* of the process in the Penitentiary. When was this possible? In certain cases, the Penitentiary could grant the petitioner a special grace that the original petition would work as testimony of the granted grace. In these cases it was thus enough that the petitioner conserve the original petition (after the case had been copied into the registers of the Penitentiary) with the signature of approval made by the officials of the Penitentiary. Because the original petition was valid with just the signature, such documents are called *sola signatura* petitions.[7]

The *iter* of the case did not end when the letter of grace was ready. The letter had to be carried back home and presented to the local bishop (or someone else to whom the issue was committed) as evidence that the supplicant had had his or her case handled and approved at the papal curia. It guaranteed that the person in question had received the papal grace (absolution, dispensation, special license, or a letter of declaration) and thus had fulfilled his or her obligations at the curia. Before the matter was resolved finally, the commissioner of the letter of grace checked that the matter and the details in the letter were correct; only then was the grace granted by the Penitentiary valid; if the details were found to be false, the grace was void. At the final stage, the scribes of the local bishop (or whoever the commissioner was), of the episcopal court, or the local notaries copied of the letter of grace into their registers, which would serve as testimony that the grace had been found correct.

At this point it might be good to remind the reader that not all letters issued by the Penitentiary were copied to the local ecclesiastical or notarial registers. There were many such documents which were of interest only to the holder of the document—such as the licenses for choosing one's confessor—and which were never copied by the local authorities. In practice, such documents as might later

7. Concerning this type of supplication see T. Frenz, *Papsturkunden des Mittelalters und der Neuzeit* (Historische Grundwissenschaften in Einzeldastellung 2; Stuttgart, 1986), 27–28; B. Katterbach, "Päpstliche Suppliken mit der Klausel der sola signatura," *Römische Quartalschrift* 31 (1924), 185–196.

have some kind of juridical (such as marriage dispensations for proving that children born from that marriage were legal) or ecclesiastical (testifying that a person with some sort of defect had been dispensed and thus could legally be ordained and practice in his office) effect were usually registered. The practice of registering documents also varied a great deal according to local practices in each diocese and territory; for example, in Italy, notarial activity was much more advanced and commonplace than in Germany or Scandinavia.

3.2. Grants and Signatures

The authority of the Penitentiary was three-fold: the ordinary faculty of the Penitentiary, the general mandates from the pope to the office, and special mandates related to certain more complicated matters, which the pope gave to the *penitentiarius maior.*

The basic way to express the approval of the supplication by the *penitentiarius maior* was with the word *Fiat.* The Cardinal Penitentiary, however, did not approve cases with just the word *Fiat,* but used more complicated formulas, which varied according to the type of the faculty he used when making the decision. *Fiat in forma* is a common wording, which means that the grace was granted on the basis of the ordinary faculty of the Penitentiary by the *penitentiarius maior* or the officials of the Penitentiary according to the formularies in use.[8] This wording refers to the typical cases brought to the Penitentiary, which were resolved in a customary way. In some cases this wording, however, meant that the Penitentiary did not grant to the supplicant all that he or she was asking for (for example, if the petitioner wanted something the regulations of canon law normally did not allow—if, for example, a priest asked to return to altar service after having killed someone), but limited the grace only to the "norm-decision" according to the formulary in use (thus, in our example, denying him the right to serve at the altar).

8. ". . . *in forma ea postulantibus, que de iure ordinarii locorum circa solutiones et dispensationes aut declarationes in forma iuris per omnia facere possunt, quia pontifices faciunt maiorem penitentiarium in Ro*[*mana*] *cu*[*ria*] *parem in facultatibus ordinariis locorum.*" BAV, Vat. lat. 3883, fol. 38r, edited in E. Göller, *Pönitentiarie* II/2, 101.

Another common wording, *Fiat de speciali,* indicates that the grace concerned issues which were reserved to the pope and were delegated to the officials of the Penitentiary or to the *penitentiarius maior* by a special papal mandate and privilege.[9] *Fiat de expresso* in its turn meant that the *penitentiarius maior* had received the competence to deal with the issue directly from the pope, *vivae vocis oraculo,* because the case was outside the ordinary faculty of the Penitentiary.[10]

Other wordings which combine forms of the above-mentioned grants also appear in the Penitentiary registers. For example, *Fiat de expresso* does not normally appear as such unless combined with *Fiat de speciali,* so that the wording used is *Fiat de speciali et expresso.* The wording *Fiat ut infra* also appears quite often; it is actually not a formula of approval, but indicates only that the matter was further delegated to the authority of other persons[11] (expressed *infra*—below the text of the petition), and that the *fiat* was granted later according to their decision.[12] The wording *Fiat ut petitur,* which does not refer to the decision of the Penitentiary but to the decision of the pope, can also be seen in the Penitentiary registers when the pope in person has signed petitions that are then directed to the Penitentiary for expedition of the papal letter.[13]

In those cases where the *penitentiarius maior* made the decision, the formula of approval was followed by the first letter, or the first

9. "*Fiat de speciali ea signantur, que specialiter pape vel communiter reservantur, et super quibus specialem mandatum habet offitium penitentiarie vel persona maioris penitentiarii commissionem specialem ex indulto vel privilegio.*" BAV, Vat. lat. 3883, fol. 38r, edited in E. Göller, *Pönitentiarie* II/2, 101.

10. "*De expresso ea signantur, que papa vive vocis expresso oraculo offitio vel persone maioris penitentiarii verbo vel rescripto concesserit.*" BAV, Vat. lat. 3883, fol. 38r, edited in E. Göller, *Pönitentiarie* II/2, 101.

11. The case was normally first given to one of the auditors, who checked the supplication from the point of view of the regulations of canon law; then the case was committed further to the local authorities, or to someone present in the curia, for giving the final judgment in the case. This formula was mostly used in *de declaratoriis* cases. See for example RPG IV, n. 1745–1845.

12. Concerning the different forms of approving, see also E. Göller, *Pönitentiarie* II/1, 27–28, and F. Tamburini, "Note diplomatiche intorno a suppliche e lettere di Penitenzieria (sec. XIV–XV)," *Archivum Historiae Pontificiae* 11 (1973), 149–208, especially 153.

13. RPG IV, n. 1596.

few letters, of his Christian name and his cardinal's title: *Fiat in forma, Phi*[*lippus*] *S*[*ancti*] *Laurentii in Lucina.*[14] When the regent signed the grants, he used the first letters of his Christian name followed by his ecclesiastical title after the formula of approval: *Fiat de speciali, Jul*[*ianus*], *episcopus Brictonoriensis, Regens.*[15] In certain cases the approval of the pope himself appears in the registers of the Penitentiary; for example, Pius II used to sign in certain of the more serious or complicated cases. In such cases, the formula of approval was the normal papal formula, i.e., *Fiat (ut petitur),* followed by the first letter of the Christian name of the pope—for example, Pius II signed petitions with *E,* which came from his secular name *E*nea Silvio Piccolomini.[16]

3.3. Commissions and Commissioners

Sometimes, especially in the *de declaratoriis* cases and in cases where the supplicant was not personally present in the curia, the details of the petition could not be clear enough for the Penitentiary, and so the office could not make a final judgment in the case (and was unable to check what was called the *veritas precum* or *veritas narrationis*—the truth of the facts reported to the Penitentiary). In these cases, the office delegated *(committatur)* the issue to a cleric *in partibus* who had to examine the case and to find out that all details were correct. Only after that would the grace be valid.

14. Philippus Calandrini was the *penitentiarius maior* during the years 1458–1476 and was the cardinal of the church of Sancti Laurentii in Lucina. E. Göller, *Pönitentiarie* II/1, 9–10.

15. Julianus de Maffeis de Vulterris, bishop of Bertinoro, was the regent of the Penitentiary during the years 1477–1505. E. Göller, *Pönitentiarie* II/1, 58; Hierarchia Catholica II, 124. Concerning the practice, see F. Tamburini, "Note diplomatiche," 153.

16. Pius II was one of the popes who quite often used his right to sign the Penitentiary supplications. Concerning signatures by the pope during the pontificate of Pius II, see K. Salonen, "The Decisions of Pope Pius II in the Penitentiary Registers," in A. Meyer, C. Rendtel, and M. Wittmer-Busch, eds., *Päpste, Pilger, Pönitentiarie: Festschrift für Ludwig Schmugge zum 65. Geburtstag* (Tübingen, 2004), 515–530. Concerning the initials of each pope, see for example: *Sussidi per la consultazione dell'Archivio Vaticano* II (Collectanea Archivi Vaticani 17. A cura di G. Gualdo; Città del Vaticano, 1989), 380–390 (Appendix II).

It was the task of the person to whom the issue was referred to check that everything was correct in the letter of the Penitentiary and in the grant that had been given. This person was the most important person in the whole supplication process, for it was he who ultimately would decide whether the grace granted to the supplicant was valid or not. If he found, when examining the case, that there was something which in his opinion was not correct, he had the authority to declare that the grace was not valid. The commissioner was also the person to whom the letter from the Penitentiary was addressed.

There were many persons to whom the cases handled by the Penitentiary could be referred: a bishop or prelate who was present in the curia; the bishop of the supplicant's diocese or his vicar *in spiritualibus;* the *penitentiarii minores;* certain local or curial officials or their deputies; abbots or other higher prelates; or local parish priests. The regulations of the Penitentiary define these matters quite strictly.[17]

Issues were most commonly referred to the *ordinarius,* the local bishop of the diocese in question, his vicar *in spiritualibus,* or the archdeacon who took care of juridical matters in the diocese. The name of this person does not appear in the entry in the Penitentiary registers, but instead the phrase *Committatur ordinario* is used. Referring the case to the local authorities was the normal way of proceeding when the supplicant was not present in the Roman curia and it was therefore impossible to verify the issue in the Penitentiary. If the supplicant was present in the curia, the matter could be referred to one of the *penitentiarii minores* in St. Peter's Church[18] or to one of the bishops present in the curia at the time the supplication was made.[19]

17. Göller gives a detailed list of officials to whom each type of case should be committed. E. Göller, *Pönitentiarie* I/2, 70–77.

18. For example ASV, *Penitenzieria Ap., Reg. Matrim. et Div.,* vol. 26, fol. 105r: *"Et committatur fratri Paulo de Roma domini nostri pape penitentiario cum dictus exponens ordinarium suum et locum delicti accedere non sit ausus. Fiat Jul."* In this case it gives the reason for which the issue was committed to the minor penitentiary, i.e., that the supplicant did not have safe access to his ordinary or to the place of the crime, where, according to canon law, he should do the public penance.

19. ASV, *Penitenzieria Ap., Reg. Matrim. et Div.,* vol. 48, fol. [561r–]562r: *"Et commictatur episcopo Milopotamensi ad presens in Romana Curia residenti."*

Commissions can be seen especially clearly in the entries of *de declaratoriis* supplications, where they are almost always explicitly written down. In declaratory cases it was important to check that the details in the *narratio* were correct, because these letters dealt with the question of whether the supplicant was or was not guilty of some crime of which he had been accused; and so, before the Penitentiary could declare that the supplicant was not guilty, it had to make sure that the details given by the supplicant were true.

Explicit commissions were used not only in *de declaratoriis* cases, but often also in cases in which the supplicant wanted to become a priest despite some corporal defect *(defectus corporis)*.[20]

3.4. Fees

Selling graces would have been impossible for the medieval Church, because this was considered simony. On the other hand, the Penitentiary did not grant graces for free (except for the poor); Christians who turned to its authority had to be ready to pay a certain fee for the services of the office. But how expensive was it for a petitioner to get a dispensation, absolution, license, or declaratory letter from the Penitentiary? The regulations of the Penitentiary, together with special tax lists, indicate how much petitioners had to pay for a letter of grace granted by the Penitentiary. Payments to the Penitentiary for a letter of absolution or dispensation do not mean that the office was selling graces, which would have been one kind of simony. The fees were officially explained by the fact that supplicants had to pay for the costs of preparing the letter, i.e., for the parchment, ink, and the material of the seal, as well as for the work of the scribes and other officials of the Penitentiary who participated in the preparation of the letter. In general, preparing a papal letter was not cheap, for—as we have seen—many persons were involved in the supplication process, and the curia was an expensive institution to maintain.[21]

20. See for example RPG IV, n. 3114.

21. Several tax lists of the Penitentiary have been preserved, and from

In principle, the Catholic Church could not serve only those who had money; absolution could not depend on money, since all Christians were equal before God. Therefore, in certain cases it was possible to have one's issue handled in the curia for free, or at least at a lower cost than normal. Turning to the Penitentiary was in any case a cheaper choice than using the other papal offices. The tax lists of the curia demonstrate that the Penitentiary granted absolutions, dispensations, and special licenses at a lower cost than other offices. Sometimes the Penitentiary even granted graces for free, as can clearly be seen in certain entries in the Penitentiary registers, in which is recorded, at the place where normally would appear the sum of fee the petitioner had had to pay, *Gratis pro Deo*[22] (for free in God's name), or *Gratis pro paupere [presente]*[23] (for free for a pauper [present in curia]).

From the lower costs of preparation of a letter of grace (in comparison with the fees of the other papal offices), and from the reduction or removal of payments, it has been concluded that the Penitentiary was the papal office intended for poor supplicants. This is not, howev-

---

them we can see how much a grace cost. We will not go into details on this question because it is not essential to this study, and because good research has already been done concerning the taxes. For example, Göller has published many tax lists and dedicated a great part of his book to taxes. E. Göller, *Pönitentiarie* II/1–2. Two more recent studies concerning the taxes of the Penitentiary have been written by W. P. Müller, "Die Gebühren der päpstlichen Pönitentiarie (1338–1569)," *Quellen und Forschungen aus italienischen Archiven und Bibliotheken* 78 (1998), 189–261, and "The Price of Papal Pardon—New Fifteenth-Century Evidence," in A. Meyer, C. Rendtel, and M. Wittmer-Busch, eds., *Päpste, Pilger, Pönitentiarie,* 457–481. Concerning the fees of the Penitentiary in general, see L. Schmugge, P. Hersperger, B. Wiggenhauser, *Supplikenregister,* 51–54.

22. ASV, *Penitenzieria Ap., Reg. Matrim. et Div.,* vol. 57, fol. 350r.

23. ASV, *Penitenzieria Ap., Reg. Matrim. et Div.,* vol. 72, fol. 369v–[370r]. It must, however, be said, that poverty is quite a relative term. A person with a lot of property could be considered poor if he, at the moment of making the supplication in the curia, did not have much money. In the Penitentiary, as well as in the papal Chancery, it was possible to get the graces for free if the person took an oath of poverty. "*. . . si etiam pauperes, minus capitur, sed non admittitur iuramentum paupertatis quoad obtinendum compositionem gratis.*" L. Celier, *Les Dataires du XVe siècle et les origines de la daterie apostolique* (Bibliothèque de l'Ecole française d'Athens et de Rome 103; Paris, 1910), 153.

er, the whole truth. According to Tamburini, the practice of reducing prices was used not only when the supplicant was very poor, but also when the officials of the Penitentiary wanted to do a favor for someone who was close to the personnel of the office or the pope.[24] However, as can clearly be seen from the tax lists, the Penitentiary was not as expensive as the other papal offices.[25] It is also known that the Penitentiary was not only cheaper than the papal Chancery, but also much quicker when it came to the composing of a letter of grace.[26] It was important that the petitioners receive the grants quickly, because it was not the intention of the Catholic Church to let excommunicated persons wait a long time before they could be absolved.

A special situation concerning the cost of a grace arose when the case was supposed to be composed with another papal office, the

24. F. Tamburini, "Il primo registro di Suppliche dell'archivio della Sacra Penitenzieria Apostolica (1410–1411)," *Rivista di storia della Chiesa in Italia* 23 (1969), 384–427, especially 416–417. For examples of the reduction of fees because of the poverty of the supplicant that can be noted in the Penitentiary registers, see: ASV, *Penitenzieria Ap., Reg. Matrim. et Div.*, vol. 4, fol. 79r: "*et quod littere gratis pro deo expediantur quia mendicus et pauper est; Fiat si iurat'*; vol. 4, fol. 99r: "*et si placet quod littere ubique gratis pro deo expediantur quia paratus de paupertate iurare, fiat si iurat.*" In both examples—for which we thank Paolo Ostinelli—there is a question about poverty, which the supplicant had to confirm by taking an oath. The Penitentiary would reduce the fees on the letters for other reasons as well, for example, persons who had a connection with the Penitentiary—officials or their relatives—could get their letters gratis. ASV, *Penitenzieria Ap., Reg. Matrim. et Div.*, vol. 64, fol. 550r: "*taxa gratis pro consanguineo scriptoris*"; vol. 64, fol. 708r: "*taxa gratis pro procuratore penitentiarie.*"

25. Here we have still to remember that the other offices in the papal curia also granted graces gratis for poor supplicants. A good study of poor supplicants was made by A. Meyer, *Arme Kleriker auf Pfründensuche: eine Studie über das* in forma pauperum-*Register Gregors XII. von 1407 und über päpstliche Anwartschaften im Spätmittelalter* (Forschungen zur kirchlichen Rechtsgeschichte und zum Kirchenrecht 20; Cologne-Vienna, 1990).

26. From the year 1497 has been preserved a document in which it is said about the Penitentiary: ". . . *Nam postposita illa ordinatione B(enedicti) XII, qua pro celeri et laudabili expeditione peregrinorum et confluentium penitentium melior excogitari non potest, imitati sunt magis ordinationem et consuetudinem cancellarie apostolice, que longior est et lucrosior, in magnum gravamen et retardationem pauperum penitentium et preiudicium penitentiariorum, ut claret ex illa ordinatione, quam ex adeo magno ingenio pulcre depingunt. . .'*; edited in E. Göller, *Pönitentiarie* II/2, 130–131. The ordination of Benedict XII had been cancelled because it produced a long and expensive procedure for the pilgrims and penitents coming to Rome.

Datary *(componat cum datario).* Certain issues which were handled in the Penitentiary were put under the control of the Datary. In practice, that meant that the supplicant had to pay more than the normal fee of the Penitentiary. It is, however, important to note that in these cases the actual cost of the grace was not higher than normal, but that the special treatment of the supplication by the Datary made the cost of the letter higher.[27] The cases in which this practice was used were not very numerous. They included, first, marriage cases in which the petitioners were related to each other by the fourth or third degree of consanguinity (or affinity);[28] second, cases in which the supplicant had entered ecclesiastical office by wrongful means and profited economically from this crime, i.e., there was a question of simony, wrong titles, etc.; and third, cases concerning the commutation of a vow (for example, to make a pilgrimage or to participate in a crusade) also had to be resolved with the Datary. Similarly, such a resolution was necessary in those cases in which the supplicant had dealt with Muslims or other infidels and sold them weapons or other forbidden products. In these cases, there was a question of personal financial profit in defiance of the regulations of the Church, and therefore the sinner had to pay the resolution fee.[29]

3.5. Restrictions in the Grants

In most cases, the grant of the Penitentiary was for that for which the supplicant had applied; only in some cases did the Penitentiary lay down extra conditions for the grant, or reduce the grace asked for because it did not have the authority to grant such a grace. In certain cases concerning excommunication, the grace was granted in such a way that the dispensation was not valid before the local authorities had absolved the petitioner from the sentence.[30]

27. Concerning these kinds of cases see L. Schmugge, P. Hersperger, B. Wiggenhauser, *Supplikenregister,* 48–51; E. Göller, *Pönitentiarie* II/1, 78–82, 179–189, and II/2, 32.

28. L. Schmugge, P. Hersperger, B. Wiggenhauser, *Supplikenregister,* 86–87.

29. L. Schmugge, P. Hersperger, B. Wiggenhauser, *Supplikenregister,* 49–51; E. Göller, *Pönitentiarie* II/1, 79–80; L. Celier, *Dataires,* 152–155.

30. ASV, *Penitenzieria Ap., Reg. Matrim. et Div.,* vol. 44, fol. 165r. A priest had

In certain cases the Penitentiary laid down other conditions which had to be fulfilled before the grace would be considered valid. For example, in cases which involved property crimes, the grace granted by the office was not valid before the petitioner had fully compensated the victim of the crime *(restitutio in integrum).*[31]

Strict regulations also applied when a priest had killed someone. According to canon law, such a priest could no longer be considered suitable for altar and sacrament service; thus the Penitentiary normally granted the priest absolution and dispensation, but would not allow him to continue in altar service. In some cases the suspension from altar service ordered by the Penitentiary was not final; the supplicant could be suspended for only a certain period, for example for six months.[32] In other cases, however, supplicants were suspended for the rest of their lives.[33] The Penitentiary also suspended for a certain period those petitioners who had been promoted to holy orders as minors, or who had celebrated the Holy Mass even though they were not qualified to do so. When these persons asked for absolution from the sentence of excommunication they had incurred in these cases, and dispensation from irregularity, they were ab-

celebrated mass despite having incurred a special excommunication sentence. He was granted absolution and dispensation, but the grant was not valid until he became absolved from the special sentence. *"Fiat de speciali postquam a speciali sententia fuerit absolutus."*

31. In the Penitentiary regulations: *"50. Nota, quod in littera, que fit sub sigillo domini cardinalis sive dominorum penitentiariorum pro presbitero, qui recepta pecunia, ut quosdam copularet matrimonialiter clandestine, seu alias est symoniacus, dicitur sic in conclusione: "remittatur cum primo absolutus a sententia, quam incurrit per constitutiones sinodales seu provinciales, et a reatu simonie et committatur dispensatio", ut habet forma. In fine vero dicitur "proviso, ut pecunia sic vitiose acquisita restituatur, ubi de iure fuerit restituenda"'* Edited in E. Göller, *Pönitentiarie* I/2, 56–57.

32. ASV, *Penitenzieria Ap., Reg. Matrim. et Div.*, vol. 9, fol. 142v. A priest had kept two sisters, one after the other, as concubines and had had children by both of them, which caused him to be excommunicated. He was absolved by the Penitentiary, but had to keep away from altar service for six months. *"Fiat de speciali et suspendatur a ministerio altaris ad sex menses."*

33. ASV, *Penitenzieria Ap., Reg. Matrim. et Div.*, vol. 14, fol. 161r–v: A priest had been in a fight with another priest, who died a short while later from the wounds. He was absolved and granted dispensation as he had requested, but the Penitentiary denied him the right to act in altar service. *"Fiat de speciali citra ministerium altaris."*

solved and dispensed, but the Penitentiary usually suspended them from altar service for one or two months.[34]

Some special formulas of approval can also be seen as a kind of restriction of the grace granted by the Penitentiary. *Fiat in forma* could mean a restriction to someone who had asked from the Penitentiary more than the official formulary would allow the Penitentiary to grant within the normal faculty of the office. *Fiat ut infra* can also be seen as a kind of restriction of the grant, because it delegated the final authority over the decision to other authorities. This practice was especially restrictive if, for example, the supplicant had tried to use the Penitentiary as a court of appeal against his superior, and the final solution of the case was referred to this same superior.

34. ASV, *Penitenzieria Ap., Reg. Matrim. et Div.*, vol. 16, fol. 245v: "*Fiat de speciali et suspendatur a ministerio altaris ad mensem unum*'; vol. 24, fol. 190v: "*Fiat de speciali et suspendatur a ministerio altaris ad duos menses.*"

4

Documents Produced by the Papal Penitentiary and Their Diplomatics

Every year the Penitentiary approved several thousand petitions that it had received in the form of supplications directed to the Holy Father. As we learned from Chapter 3, the process produced different types of documents. In practice we can divide the documents produced by the Penitentiary into three groups: supplications (both original petitions and their copies), letters issued by the Penitentiary (both the originals and their copies), and the so-called *litterae ecclesiae* documents. These documents can be found in the Vatican Secret Archives (supplications) and in various local archives throughout christendom (letters and *litterae ecclesiae*).

The original supplications were normally considered unnecessary and were thrown away when the petition process was over, the case had been registered into the registers of the Penitentiary, and the petitioner had received the letter of grace composed as a result of the supplication. Some original supplications have been preserved, and in rare cases they can be found in local archives. In most cases, original petitions found locally are documents in the form of *sola signatura* supplications. This means that the signature *(sola signatura)* of the approver of the case functioned as testimony that the case had been approved in the papal curia, and no papal letter of grace was ever produced. In the papal archives as well, some original supplications from the Penitentiary are preserved. Why these petitions were not thrown away is not clear. The marks in the margins of these documents show that these supplications had been copied into the registers, and thus could have been considered useless and destroyed.

For the entire Middle Ages, incoming supplications which were handled and approved by the Penitentiary were registered in the registers of supplications of the Penitentiary. In these register volumes we find entries that are abbreviated copies of incoming and approved supplications. The entries summarize the contents of the petitions; they include the decisions of the Penitentiary and the dates of approval. Thanks to these registers, which, from the second half of the fifteenth century onwards are very well preserved, we have a large collection of cases handled by the Penitentiary.[1] In a few of the Penitentiary registers, some of the original letters issued by the Penitentiary are also copied.

In addition to the Penitentiary sources kept in the Vatican Secret Archives, numerous letters issued by the Penitentiary can be found in local archives all over christendom.[2] These letters do not look like normal papal letters, for they were not issued in the name of the pope but in the name of the Cardinal Penitentiary, for which reason scholars often have difficulty in identifying these documents as letters of the Penitentiary. In fact, these letters are quite often defined in archival catalogues as "letter of grace (or a dispensation or absolution) granted by a cardinal."

Let us, however, take a closer look at these different source types, beginning with the most unusual type of Penitentiary document, the *littera ecclesiae,* and proceeding in chronological order with the different documents produced by the Penitentiary during the supplication process: original petitions, entries in the Penitentiary registers, original letters in the local archives, and finally, copies of the letters of the Penitentiary, first in the Penitentiary registers and second in local archives.

1. On the preserved volumes, see K. Salonen, *Penitentiary,* 425–426.

2. L. Schmugge, "Penitentiary Documents from outside the Penitentiary," in G. Jaritz and T. Jørgensen, K. Salonen, eds., *Long Arm,* 161–169.

When dealing with documents concerning the Penitentiary, we must keep in mind that all documents handed over to the Penitentiary *(supplicationes)*, or written by officials of the Penitentiary *(litterae)* were formally similar to the official curial style *(stilus curiae)* of preparing documents that was required for documents composed in the other papal offices. In order that documents might be composed in the correct manner, there were special Penitentiary manuals giving very strict instructions about how the documents were to be written. For example, the manuals indicated the kinds of abbreviations which could be used in the letters, and which words had to be abbreviated. The regulations were very strict concerning where certain phrases had to be placed in the documents, and which words could be divided at the ends of lines and which could not.[3] Following the manuals and using correct phraseology when composing Penitentiary letters were very important, for it was the only way to avoid forgeries.[4]

4.1. *Litterae ecclesiae*

The *litterae ecclesiae* were letters that the minor penitentiaries could issue to those who confessed their sins to them in the main basilicas in Rome. These letters, which were not copied into the Penitentiary registers, do not reveal the kinds of sins confessed—since that remained under the seal of confession—but contain only testimony that the person named in the letter has confessed his sins in Rome and been absolved by the minor penitentiary in whose name the *littera ecclesiae* was issued. These letters could also be considered a kind of souvenir from Rome for those Christians who visited the Holy See in the Middle Ages. Nowadays the pilgrims can receive a similar kind of letter known as certificate of a pilgrimage.

The *litterae ecclesiae* were not registered—or, at any rate, no such

3. For more detail on this see E. Göller, *Pönitentiarie* I/2, 78–81.

4. Concerning different kinds of forgeries in the Middle Ages, see *Fälschungen im Mittelalter* (Internationaler Kongreß der Monumenta Germaniae Historica München, 16.–19. September 1986, Bde I–V; Monumenta Germaniae Historica, Schriften 33, I–V; Hannover, 1988).

registers, or even any mention of them, have survived to our day. We know that the minor penitentiaries were very busy, and that numerous such letters were issued on a daily basis; nevertheless, no traces of such documents can be found in the Vatican Secret Archives. In order to find such documents, we would have to look into the local archives; but, alas, finding *litterae ecclesiae* in the local archives is quite difficult, since these letters were strictly personal and did not contain any details important for persons other than the holder of the letter. Thus, after the death of the person who had received the letter, it was considered useless and, in most cases, thrown away.

A very rare surviving example of a *littera ecclesiae* can be found in the Swedish National Archives in Stockholm.[5] The contents of this letter will be discussed in the second part of this book, but in brief, the letter testifies that on the 5th of August 1449 a certain Nanne Kärling, present in Rome, was absolved from all his sins by the German minor penitentiary Johannes Calp.

The *litterae ecclesiae* look very modest and plain. They were prepared on parchment, making them quite durable. The letters are also quite small in size; for at least the letter preserved in Sweden, maximum letter size is about 19 cm x 12.5 cm. It is bound with a hemp cord which carries the red wax seal of the Penitentiary. On the plica of the document the name of the scribe who prepared the document is written. Apart from the scribe's name and the text itself, only one kind of information is given in the *litterae ecclesiae* about the process these letters had to go through in the Penitentiary: in the left margin, on the level of the first line, is written *"bene."* This means that someone had checked the letter after its preparation and seen that all details were correct.

All letters follow the same formularies. They begin with the general phrase *"Universis presentes litteras inspecturis,"* which states that the information in the letter was directed "to whom it may concern." After that comes the name of the minor penitentiary who

5. Stockholm, Riksarkivet, Or. Perg. (5.8.1449). See also the first document published in Part II of this book.

had heard the confession, in this case *"Johannes Calp, domini pape penitentiarius"* (a German minor penitentiary), followed by the general phrase of salutation *"Salutem in domino."* These three parts belong to the "protocol"—the first part of the letter, which had to be present in any official letter issued in the Middle Ages.

After the protocol, the second part of the letter, known as the *corpus,* begins. This part begins with the *narratio,* which contains all the necessary information for that particular letter. In this case the *narratio,* which begins with the word *"Noverit,"* tells that Nanne Torberni Kärling from the Diocese of Skara had personally visited Rome and the Holy See *(limina beatorum apostolorum Petri et Pauli de urbe ac sedem apostolicam . . . personaliter visitantem),* and had confessed his sins and been absolved by the above-mentioned minor penitentiary. The letter continues with the second part of the *corpus,* called the *dispositio,* in which the minor penitentiary refers to the authority he had received from the pope and on the basis of which he had been able to absolve the person in question *(. . . auctoritate domini pape absolvimus et iniunximus ei super ipsis auctoritate predicta . . .).*

The letter ends with the *eschatocol,* in which the minor penitentiary refers to his authority as manifested by the seal of the Penitentiary *(Presentes inde sibi litteras sigillo officii penitentiariorum sigillatas in testimonium concedentes).* At the end of the letter we find the *datatio,* which contains both the place and the date of the approval. In this case the letter is dated the 5th of August of the third pontifical year of Pope Nicholas V, 1449, in Rome at St. Peter's Church *(Datum Rome apud sanctumpetrum nonas augusti pontificatus domini Nicolai pape V anno tertio.).*

4.2. Supplications

As we learned above, the first stage of the supplication process in curia was the preparation of the petition, which was normally the task of the proctor of the supplicant. It was important to use the services of an expert, for the correct preparation of the petition required knowledge of canon law and of the curial writing style.

Two different kinds of documents which can be used when

studying the supplications presented to the Penitentiary have survived: the original supplications, and the entries in the Penitentiary registers. The original supplications show us *in extenso* what the petitions looked like and the kind of phraseology used, while the medieval Penitentiary registers contain only abbreviated copies of the original supplications.

4.2.1. The form of the original supplications

Supplications made to the Penitentiary were supposed to be written on paper and be composed according to the curial practice and style. The text of every petition consists of two parts: the first part, called the *expositio,* contains the opening phraseology as well as the part in which the petitioner explains the facts of his problem; the second part of the petition text, called the *supplicatio* or *petitio,* contains the request itself. According to curial practice, petitions were always directed to the pope, even though the case was later handled by someone other than the pope himself. Let us now take a closer look at the form of the original supplication.[6]

The *expositio* of the supplications is expressed in the following way: *Exponit(ur) Sanctitati Vestre (pro parte) N.N.* In the place of N.N., the first name and family name (or the patronymic) of the supplicant(s), his/her social status, and the name of his/her home diocese are given. The *expositio* could be in the active *(exponit)* or the passive *(exponitur pro parte)* form. It seems that it was common to use the active form when the supplicant was personally present in the curia at the moment of presenting the supplication, while the passive form was used when the petitioner was not in the curia; because of the small number of original supplications preserved, however, this has not yet been proved for certain. In any case, the absence or presence of the supplicant was an important matter and can be seen in the phraseology of the letters issued by the Penitentiary, but this difference cannot be proved based only upon the supplications.

6. Readers are invited to compare the information here to Illustration 2 in Part II, Chapter 2 of this book.

The opening phraseology is followed by the *narratio,* which is the part of the supplication revealing what the supplicant had done and the reason for which he had had to turn to the Penitentiary. This part is normally rather short and formulaic and does not contain any extra information beyond what was necessary for the handling of the case in the curia. The narration is long and detailed only in the *de declaratoriis* supplications, in which the details were important for proving the innocence of the supplicant.

The *expositio* is followed by the second obligatory part of the petition, the *supplicatio*—i.e., the part in which the supplicant expressed what kind of grace he was requesting. The phraseology used in the Penitentiary petitions begins thusly: *Supplicat(ur) igitur Sanctitati Vestre (pro parte).* After this, the supplicant made clear what kind of grace he needed, i.e., an absolution, a dispensation, a declaration, and/or a special license.

These were thus the parts that are always repeated in the same order in each supplication. Those original supplications which have been preserved to our day either in local archives or in the Vatican Archives also contain other information which does not belong to the actual text of the petition and, consequently, was not written by the proctor. This extra information refers to the handling of the supplications in the Penitentiary. In what follows will be discussed the kinds of additions that can be found in the original petition conserved in the National Library in Helsinki (see Illustration 2 and the description of the document in Part II). These additions can be generalized to all original petitions.

The first addition to the text of the original petition that we find in the document is the formula of approval (i.e., the *Fiat,* according to the need for different formulas, which were explained in Chapter 3 above), found immediately after the text of the petition, as well as the name and position of the person who made the decision. In the example document it reads: *Fiat de speciali, A*[*ntonius*] *episcopus Aprutinus, regens.*

In the lower part of the original petition there appears another addition to the original text. Here we find the place and the date of approval, written in the Roman style with *calends, ides,* or *nones,* followed by the pontifical year of the reigning pope. In this case we read in the document: *Datum Senis xii kal. Augusti Anno ij.* (Dated in Siena, the 21st of July of the second pontifical year [of Pius II]; i.e., 1460).[7] Since the name of the ruling pope is not expressed in the document, it is sometimes difficult to ascertain which year the document is dated. In such cases, we can try to identify the pope, for example, on the basis of the place at which the document was dated. Medieval popes did not necessarily reside all the time in Rome, but traveled a great deal; for this reason, the place of approval can sometimes help in identifying the correct pope and year. For example, in this case we know that Pope Pius II resided in Siena during the summer of 1460, which was his second pontifical year; no other pope visited Siena in the summer of their second pontifical year.

After the date of approval, we can see in the document a name; in our example, *C. de Regio*. In other papal offices it was the task of the datary to put the date on the documents.[8] The sources of the Penitentiary, however, do not say anything about a datary of the Penitentiary prior to the pontificate of Alexander VI; in fact, it would seem that the Penitentiary had no datary of its own, but that the *auditor* of the Penitentiary also handled the role of datary, i.e., signed the petitions after the date. The signature of *C. de Regio* proves this to be true, for we know from other sources related to the Penitentiary that Coradinus de Regio was a Penitentiary *auditor*.[9] Thus the signature after the date must be that of the *auditor*, if not that of someone else signing on his behalf—it is known that he sometimes delegated this task to someone else.[10] Perhaps there was no need to install a separate datary for the Penitentiary, for in the Penitentiary the date did not play as important a role as it did in the Chancery, where the date could be most important, especially in petitions for

7. Concerning the chronology of medieval diplomatics, see for example L. E. Boyle, "Diplomatics," in J. M. Powell, ed., *Medieval Studies: An Introduction* (Syracuse, NY, 1992), 82–113.

8. B. Katterbach, *Specimina Supplicationum ex Registris Vaticanis* (Subsidiorum Tabularii Vaticani, Volumen II Extra: Rome, 1927), VI. Léonce Celier also talks about the datary of the Penitentiary (L. Celier, *Dataires*, 91).

9. ASV, *Penitenzieria Ap., Reg. Matrim. et Div.*, vol. 16, fol. 70r and 74r.

10. E. Göller, *Pönitentiarie* II/1, 3, 63, 83.

a benefice (*prius in data, potius in iure*—the earlier the date, the more powerful the rights).

In the upper left-hand corner of the document we find the third piece of additional information: a summary of the content of the supplication,[11] which in the example (a marriage matter) is: *De contracto scienter et non consumato in 4° affinitatis* (Concerning a marriage contracted, but not consummated, the couple knowing they were related to each other by the tie of the 4th degree of affinity). The documents do not contain any information about the writer of the summary, nor do the Penitentiary manuals or instructions say anything regarding this; however, there are not many possibilities as to who it could have been. One of the possibilities is that, since it was the *auditor*'s task to receive the incoming petitions in the first place and to prepare the petitions for the audience of the Cardinal Penitentiary or the regent,[12] it seems quite logical that he could also have written the summary that facilitated the handling of the case. The writer could not have been the proctor who formulated and wrote the petition, for the summaries are not written with the same ink or in the same handwriting as the petitions.

On the back side of the document, called the *verso*, we find the name of the proctor who took care of the case. It was very important to also note on the petition who the proctor was, as all responsibility regarding the facts of the case rested with him. Besides preparing the text of the petition, the proctor followed the entire petition process in the Penitentiary and was the primary person responsible for ensuring that all details in the letter issued by the Penitentiary as a result of the petition were correct. In the case in question here, this was a German proctor named Johannes Weythas.[13]

In the original supplications preserved in the Vatican Secret Ar-

11. The same practice was also in use in other supplications presented to the other offices of the papal curia. See B. Katterbach, *Specimina Supplicationum,* VI and Tab. XIII.

12. E. Göller, *Pönitentiarie* II/1, 85.

13. National Library of Finland, *Scheelska samlingen.* Concerning procurator Johannes Weythas see for example L. Schmugge, P. Hersperger, B. Wiggenhauser, *Supplikenregister,* 45; L. Schmugge, *Kirche, Kinder, Karrieren,* 101–103, 238.

chives from the first quarter of the sixteenth century, in the lower parts of the documents, on the right-hand side, is indicated "R," or "R^{ta}" *(registrata).* A similar, although much larger, sign can be found in slightly later documents from the middle of the sixteenth century, on the reverse side of the original supplications. This sign is the mark of registration, and indicates that the supplication had been copied into the Penitentiary registers. Marking the registered documents with a registration mark such as "R" was a common procedure for all petitions approved in the papal curia, not just in the Penitentiary.[14]

The original supplications also contain notes referring to the fees of the office. In the left margin of the supplication is written the month in which the handling fee had been paid; under this we find the amount the supplicant had paid to have the letter of grace prepared.

The original supplications kept in the Vatican Secret Archives also have a hole in the lower part of the folio. These holes probably indicate the manner in which the supplications were preserved before and after registration: they must have been kept on wooden or metal sticks while awaiting their turn to be registered. A similar method was also used in the Datary.

Concerning the *datatio* of the original supplications, according to the manual of Walter Murner of Strasbourg, there were two different ways of marking the date. If the supplication was registered in the registers of the Penitentiary, the letter was dated according to the day on which the grace was granted; if the supplication was not registered, the date given was the day on which the letter of the Penitentiary was composed.[15]

In rare cases the original supplication was validated as a *sola signatura* supplication. This kind of supplication was sufficient to prove

14. B. Katterbach, *Specimina Supplicationum,* VI.

15. *"Nota, quod in litteris . . . quarum supplicationes non registrantur, ponenda est data illius diei, qua presenta*[*n*]*tur scriptoribus vel qua scribuntur." "Item datam in supplicatione registrata notatam ponant in littera iuxta stilum officii."* Edited in E. Göller, *Pönitentiarie* I/2, 87–88. See also F. Tamburini, "Note diplomatiche," 154.

that the grant had been given and did not require the issuing of a *littera*. Since *sola signatura* supplications were a special favor granted only to certain petitioners, they were not common. In the Penitentiary registers one sometimes comes across phrases which indicate that the supplicants received their supplication *sola signatura*, but these remarks are very rare.[16]

4.2.2. The copies of petitions recorded into the Penitentiary registers

The register volumes of the Penitentiary contain entries which are more or less abbreviated copies of the original supplications handled in and approved by the office. These entries were copied into the registers of the Penitentiary one after another, with the text running down the middle of the page. In the left margin the place and day of approval of the supplication is mentioned, and in the right margin the name of the home diocese of the supplicant is given. In some earlier register volumes the name of the proctor is also mentioned in the right margin, but this practice was not common throughout the late Middle Ages. Mention of the name of the proctor became common again in the later volumes, from the pontificate of Julius II (1503–1513); in these later volumes, the name of the proctor is given above each entry together with the sum of the tax the supplicant was supposed to pay for the letter of grace.[17]

Because the medieval registers of the Penitentiary contain copies of the petitions, the entries have the same form as the supplications; the entries in the pages of the Penitentiary registers do not, however, entirely match the original petition texts. The preserved original supplications have allowed us to compare the original petitions with the texts copied into the registers; this comparison shows that the entries in the registers are—sometimes very much—shorter than the texts in the original supplications.

16. For supplications signed *sola signatura* see RPG V, n. 1284, 1285, 1441, 1476, and 3845.

17. Some earlier volumes, for example from the pontificates of Pius II and Sixtus IV, also contain information concerning proctors, but the names of proctors have been copied systematically only since the pontificate of Julius II.

In fact, the scribes did not copy the supplications word for word, but included in the entries only the juridically important facts—which reflects the writers' knowledge of canon law and the faculty of the Penitentiary. In any case, all important details which would have been needed when the officials of the Penitentiary made their decision concerning the issue are present in the entry: the name(s) of the supplicant(s), a short description of what was wrong, and what the supplicant(s) requested, as well as the decision of the Penitentiary and the name and title of the person who made the decision. On the other hand, any details which did not help in resolving the case were left out; for example, the formulary of the supplication and mention of the pope, i.e., *Supplicat(ur) igitur Sanctitati Vestre (pro parte) . . .* , along with all other unnecessary phraseology which was always repeated in the petitions, but did not have any significance.

At the end of each entry in the Penitentiary records, the decision of the Penitentiary is mentioned, together with the name and title of the person who had made the decision. This is a very important fact, because all letters granted by the Penitentiary were issued in the name of the Cardinal Penitentiary; consequently the original letters do not reveal who in the Penitentiary actually made the decision, and thus the supplications are the only way to know who was responsible for the decision making. At the ends of entries, copied under the title *de declaratoriis*, are also mentioned the name of the person(s) to whom the matter was referred for further examination, as well as the name of the *auditor* who had taken care of the legal matters of the case. These names are sometimes also given in the original letters.

When studying and analyzing the copies of the petitions recorded in the Penitentiary registers, we have to keep in mind that scribes did not all abbreviate the supplications in the same way, even though the main principles were the same; it is possible to note slight differences in which one scribe has copied what others did not consider to be of sufficient importance.

4.3. The Letters of the Penitentiary

In contrast to other papal offices, such as the Apostolic Chancery and Apostolic Chamber, the Penitentiary, up until 1570, did not register the outgoing letters *(litterae)* that the office issued to petitioners throughout christendom. The original letters issued by the office were simply sent out *in partibus* to the recipients without any trace being left in the office. Documents issued by the Penitentiary normally had a minute probability of surviving, which means that our knowledge of the Penitentiary depends largely on the petitions.[18]

Fortunately, the original letters of the Penitentiary are not the only possibility for the study of documents produced by the office. In some instances it is possible to find copies of the original letters among the entries in the registers of the Penitentiary as well as in the local episcopal or notarial registers. The original letters were almost always presented to the ecclesiastical authorities back home, and thus were often copied into episcopal or notarial registers, once local officials had made a decision concerning the case. Let us now take a closer look at the kinds of documents still to be found in different places.

4.3.1. The original letters of the Penitentiary in local archives

The most important documents for the study of the administrative procedure (Geschäftsgang) of the Penitentiary are of course the original letters issued by the office. These letters offer us the possibility of understanding exactly how the letters were prepared, who the officials employed in producing them were, and the kinds of marks they contain. As stated above, finding these letters is not very easy, for the great majority of the original letters produced by the Penitentiary have been lost over the years; some have been thrown away after the death of the person in question, some were destroyed in fires, and some were simply eaten by mice or damaged by humidity. Nevertheless, there are still numerous original letters of the

18. Regarding this methodological problem see A. Esch, "Überlieferungs-Chance und Überlieferungs-Zufall als methodisches Problem des Historikers," *Historische Zeitschrift* 240 (1985), 529–570.

Penitentiary in local archives and collections all over Europe; scholars just need the patience to look for them.

As with late medieval charters and documents in general, too little attention has been paid to Penitentiary documents; only recently has interest in such documents begun to grow.[19] Along with the supplications, historians are now able to trace the *litterae*. Let us take as one example the *Repertorium* of papal documents in northern Germany published by Brigide Schwarz;[20] with the help of this work's index, all documents concerning the Penitentiary which have been preserved in the archives of Lower Saxony and Bremen can be found.[21]

If we look at some of the *litterae* listed in this publication, we can see how the Penitentiary registers kept in the Vatican Secret Archives can be matched with the originals *in partibus*. Let us take as an example the supplication for dispensation from illegitimate birth *(defectus natalium)* for a certain cleric named *Theodericus Valdendinch* from the Diocese of Verden, which was accepted and copied in the Penitentiary registers in the Holy Year 1450.[22] The corresponding original letter, as we learn from the *Repertorium*, can be found in the Staatsarchiv Lüneburg.[23] In the letter issued by the Penitentiary, the name of the petitioner reads *Dietrich Welderdingh;* this difference in orthography, however, is no surprise, and can easily be explained. In the register of the Penitentiary we find the Christian name of the supplicant converted into Latin form—the German name Dietrich is correctly Latinized as Theodericus. The slight difference in the fami-

19. A valuable contribution to our knowledge of Penitentiary originals has been made by S. Weiss, *Kurie und Ortskirche. Die Beziehungen zwischen Salzburg und dem päpstlichen Hof unter Martin V. (1417–1431)* (Bibliothek des Deutschen Historischen Instituts in Rom 76; Tübingen, 1994). See, for example, page 451 with footnote 18, in which five originals from Austrian archives are mentioned.

20. B. Schwarz, ed., *Regesten der in Niedersachsen und Bremen überlieferten Papsturkunden 1198–1503* (Veröffentlichungen der historischen Kommission für Niedersachsen und Bremen XXXVII: Quellen und Untersuchungen zur Geschichte Niedersachsens im Mittelalter 15; Hannover, 1993).

21. B. Schwarz, *Regesten*, 638: Pönitentiarie.

22. Concerning the entry in the Penitentiary register, see RPG II, n. 1478.

23. B. Schwarz, *Regesten*, 438, n. 1754.

ly name is definitely an error of the scribe who copied the entry into the Penitentiary register and did not succeed in copying the name in its correct form. At any rate, there can be no doubt that the registered supplication and the *littera* in Lüneburg match, for similar kinds of errors in registration have also been found elsewhere. We also have to keep in mind that there was no established orthography for names in the Middle Ages; therefore, variation in the names of persons and places such as that presented above is very common. Sometimes we even find variations of a name within a single document.

Because the original letters of the Penitentiary contain a great deal of important extra information which cannot be found in the petitions, those letters which have survived are of extraordinary importance for historical research. Especially important are those from the period prior to 1448, as there are no surviving register volumes—except for some fragments—before the pontificate of Nicholas V. This means that the original letters, or their copies, are the only testimony we have to the activity of the papal Penitentiary before the middle of the fifteenth century.

4.3.2. The copies of the original letters

As we mentioned above, the original letters are not the only testimonies of the activity of the Penitentiary; sometimes we also find copies of the original letters in local archives, as well as in the Penitentiary records among the supplications. Quite often these copies are very exact, even the marks in the margins having been repeated, and not just the plain text. The exact transcription of all possible detail is very important for the best possible study of the Penitentiary.

Although the registers of the papal Penitentiary kept in the Vatican Secret Archives officially contain only supplications, several *litterae* have been copied into some volumes from the second half of the fifteenth century. The practice of copying *litterae* into the supplication registers seems to have decreased after the pontificate of Paul II (1464–1471). From the long pontificate of Sixtus IV (1471–1484), which produced 13 volumes of registered supplications, only five *litterae* have been copied into the registers.[24] The reason for this extraordinary fact is very difficult to ascertain, but their existence is a good thing, for they give us very important information on the personnel of the Penitentiary involved in the supplication process.

The texts of the original letters copied into the registers of the Penitentiary were carefully transcribed, and they contain every name which had been written in the original letter; we therefore get all the names of the officers involved in preparing the littera, from the proctor to the signer.

Copies of the original letters can also be found in registers kept by local authorities such as notaries and bishops. The notarial and episcopal registers often describe and duplicate the original letters in detail, for it was very important for them to know exactly what the original letter looked like. Before registering the documents, the local authorities studied them very carefully in order to avoid forgeries, which were rather common in the Middle Ages. Once they had determined that a letter brought to them was authentic, they copied it into their registers as carefully as they could, so that nobody could claim later on that the document or copy was not authentic.

Unfortunately, numerous medieval episcopal, as well as notarial, registers were lost over the centuries; fires and foreign military troops did their best to prevent the survival of such documents. Despite such disasters, there are still numerous medieval registers in local archives in different parts of Europe, many of which remain unstudied.[25]

Copies of the documents produced by the Penitentiary can sometimes be found within other medieval, or later, documents. If, for

24. We want to mention at least one of them, to be found in ASV, *Penitenzieria Ap., Reg. Matrim. et Div.*, vol. 28, fol. 287v–288r: Letter of the Cardinal Penitentiary Julianus [della Rovere] for Baptista de Xanctoris from Viterbo (Italy) dated 12th of June 1479. See also for example the final letter in Register 17 directed to the bishop of Utrecht, which is printed fully in RPG V, n. 2126.

25. Paolo Ostinelli has studied the notarial registers of the diocese of Como in northern Italy, while the English episcopal registers are—at least partly—edited. In both registers can be found copies of several letters of the Penitentiary. P. Ostinelli, *Penitenzieria Apostolica. Le suppliche alla Sacra Penitenzieria Apostolica provenienti dalla diocesi di Como (1438–1484)* (Materiali di storia ecclesiastica lombarda (secoli XIV–XVI), 5; Milano, 2003).

example, the Penitentiary documents were used as testimony in the ecclesiastical or secular courts, the contents of the documents were often copied into the documents concerning the proceedings of the court. Finding such documents requires a great deal of work and reading through numerous documents, but this can reveal some unknown, earlier Penitentiary documents.[26]

4.3.3. The form of the original letters of the Penitentiary

The form in which papal letters were to be composed was very strictly regulated. The regulations concerning the composition of the letters of the Penitentiary were twofold: the general regulations for the whole curia, and the special regulations for the Penitentiary. Letters composed by the Penitentiary had to be written according to the general rule of the *stilus curiae.* The special rules for the Penitentiary, in their turn, were more concerned with minor details than with the general form of the letter. According to the Chancery regulations of the papal curia, papal letters were supposed to be made up of three parts: *protocol, corpus,* and *eschatocol.*[27]

The *protocol* in letters granted by the Penitentiary—just as in any papal letter—consisted of three parts: *intitulatio, inscriptio,* and *salutatio.* The *intitulatio* consisted of the name and title of the Cardinal Penitentiary who was the official author of the letter (all letters of grace granted by the Penitentiary were issued in the name of the *penitentiarius maior* regardless of who had made the decision in the case). The *inscriptio* in its turn consisted of the name and the title of the addressee (possibly the supplicant himself, the local bishop, or some other authority to whom the issue was referred), for example: *Dominicus miseratione divina tituli sancte crucis in Jerusalem presbiter car-*

26. Such documents exist at least in the Swedish National Archives: Stockholm, Riksarkivet, Or. Perg. 14.6.1476. See for example K. Salonen, "Fallet Nanne Kärling: Att kombinera biografiska uppgifter ur olika arkiv," in *Ny väg till medeltidsbreven* (Från ett medeltidssymposium i Svenska Riksarkivet 26–28 november 1999: Skrifter utgivna av Riksarkivet 18; Västervik, 2002), 99–106.

27. The same division into three parts was used in all kinds of documents. Concerning medieval diplomatics, see for example L. E. Boyle, "Diplomatics," 98. Concerning diplomatics in papal documents, see also T. Frenz, *Papsturkunden.*

dinalis (the *intitulatio*), *discreto viro Wenceslao de Crumlow . . . administratori ecclesie Pragensis* (the *inscriptio*).[28] The order of these can also be reversed, so that the *inscriptio* comes first, and then the *intitulatio: Venerabili in Christo patri*[29] *Dei gratia episcopo Lucano vel eius in spiritualibus vicario* (the *inscriptio*), *Philippus miseratione divina episcopus Portuensis* (the *intitulatio*).[30] They are in both cases immediately followed by the formula of the greeting, the *salutatio: Salutem et sinceram in Domino caritatem,* or in some cases *Salutem in Domino.*[31]

Then follows the most important part of the letter, the *corpus,* in which are repeated all important details concerning the petition. The *corpus* also consists of several different parts: the *arenga, narratio, dispositio, clausulae,* and *sanctiones,* as well as the mention of the seal. The first part, the *arenga,* is a rhetorical preparation for the issue; in Penitentiary documents there were several different kinds of *arengae,* depending on the issue in question.[32] The *arenga* also changed over the course of time, and can be missing altogether.[33] The fol-

28. See the text of the letter of the Penitentiary related to the marriage dispensation for Michael Genczss and Katerina Lapka in Part II. Chapter 2 of this book.

29. There are several different ways of expressing the title of the supplicant. In cases where the papal letter is addressed to a cardinal, the phrase is *Reverendo in Christo patri;* where it is addressed to an archbishop or bishop the phrase is *Venerabili in Christo patri;* when the addressee is any other man it is *Dilectus filius;* when a woman, *Dilecta in Christo filia.* See F. Tamburini, "Note diplomatiche," 179–180; T. Frenz, *Papsturkunden,* 35.

30. See the text of the letter of the Penitentiary related to the marriage dispensation for Johannes Vitalis and Lucia Baldassaris Bartolomei in Part II, Chapter 2 of this book.

31. F. Tamburini, "Note diplomatiche," 180; M. Meyer, *Die Pönitentiarie-Formularsammlung des Walter Murner von Strassburg* (Spicilegium Friburgense 25; Freiburg i. Ü., 1979), 133–134.

32. On the different kinds of *arenga* see Meyer, *Pönitentiarie-Formularsammlung,* 134–138. An example can also be found in the text of the letter of the Penitentiary related to the marriage dispensation for Michael Genczss and Katerina Lapka in Part II of this book: *"Sedis apostolice providentia circumspecta nonnumquam rigorem iuxta mansuetudinem temperat et quod sacrorum canonum prohibent instituta de gratia benignitatis indulget prout personarum et temporum qualitate pensata id in Deo salubriter expedire cognoscit."*

33. See the text of the letter of the Penitentiary related to the marriage dispensation for Johannes Vitalis and Lucia Baldassaris Bartolomei in Part II of this book., in which the *salutatio* is immediately followed by the *narratio.*

lowing part, the *narratio*, which differed somewhat according to the presence or absence of the supplicant in the curia, contained the details of the case: what the supplicant had done, and why he had turned to the Penitentiary. If the supplicant was not present in the curia at the moment of making the supplication, the *narratio* in the letter of the Penitentiary began: *Ex parte N.N. nobis oblata petitio continebat* . . .[34] If the supplicant was present the phrase was: *Sua nobis N.N. lator presencium petitione monstravit* . . . After this phrase, the details of the issue and the supplication itself were presented. These were copied almost directly from the text of the supplication. If the supplicant was not present in the curia the *narratio* ended with the phrase: . . . *(super quibus) supplicari fecit humiliter dictus exponens sibi super hiis per Sedem Apostolicam misericorditer provideri.* If he was present the phrase was usually: . . . *super quibus supplicavit humiliter dictus exponens sibi super hiis per Sedem Apostolicam misericorditer provideri.*[35]

The next part of the papal letter was the *dispositio*. This is the heart of the letter, and concerns the sentence or the decision of the Penitentiary based on the facts mentioned in the *narratio*. When a petition had been approved according to the general authority of the Penitentiary, the formula of the *dispositio* began as follows: *Nos igitur . . . auctoritate domini pape cuius penitentiariae curam gerimus* . . .[36] If the decision of the Penitentiary was made by a special faculty from the pope, the phrase continued: . . . *et de eius speciali mandato super hoc vivae vocis oraculo nobis facto* . . . .[37] In cases where the Penitentiary had made its decision according to an expressed mandate from the pope, the phrase was: . . . *et de eius speciali et expresso mandato super hoc vive vocis oraculo nobis facto* . . .[38] Another, but very rare, phrase, . . . *et de eius*

34. See the text of the letter of the Penitentiary related to the marriage dispensation for Johannes Vitalis and Lucia Baldassaris Bartolomei in Part II of this book.: "*Ex parte Johannis Vitalis laici et Lucie Baldassaris Bartolomei mulieris de Fabricis vestre diocesis nobis oblata petitio continebat* . . .'

35. F. Tamburini, "Note diplomatiche," 181; M. Meyer, *Pönitentiarie-Formularsammlung*, 134–143.

36. See the text of the letter of the Penitentiary related to the confessional letter granted to Henricus Sartoris in Part II, Chapter 2 of this book.

37. See the text of the letter of the Penitentiary related to the illegitimacy dispensation for Conradus Fischer in Part II, Chapter 2 of this book.

38. See the text of the letter of the Penitentiary related to the dispensation

commissione in talibus generaliter nobis facta . . .[39] can be found in very special cases which were normally beyond the authority of the Penitentiary. If the case was further referred to the local or curial authorities, this fact was mentioned immediately after the decision using the phrase: . . . *circumspectioni vestre committimus* . . .[40] At the end of the *dispositio* is written the decision of the Penitentiary, i.e., the declaration, dispensation, absolution, or concession of a special license. The *dispositio* is followed by the clauses which defined the validity of the document and made it clear that the Penitentiary had satisfied the supplicant concerning all the matters mentioned in the letter. In this part the phraseology varies a great deal between different kinds of cases. In the case of a simple marriage dispensation, the phraseology is the following: . . . *huiusmodi quod ex premissis provenit non obstante in eorum sic contracto matrimonio libere et licite valeant remanere misericorditer dispensetis, dummodo dicta N.* (name of the woman) *propter hoc ab aliquo rapta non fuerit prolem susceptam si qua sit et suscipiendam exinde legitimam decernentes.*[41] After that there now and then came a phrase referring to the seal of the Penitentiary: *In huius rei testimonium presentes litteras sigilli nostro munitas duximus concidendas.*[42]

The last part of the letter was the *eschatocol,* which included the *datatio.* The date of approval of the supplication had to be written into the papal letter according to strict rules, which appear in the Penitentiary statutes.[43] First was given the place at which the supplication was approved, then the phrase which made it clear that

---

to change from one monastery to another for Barbara de Rischach in Part II, Chapter 2 of this book.

39. F. Tamburini, "Note diplomatiche," 181–182; M. Meyer, *Pönitentiarie-Formularsammlung,* 145.

40. M. Meyer, *Pönitentiarie-Formularsammlung,* 146–148. See the text of the letter of the Penitentiary related to the dispensation to change from one monastery to another for Barbara de Rischach in Part II of this book.

41. See the text of the letter of the Penitentiary related to the marriage dispensation for Johannes Vitalis and Lucia Baldassaris Bartolomei in Part II of this book.

42. Regarding the phraseology concerning the seal, see M. Meyer, *Pönitentiarie-Formularsammlung,* 148–149.

43. *"Item quotitas kalendarum, nonarum et yduum non debet scribi per litteras, ut primo kal., secundo non., tertio ydus, sed per numerum: IV kal, III non., IV ydus etc.*

the Penitentiary had made the concession, and finally the day, the month, and the year of the pontificate of the ruling pope: *Datum Rome apud Sanctum Petrum sub sigillo officii penitentiarie .viii. idibus aprilis pontificatus domini Julii pape II anno nono.*[44]

In addition to the normal text, which consisted of the four above-mentioned parts, letters granted by the Penitentiary also contained other notes which were written during the supplication process. In the upper margin, above the text, we can see a phrase written by the *corrector: Videat eam N.N. / dominus regens / dominus auditor.* "N.N." refers to the name of the *penitentiarius maior;* the others refer to the *regens* and the *auditor* to whom the case was committed as an expert in canon law. If the approver found that the letter was correct, he wrote in the left margin at the level of the fifth line of the letter *Visa per me,* and in the right margin at the same level his name and title. If the signer was a bishop or abbot, he wrote the first letters of his Christian name and then his ecclesiastical title, for example *Jo*[*hannem*] *ep*[*iscopum*] *Nucerin*[*ensem*]. If the approver, on the other hand, was an official of the Penitentiary, he wrote his first name, surname, and title: *A.*[*nthonium*] *de Grassis, auditorem.* When there was no need for the intervention of the *auditor,* the *corrector* wrote in the left margin *Bene.*[45]

Down in the lower left-hand corner, which remained under the fold, two or three names appear. In the upper line was written the

---

Item quotitas annorum pontificatus pape scribitur per litteras ut 'pontificatus domini Urbani pape VI anno primo vel tertio' . . . ," edited in E. Göller, *Pönitentiarie* I/2, 80.

44. See the text of the letter of the Penitentiary related to the procession matter in Cologne in Part II, Chapter 2 of this book. Regarding the dating system in the Penitentiary, see also M. Meyer, *Pönitentiarie-Formularsammlung,* 151. First is the place: *Rome apud Sanctum Petrum,* then the reference to the Penitentiary: *sub sigillo officii penitentiarie* and finally the actual date—first the day in the form of kalends *(kalendae),* ides *(idus)* or nones *(nonae),* then the month and finally the year in the form of pontifical year, i.e., the year of the pope's pontificate: *viii. idibus aprilis* (6.4.) *pontificatus domini Julii pape .ii. anno nono* (i.e., the 9th pontifical year of Julius II, 1511–1512, in which 6.4. means that the year was 1512). Concerning the chronology see, for example, R. D. Ware, "Medieval Chronology," in J. M. Powell, ed., *Medieval Studies,* 252–277.

45. F. Tamburini, "Note diplomatiche," 185. Examples from Swedish National Archives: Stockholm, Riksarkivet, Or. Perg., 14.2.1484, and 8.3.1488. See also E. Göller, *Pönitentiarie* I/2, 85.

name of the *distributor* (who also acted as *taxator*) with the amount of tax which the supplicant had to pay to the Penitentiary. This amount is cleverly written in the middle of the *distributor-taxator*'s name; for example F. Rosextursa (i.e., F. Rosa, with the amount of the tax, 6 *tournois*).[46] The second name below the first one was the name of the *computator,* who also took part in the taxation.[47] The third name, which is not present in all the letters, could be the name of the procurator; certainly the name *Ge. Homines,* which appears in one Swedish letter,[48] is the name of one well-known procurator. The issue is not, however, so simple, for in this case the proctor had not been *Homines* but another man, named *Gebellon* (which is apparent from the signature of the procurator in the letter). Tamburini does not know of any third signature in this context; however, he refers in this context to Göller, who knows that under the fold there had been, at least in the time of Sixtus IV, also the name of the procurator.[49] Thus we can conclude that the third name under the fold is not necessarily the name of the proctor who took care of the case, but could be the name of a proctor who had had something to do with the case. It is possible that the element common to all three was payment to the office, since the other two signatures refer to persons connected with the fees.

On the lower right-hand side, above the fold, are written the name and surname of the scribe who had composed the letter. If the letter of the Penitentiary was a so-called *littera clausa,* the proctor signed his name above the fold, but on the left-hand side; if the letter was a normal papal letter, the proctor signed his name on the *verso* of the letter.[50] Often there also appears on the *verso* of the letter the name of the person to whom the letter was supposed to be given; however, this name was probably not written by the officials of the Penitentiary.

46. See the text of the letter of the Penitentiary related to the murder case in the diocese of Skara in Part II, Chapter 2 of this book.

47. F. Tamburini, "Note diplomatiche," 186–187.

48. Stockholm, Riksarkivet, Or. Perg., 31.10.1509.

49. F. Tamburini, "Note diplomatiche," 187, footnote 31; E. Göller, *Pönitentiarie* II/1, 65, 84; II/2, 82, 102.

50. F. Tamburini, "Note diplomatiche," 187–188.

Part II

Documents

List of Documents and Illustrations

The following list gives the documents presented in Part II and the page on which each text begins. The illustrations corresponding to these documents are numbered in parentheses below and begin on page 165. High-resolution color images of the same illustrations can be viewed on the CD-ROM in the pocket inside the back cover of this book; or at this web address: http://cuapress.cua.edu/BOOKS/Supplementary/SalonenSchmugge/index.html. On screen, these images can be enlarged to increase the legibility and reveal even minor details of the manuscripts.

1

Litterae ecclesiae

The letter reproduced below is a rare example of the *litterae ecclesiae*—i.e., letters issued by minor penitentiaries to those Christians who confessed their sins to them in the main basilicas in Rome. The person in question is Nanne Torberni Kärling[1] (Nanne, son of Torbern Kärling), a Swedish layman from the Diocese of Skara. He arrived in Rome in the autumn of 1449, where he stayed until early spring 1450. The other person mentioned in the letter, Torstein Kärling, was the late brother of Nanne.

The letter attests that Nanne had confessed his sins and been absolved by the German minor penitentiary Johannes Calp. Nanne was obliged to turn to a German-speaking confessor, since at that point the papal curia no longer employed a special confessor for Christians speaking Scandinavian languages. The document was probably produced and handed over to him very soon after the confession.

This letter, together with some other documents, among which were other papal letters granted to Nanne during his stay in Rome, has survived to our day in the collections of the Swedish National

1. In the document, his family name—Kärling—is spelled in the form Clericus (Clericum – Clerici). This is not to be confused with the Latin word *clericus* meaning "a cleric."

Archives, probably because of a long litigation process before the episcopal court in Sweden in which Nanne and his family had to fight against his sister over inheritance upon their parents' death.[2]

DOCUMENT 1. Nanne Torberi Kärling Is Absolved by Johannes Calp (Illustration 1).[3]

Note: In this and all following texts, forward slashes indicate the end of a line in the original document.

Universis presentes litteras inspecturis, Johannes Calp domini pape penitentiarius, salutem in Domino. Noverit /2/ universitas vestra quod nos Nannonem Torberni Clericum Scharensis diocesis latorem presencium, limina /3/ beatorum apostolorum Petri et Pauli de urbe ac sedem apostolicam pro se et anima cuiusdam Torstani /4/ Clerici laici dicte diocesis personaliter visitantem, a peccatis suis omnibus auctoritate domini pape absolvimus /5/ et iniuximus ei super ipsis auctoritate predicta penitentiam quam secundum Deum anime sue saluti /6/ vidimus iniungendam, presentes inde sibi litteras sigillo officii penitentiariorum sigillatas in testi/7/monium concedentes. Datum Rome apud Sanctumpetrum nonas augusti pontificatus /8/ domini Nicolai pape V anno tertio.

In the left margin: Bene
In the plica: Jo. de Caraczolis[4]
There is no information on the Penitentiary on the *verso*.
Seal of the Penitentiary, red wax, white and red hemp cord.

2. For details of the case of Nanne Kärling, see M.-L. Nordmark, "Nanne Kärling, munk och frälseman: Studier kring en medeltida arvsprocess," *Kyrkohistorisk Årsskrift* 42 (1942), 124–153; K. Salonen, *Penitentiary,* 57, 311–312, 402–405; K. Salonen, "Fallet Nanne Kärling, Att kombinera biografiska uppgifter ur olika arkiv," in *Ny väg till medeltisbreven* (Från ett medeltidssymposium i Svenska Riksarkivet 26–28 november 1999. Skrifter utgifna av Riksarkivet 18; Stockholm, 2002), 99–106.

3. Stockholm, Riksarkivet, Or. Perg. (5.8.1449).

4. Johannes de Caraczolis is the name of the scribe who composed the document.

English translation:

To all who will read the present letter, Johannes Calp, the Penitentiary of the Lord Pope, sends his greeting in the Lord. Let it be known to all of you that we have absolved Nanno Torberni Kärling from the Diocese of Skara and the bearer of the present letter, who is personally visiting the threshold of the Holy Apostles Peter and Paul in the city and apostolic seat, on his own behalf and on behalf of a certain Torstanus Kärling, a layman of said diocese, from all of his sins by the authority of the Lord Pope, and with regard to them, by the aforementioned authority, we have imposed a penance on him which we saw fit to be imposed for the well-being of his soul before God, granting him the present letter which has been sealed as testimony with the seal of the office of the penitentiaries. Given in Rome at St. Peter's on the 5th of August, in the 3rd year of the pontificate of Lord Pope Nicholas V.

2

Different Types of Absolutions, Dispensations, Licenses, and Declarations

1. Matrimonial Dispensations

Matters of marriage have already been discussed in the first part of this book; we will not repeat the details here again, but will go directly to the cases we want to present. We have here three different cases, in which different kinds of documents have been preserved. Even though most of the letters of the Penitentiary were considered unnecessary and were therefore thrown away after the death of the supplicant(s), letters referring to marriage dispensations could be useful later. They could be used as testimony of the legality of children born of the marriage, after the death of their parents. These letters could be especially important in cases in which close relatives tried to prevent the offspring of the deceased couple from inheriting family property by claiming that they were illegitimate because their parents were not properly married. This could be the reason for which some examples of this kind of letter still exist in local archives.

The first case we want to present is the case of Philippus Yverson and Helena Henrici. We have two surviving documents: the original supplication, preserved in the collection of Paulus Scheel (who was the dean of the cathedral chapter of Turku) and now kept in the National Library of Finland, and an abbreviated copy of the supplication in the Penitentiary registers.

This document was preserved in Finland and was in the archives of the dean because Conradus Philippi, the son of the couple who received the dispensation, later became a member of the cathedral chapter of Turku. It is possible that before his nomination he had to present a document showing that he was born of a legal marriage. The document states that Philippus Yverson and Helena, daughter of Henrik, who had contracted a marriage despite knowing that they were related to each other by the fourth degree of affinity, had been absolved and dispensed by the Penitentiary in July 1460. This dispensation had probably been procured by Bishop Konrad Bitz of Turku. It is known that Bishop Konrad visited Siena for his consecration at the time the marriage dispensation for Philippus and Helena was granted. Bishop Konrad had a special interest in the case, for the female supplicant was the daughter of his cousin.[1]

The existence of an original supplication in the local archives is extremely rare, and it probably is a *sola signatura* supplication. This means that the Penitentiary never issued a letter of grace on the basis of its decision, and that the original petition with the signature of the official of the Penitentiary functioned as testimony of the decision. Such a favor is not recorded in the Penitentiary records, but this seems to have been the case; otherwise, it would have been strange that the letter issued by the Penitentiary did not survive, while the supplication, which would have been unnecessary after the issuing of a letter of grace, did.

The survival of both an original supplication and the entry in the Penitentiary registers allows us to compare these two documents, in order to see what information was copied into the entries and what was left out. The documents edited below show the fascinating way in which the entries in the Penitentiary registers really are very abbreviated copies of the original supplications. The scribes reduced the text of the original petition, consisting of 113 words, into an entry of only 25 words. With this example we can also prove that

1. On this case, see K. Salonen, *Penitentiary*, 94, 253, 258, 429–430; see also E. Anthoni, "En påvlig dispens för äktenskap i förbjudna led," *Historisk Tidskrift för Finland* 37 (1952), 91–93.

only the most important details were copied into the entries in the Penitentiary registers: the names of the supplicants and their home diocese, the impediment, the kind of grace requested, the date and the decision made by the Penitentiary and the name of the decision maker. All other information has been left out. This demonstrates that the scribes of the Penitentiary needed to have knowledge of both canon law and the decision-making process of the office.

DOCUMENT 2. Philippus Yverson and Helena Henrici: Original Supplication (Illustration 2)[2]

Exponitur sanctitati vestre pro parte devotorum vestrorum Philippi Yverson armigeri et Helene filie Henrici mulieris coniugum /[2]/ Aboensis diocesis quod ipsi olim scientes se quarto affinitatis gradu invicem fore attinentes matrimonium inter se publice /[3]/ per verba de presenti contraxerunt carnali copula minime subsecuta. Cum autem, pater sancte, prefati exponentes in dicto /[4]/ matrimonio sic contracto absque speciali dispensatione sedis apostolice remanere non possint, supplicatur igitur /[5]/ sanctitati vestre pro parte dictorum coniugum quatenus ipsos ab huiusmodi excessibus absolvere cum eisque ut impedimento predicto non /[6]/ obstante in eorum sic contracto matrimonio libere et licite remanere possint et valeant misericorditer dispensare dignemini /[7]/ prolem ex inde suscipiendam legitimam decernentes de gratia speciali. Fiat de speciali, A[ntonius] episcopus Aprutinus, Regens.[3]

Datum Senis xij kalendas augusti anno ij°, C. de Regio.[4]

In the upper left corner: De contracto scienter et non consumato in quarto affinitatis.[5]

2. National Library of Finland, Scheelska samlingen.

3. *"Fiat . . . Regens'* is in different handwriting—probably that of the regent himself—and darker ink than the text of the supplication.

4. Dated in Siena, on the 21st of July 1460. *"Datum . . . Regio'* is in different handwriting—probably that of the auditor who had taken care of the supplication—and lighter ink than the text of the supplication.

5. *"De . . . affinitatis'* is in different handwriting—probably that of the *audi-*

On the *verso:* Jo. Weythas.[6]
Other notes are more recent archival references.[7]

English translation:

It is set forth to your Holiness by your devotees squire Philippus Yverson and wife Helena, daughter of Henricus, spouses from the Diocese of Turku, that they some time ago, knowing themselves to be mutually constrained by affinity of the fourth degree, publicly contracted a marriage between themselves through words of present intent, which was not followed by carnal union. Since, however, Holy Father, the aforementioned petitioners may not remain in the mentioned matrimony, which was contracted without a special dispensation from the Apostolic See, Your Holiness is therefore beseeched on behalf of the aforementioned spouses to mercifully deign to absolve them from such transgressions, and—notwithstanding the aforementioned impediment—to deign to grant dispensation to them by special grace so that they might be able and have the power to remain freely and lawfully in their marriage thus contracted, and to regard the offspring resulting from it as legitimate. So be it by special mandate, Antonius, bishop of Teramo, regent.

---

tor—and lighter ink than the text of the supplication. The hand could be the same as for the date. This testifies to the practice of abbreviating the contents of the case into a few words for the handling of the case.

6. Johannes Weythas was a German proctor active in the Penitentiary. About him, see L. Schmugge, P. Hersperger, B. Wiggenhauser, *Supplikenregister,* 45–47.

7. The document is published in R. Hausen, ed., *Finlands medeltidsurkunder,* n. 4948 with the wrong date, 21.7.1502. The error in dating the document in the edition stems from the fact that the editor did not know what kind of document this was. He recognized that it was a matter of a dispensation issued through the papal curia, but he did not understand that it concerned the Penitentiary, and that the signer of the case was the regent of the Penitentiary. The editor wrongly interpreted the initial of the regent of the Penitentiary, "A' (Antonio de Fatatis de Ancona, bishop of Teramo), to be the initials of Pope Alexander VI, and therefore dated the document as belonging to that pontificate and thus as being from the year 1502.

DOCUMENT 3. Philippus Yverson and Helena Henrici: Enregistered Summary (Illustration 3)[8]

In the left margin: Senis vii idus julii[9]
In the right margin: Aboen. dioc.

Philippus Yverson armiger et Helena /²/ Henrici mulier Abuensis diocesis 4° affinitatis /³/ gradu coniuncti petunt similem gratiam sibi /⁴/ fieri. Fiat de speciali, A[ntonius] episcopus Aprutinus, Regens.

English translation:

Squire Philippus Yverson and Helena, daughter of Henricus, from the Diocese of Turku, who are connected by affinity of the fourth degree, seek to have the same grace granted to them. So be it by special mandate, Antonius, bishop of Teramo, regent.

From the second marriage case we want to present, there is only one surviving document. Even though the document cannot be compared to other documents, this case merits inclusion in this book because it gives an idea of the ways in which original documents were sometimes preserved until our times. The document—the original letter of Cardinal Penitentiary Domenico Capranica to the bishop of Lucca in Italy—is currently preserved in the University Library of Bonn.

It is very curious that a document concerning a marriage in an Italian diocese ended up in the collections of a German library. The reason for this extraordinary event is that the document was used as

8. ASV, *Penitenzieria Ap., Reg. Matrim. et Div.,* vol. 8, fol. 63v.

9. Siena, 9th of July 1460. The date differs from the date written in the supplication, which must be the correct one. In the register it is probably a question of error on the part of the writer, because a little further up on the same folio there is another entry from Finland that is dated similarly vii idus julii. It is possible that the writer has mistakenly put the same date for both Finnish entries, even though they were not handled by the office on the same day.

the cover for a manuscript belonging to the collection of the University Library of Bonn. It was very common for parchment documents to be recycled and used in covering or binding a book once the document itself was no longer of use—in this case, probably after the death of the persons in question. Parchment was a very strong material and was very good in protecting manuscripts from dirt.

The document contains a marriage dispensation for Johannes Vitalis and Lucia Baldassaris Bartolomei of the Diocese of Lucca. The couple had been legally and publicly married in ignorance of the existence of a marriage impediment. Afterwards they learned that they were bound to each other by the impediment of spiritual relationship, because the father of Johannes was the godfather of Lucia; the couple therefore requested a dispensation allowing them to remain in their marriage despite the existence of the impediment. In addition, they requested legitimization for their children. The Penitentiary granted them the grace they were asking for and referred the final decision in the matter to the bishop of Lucca, to whom the letter of grace, issued in the name of the Cardinal Penitentiary Domenico Capranica, is addressed. The decision is dated in Rome on the 13th of February 1454.

This document is also important in another way. As marriage dispensations were not recorded in the registers of the Penitentiary during the pontificate of Pope Nicolas V, this document is thus a rare testimony of the marriage dispensations that were granted by the Penitentiary during his papacy.

DOCUMENT 4. Johannes Vitalis: Dispensation in the Penitentiary Register (Illustration 4)[10]

Venerabili in Christo patri Dei gratia episcopo Lucani vel eius in spiritualibus vicario, Dominicus miseratione divina tituli sancte crucis in /2/ Jerusalem presbiter cardinalis, salutem et sinceram in

10. University Library of Bonn, S 327. We thank Dr. Stieldorf for having provided us with a photocopy of the letter.

Domino caritatem. Ex parte Johannis Vitalis laici et Lucie Baldassaris Bartolomei /[3]/ mulieris de Fabricis vestre diocesis nobis oblata petitio continebat quod ipsi olim ignorantes aliquod impedimentum inter eos existere, /[4]/ quominus possent invicem matrimonialiter copulari, matrimonium inter se per verba legitima de presenti publice contraxerunt illudque /[5]/ carnali copula nondum consumarunt. Postmodum vero ad eorum pervenit notitiam quod pater dicti Johannis prefatam Luciam de sacro fonte /[6]/ levavit. Verum quia, si divortium fieret, inter eos gravia exinde damna et scandala possent verisimiliter exoriri, supplicari fe/[7]/cerunt humiliter prefati exponentes coniuges eis super hiis per sedem apostolicam misericorditer provideri. Nos igitur cupientes ipsorum /[8]/ coniugum animarum providere saluti et huiusmodi damnis et scandalis, quantum cum Deo possimus, obviare, auctoritate domini pape, cuius /[9]/ penitentiarie curam gerimus et de eius speciali et expresso mandato super hoc vive vocis oraculo nobis facto, circumspectioni vestre /[10]/ committimus quatenus, si est ita, cum ipsis coniugibus, quod impedimento cognationis spiritualis huiusmodi, quod ex premissis provenit, non /[11]/ obstante in eorum sic contracto matrimonio libere et licite valeant remanere, misericorditer dispensetis, dummodo dicta Lucia propter hoc /[12]/ ab aliquo rapta non fuerit, prolem susceptam, si qua sit, et suscipiendam exinde legitimam decernentes. Datum Rome apud /[13]/ Sanctumpetrum sub sigillo officii penitentiarie idibus februarii pontificatus domini Nicolai pape V anno septimo.

In the upper margin: Videat eam Reverendus dominus Cardinalis.
In the left margin at the height of the fifth line: [Visa] per me
In the right margin at the height of the fifth line: Card. +[11]
Under the plica: Ful quatuordecim tur. co;[12] De Leys[13]
The seal is missing.

11. Signature of the Cardinal Penitentiary Domenico Capranica.

12. Fulco is the name of the person who acted as *referendarius-taxator* in this case, and the tax was 14 *tournois.*

13. De Leys is the name of the person who acted in this case in the role of *computator.*

English translation:

Dominicus, by divine mercy Cardinal Priest of the church of the Holy Cross in Jerusalem, [sends] greeting and sincere love to the venerable in Christ, by the grace of God bishop of Lucca, or to his vicar in spiritual affairs. A petition brought to us by Johannes Vitalis, a layman, and Lucia Baldassaris Bartolomei, woman from Fabrica, both of your diocese, stated that they once, ignorant that there existed an impediment between them preventing them from mutually joining in marriage, publicly contracted a marriage between themselves through legitimate words of present intent, and which they did not yet consummate by carnal union. Afterwards, however, it came to their attention that the father of the mentioned Johannes acted as a godparent to the aforementioned Lucia. However, since if they were divorced a grave harm and scandal could possibly come of it, the aforementioned married petitioners beseech that in this regard the Apostolic See mercifully provide them grace. We, therefore, wanting to provide for the well-being of the souls of these spouses and to prevent such harm and scandal as with God we are able, by the authority of the Lord Pope, who has entrusted the administration of the Penitentiary to us, and by his special mandate given to us in person in this regard, commit to your consideration that, if it be so, you mercifully grant dispensation to these spouses so that they might be able to remain in their marriage thus contracted freely and lawfully despite such an impediment of spiritual relationship which arises from the aforementioned, provided that the mentioned Lucia has not been seized by anyone because of this, and judging the existing offspring, if there is any, and any yet to come, to be legitimate. Given in Rome at Saint Peter's by the seal of the office of the Penitentiary on the 13th of February, in the 7th year of the pontificate of Lord Pope Nicolas V.

The third marriage case we have chosen as an example offers us another opportunity to compare two different kinds of documents concerning one marriage matter: the petition registered in the Penitentiary registers, and a copy of the original letter of the Penitentiary, preserved in a copy book in the archives of the Prague Metropolitan Chapter.

The protagonists in this case, Michael Genczss and Katerina Lapka, came from the Diocese of Prague. They explain in their supplication that they had married without knowing that Michael's first wife had been related to Katerina by the third degree of consanguinity. After some time they were informed of the marital impediment, and Wenceslaus of Crumlau, *decretorum doctor* and dean of the Prague cathedral chapter (at that time there was no regular bishop in Prague because of the Hussite wars), took Michael and Katerina before his court and separated them. They obeyed his sentence and separated, but for the sake of their children they decided to turn to Pope Calixtus III and ask for a dispensation and permission to marry again, as well as to have their children legitimized.

The Cardinal Penitentiary Domenico Capranico approved their petition on the 24th of May 1455. The same day a letter of grace was also issued, addressed to Wenceslaus of Crumlau, who was supposed to take care of the case back in Prague. Wenceslaus must have acted in the matter, because we can now find a copy of the original letter in the archives of the Prague Metropolitan Chapter.

DOCUMENT 5. Michael Genczss and Katerina Lapka: Petition in Registers (Illustration 5)[14]

In the left margin: viiii kal junii[15]

Exponitur sanctitati vestre pro parte devotorum vestrorum Michaelis Gentzss et K[a]terine Lapka laicorum /[2]/ coniugum quod ipsi olim ignorantes, quod quondam uxor prima dicti Michaelis esset coniuncta K[a]terine /[3]/ tercio consanguinitatis gradu, matrimonium per verba de presenti in facie ecclesie de facto contraxerunt carnali copula /[4]/ et prole subsecuta. Postmodum ad notitiam dictorum Michaelis et Caterine atque ipsius ordinarii videlicet Wenezeslai /[5]/ de Crumlare decretorum doctori decani et administratori ecclesie Pragensis notitiam /[6]/ devenit ipsos Michaelem et Catherinam tertio affinitatis gradu fore coniunctos. Idem decanus /[7]/ eos coram se fecit ad iudicium evocari et servatis servandis ipsos Michaelem et K[a]ter-

14. ASV, *Penitenzieria Ap., Reg. Matrim. et Div.*, vol. 6, fol. 175r. An abstract of this case is also published in RPG III, n. 1688.

15. The 24th of May 1455.

inam /[8]/ per suam diffinitivam sententiam ab invicem separavit et divortiavit, cui sententie ipsi Michael /[9]/et K[a]terina par[u]erunt cum effectu. Cum autem in favorem prolis - - - - /[10]/ Cum autem in favorem prolis ex predicto matrimonio suscepte et propter alias causas desidere[n]t etiam de novo /[11]/ matrimonialiter copulari et si divortium fieret etc. Supplicant etc. non obstante impedimento huiusmodi inter se /[12]/ possint contrahere et in sic contracto licite remanere dispensari cum eis misericorditer dignemini prolemque exinde etc. /[13]/ de gratia speciali. Fiat de speciali et expresso, D. S. +[16]

English translation:

It is set forth to your Holiness by your devotees Michael Genczss and Katerina Lapka, lay spouses, that they once, unaware that the former first wife of the said Michael was connected to Katerina by consanguinity of the third degree, contracted a de facto marriage through words of present intent in the presence of the congregation which was followed by a carnal union and offspring. Afterwards it came to the attention of the said Michael and Katerina, and to the attention of their ordinary, namely Wenceslaus of Crumlau, doctor in canon law, dean and administrator of the church of Prague, that the same Michael and Katerina were connected by affinity of the third degree. This same dean had them called before him for judgment and, having observed all that was to be observed, he mutually separated and divorced the same Michael and Katerina through his definitive sentence, to which sentence the same Michael and Katerina submitted with effect. Since however, for the benefit of the offspring - - - - Since however, for the benefit of the offspring begotten from the aforementioned matrimony, and for other causes, they wish to be joined in marriage again, and if there were a divorce etc., they beseech etc. that despite such an impediment you mercifully deign to grant them dispensation by special grace so that they might be able to contract a marriage between themselves and to remain lawfully in one thus contracted, and that the offspring from it etc. So be it by special and expressed mandate, D[ominicus Cardinal Priest of] S[ancte] Crucis [in Jerusalem].

16. D. S. + is Domenicus Capranica, Major Penitentiary, Cardinal of the Roman church of the Holy Cross in Jerusalem.

DOCUMENT 6. Michael Genczss and Katerina Lapka: Letter in Prague Archives (Illustration 6)[17]

Dominicus miseratione divina tituli sancte crucis in Jerusalem presbiter cardinalis, discreto viro Wen[cesla]o de /²/ Crumlow decretorum doctori decano ac administratori ecclesie Pragensis, salutem in Domino. Sedis /³/ apostolice providentia circumspecta nonnumquam rigorem iuxta mansetudinem temperat et, quod sacrorum canonum /⁴/ prohibent instituta, de gratia benignitatis indulget, prout personarum et temporum qualitate pensata id in Deo sa/⁵/lubriter expedire cognoscit. Quare ex parte Michaelis Genzss laici et Katherine Lapka mulieris /⁶/ Pragensis diocesis nobis oblata petitio continebat quod ipsi olim ignorantes aliquod impedimentum inter eos /⁷/ existere, quominus possent invicem matrimonialiter copulari, matrimonium inter se per verba legittime de presenti /⁸/ publice iuxta morem patrie contraxerunt illudque per carnalem copulam consumarunt et prolem procre/⁹/arunt. Postmodum vero ad eorum et tui notitiam pervenit quod tertio affinitatis gradu se invicem /¹⁰/ attinent, propter quod tu iuridice procedens eos coram te ad iudicium evocari fecisti et servatis servandis /¹¹/ eosdem Michaelem et Katherinam ab invicem separasti per tuam sententiam diffinitivam ac divorciasti, /¹²/ cui sententie divorcii dicti exponentes humiliter cum effectu paruerunt. Cum autem prefati exponentes /¹³/ in favorem prolis huiusmodi et propter certas alias legittimas causas desiderent de novo invicem /¹⁴/ matrimonialiter copulari et, si sic divorciati perpetuo remanerent, gravia damna et scandala exinde /¹⁵/ verisimiliter exoriri possent, quare supplicari fecerunt humiliter iidem exponentes eis super hiis /¹⁶/ per sedem predictam de oportune dispensationis gratia misericorditer provideri. Nos itaque cupientes /¹⁷/ quatenus damnis et scandalis obviare eorumque in hac parte supplicationibus inclinati, auctoritate domini /¹⁸/ pape, cuius penitentiarie curam gerimus et de eius speciali et expresso mandato super hoc vive vocis /¹⁹/ oraculo

17. Archiv prazske metropolitni kapituly, Cod. VI-5, fol. 62v. We thank Zdenka Hledíková, director of the Istituto Storico Ceco di Roma, for indicating the existence of this document to us.

nobis facto, discretioni vestre, cum ad presens iurisdictionem ecclesiasticam ecclesie Pragensis /[20]/ exerceas, committimus quatenus, si est ita, cum ipsis Michaele et Katherina, quod impedimento /[21]/ affinitatis huiusmodi non obstante possent inter se de novo matrimonium libere contrahere et /[22]/ in eo postquam contractum fuerit licite remanere, misericorditer dispensari, dummodo dicta Katherina /[23]/ propter hoc ab aliquo rapta non fuerit prolem susceptam et suscipiendam exinde legittimam /[24]/ decernentes. Datum Rome apud Sanctum Petrum sub sigillo officii penitentiarie viiii kalendas junii pontificatus /[25]/ domini Calixti pape tercii anno primo.

At the level of the fifth line, the scribe has copied in the left margin reference to the checking of the original letter: *Visa per me*. However, the corresponding reference to the name of the Cardinal Penitentiary in the right margin has not been copied to the register.

English translation:

Dominicus, by divine mercy the Cardinal Priest of the church of Sancte Crucis in Jerusalem, [sends] greeting in the Lord to the distinguished man, Wenceslaus of Crumlau, doctor in canon law, dean and administrator of the church of Prague. The circumspect foresight of the Apostolic See sometimes combines severity with clemency and grants, through the favor of benignity, what the regulations of the holy canons prohibit in the manner in which the See recognizes this to be wholesomely advantageous before God after it has considered the quality of the people and the times. The petition brought to us on behalf of layman Michael Genczss and a woman Katerina Lapka, from the diocese of Prague, contained that they once, ignorant of any impediment existing between them which would prevent them from joining in matrimony, publicly contracted a marriage between themselves through legitimate words of present intent according to the custom of their land, and consummated it through carnal union and procreated offspring. Afterwards, however, it came to their and your notice that they are mutually constrained by affinity of the third degree, for which reason, proceeding juridically, you had them called before yourself for judgment and, having observed all that was to be observed, you mutually separated the same Michael and Katerina through your definitive sentence and divorced them, to which divorce sentence the mentioned petitioners humbly submitted with effect. Since, however, the aforementioned petitioners wish to join mutually in marriage again for the benefit of the offspring and for certain other legitimate causes, and since, if they were to remain perpetually thus divorced, grave harm and scandal could possibly come of it, therefore the same petitioners have humbly beseeched that in these regards the Apostolic See mercifully provide [grace] to them by the grace of suitable dispensation. We, therefore, wanting to prevent such harm and scandal and being inclined toward their appeals in this respect, by the authority of the Lord Pope, who has entrusted the administration of the Penitentiary to us, and by his special and expressed mandate given to us in person on this account, commit to your discretion, since you now exercise ecclesiastical jurisdiction in the church of Prague, that, if it be so, [you mercifully grant dispensation] to the same Michael and Katerina so that, despite such an impediment of affinity, they be able to contract matrimony again freely between themselves and to remain in it lawfully after it has been contracted, provided that the mentioned Katerina has not been seized by anyone because of this, and judging the existing offspring, and any yet to come, to be legitimate. Given in Rome at Saint Peter's by the seal of the office of the Penitentiary on the 14th of May, in the 1st year of the pontificate of Lord Pope Calixtus III.

2. Dispensation from Illegitimate Birth

As was explained in the Part I of this book, there were almost 38,000 people from all over Latin West who, in the years 1449–1533, turned to the Penitentiary for a dispensation from illegitimacy. Information on such persons exists, however, for the most part only in the folios of the registers of the Penitentiary. A very few original letters have been preserved to the present time, for when the candidate for the priesthood who was requesting a dispensation from his illegitimacy died, there was no further need to conserve such a document. Since they were no longer of any importance—unlike marriage dispensations, which, on the contrary, might continue to be of some value—these letters were often thrown away.

We will now present two different kinds of decisions of the Penitentiary in matters of illegitimacy: a dispensation from illegitimacy in simple form, and an *ubi pater* dispensation. Two documents survive from each of the chosen cases: the entry in the Penitentiary register and the letter of grace.

A Simple Dispensation

The case of Conradus Fischer from the Diocese of Constance, Germany, is a simple dispensation from illegitimacy. Two different documents exist for this case: a very much abbreviated copy of the petition is registered among the Penitentiary entries, and the original letter of the Penitentiary—showing the full formulary of this kind of dispensation—is preserved in the Generallandesarchiv Karlsruhe.

According to these documents, a certain Conrad (in German Konrad) Fischer from the Diocese of Constance asked to be dispensed from defect of birth so that he could receive ecclesiastical orders despite being an illegitimate son. His father was an ordained priest and his mother—typically for such relationships—an unmarried woman. The Cardinal Penitentiary, Philippus Calandrini, made a positive judgment in this case on the 26th of September 1459. In the letter of grace addressed to the bishop of Constance, he stated that the bishop could ordain Conrad to priesthood if he found that Conrad would be a valuable person and did not follow in "his father's footsteps."

Document 7. Conrad Fischer: Entry in the Penitentiary Register (Illustration 7)[18]

In the left margin: Mantue vi kalendas octobris[19]
In the right margin: Constan. dioc.
In the right margin: J. Weythas[20] (the name of the proctor)

Corandus Fischer scolaris Constanciensis diocesis supplicat /2/ quatenus secum super deffectu [*sic!*] natalium, quem patitur /3/ de presbitero et soluta genitus, ut eo non obstante deffectu [*sic!*] /4/ ad omnes etiam sacros et presbiteratus ordines possit promoveri /5/ et beneficium ecclesiasticum obtinere, dispensari dignemini. Fiat de speciali, /6/ Phi[lippus] Sancti Laurencii in Lucina.

18. ASV, *Penitenzieria Ap., Reg. Matrim. et Div.*, vol. 7, fol. 324v. A summary of the case is published in the RPG IV, n. 1999.

19. Mantova, 26th of September 1459.

20. Johannes Weythas was a German proctor who took care of the case.

English translation:

Conrad Fischer, a scholar from the Diocese of Constance, appeals, concerning a defect of birth which he suffers as the son of a priest and an unmarried woman, that despite that defect you deign to grant him dispensation so that he may be ordained to all sacred and priestly orders and obtain an ecclesiastical benefice. So be it by special mandate, Philippus of Sancti Laurentii in Lucina.

DOCUMENT 8. Conrad Fischer: Original Letter (Illustration 8)[21]

Venerabili in Christo patri Dei gratia episcopo Constantiensi vel eius vicario in spiritualibus, Philippus miseratione /[2]/ divina tituli Sancti Laurentii in Lucina presbiter cardinalis, salutem et sinceram in Domino caritatem. Ex parte Conradi /[3]/ Fischer scolaris vestre diocesis nobis fuit humiliter supplicatum, ut cum eo, qui sicut asseritur ascribi desiderat /[4]/ militie clericali, super defectu natalium, quem patitur de presbitero genitus et soluta, quod huiusmodi non obstante de/[5]/fectu ad omnes possit etiam sacros ordines promoveri et beneficium ecclesiasticum obtinere, etiam si curam /[6]/ habeat animarum, sedes apostolica dispensare misericorditer dignaretur. Nos igitur, auctoritate domini pape, cuius penitentiarie curam /[7]/ gerimus et de eius speciali mandato super hoc vive vocis oraculo nobis facto, circumspectioni vestre commit/[8]/timus quatenus, si est ita, consideratis diligenter circumstantiis universis, que circa ydoneitatem persone /[9]/ fuerint attendende, si paterne non est incontinentie imitator sed bone conversationis et vite sufficientisque /[10]/ litterature, super quibus vestram conscientiam oneramus, aliaque sibi merita suffragantur ad huiusmodi /[11]/ dispensationis gratiam obtinendam, cum eo super petitis misericorditer dispensetis, ita tamen quod idem scolaris, /[12]/ prout requiret onus beneficii, quod eum post dispensationem hui-

21. Karlsruhe, Generallandesarchiv, B IV 1650 (26.9.1459); see Rieder (ed.), *Regesta Episcoporum Constantiensium,* vol. 4, Nr. 12.284, p. 259. Tamburini, Suppliche e lettere p. 195. L. Schmugge, P. Hersperger, B. Wiggenhauser, *Supplikenregister,* 39–41. E. Göller, *Pönitentiarie* II/1, 88.

usmodi obtinere contigerit, se faciat /13/ statutis a iure temporibus ad ordines promoveri et personaliter resideat in eodem, alioquin dicte dispensa/14/tionis gratia quoad ipsum beneficium nullius penitus sit momenti. Datum Mantue sub sigillo officii /15/ penitentiarie vi kalendis octobris pontificatus domini Pii pape II anno secundo.

On the *verso:* "Disen brif sol man gen her Cünraten zo Costenz zue den schotzen" (This letter has to be given to Master Conrad in Constance in the monastery of the Scotsmen).[22]

English translation:

Philippus, by divine mercy Cardinal Priest of Sancti Laurentii in Lucina, sends his greeting and sincere love in the Lord, to the venerable in Christ, by the grace of God bishop of Constance, or to his vicar in spiritual affairs. We were humbly appealed to by Conradus Fischer, a scholar of your diocese, that the Apostolic See mercifully deign to grant dispensation to him who, as is claimed, desires to be included among the clergy, concerning a defect of birth, which he suffers as the son of a priest and an unmarried woman, so that despite such a defect he be able to be promoted to all, even sacred, orders and obtain an ecclesiastical benefice even if it includes cure of souls. We, therefore, by the authority of the Lord Pope who has entrusted the administration of the Penitentiary to us, and by his special mandate given to us in person on this account, commit to your consideration that, if it is so, you consider diligently all the circumstances which mark the suitability of a person, [and] if he is not an imitator of paternal incontinence but of good behavior and sufficient in age and learning—concerning which we burden your conscience—and [if] other merits recommend him for obtaining the grace of such dispensation, you mercifully grant him dispensation concerning this appeal, in such a way, however, that the same scholar, since he requests the burden of benefice, which he is able to obtain after such a dispensation, should have himself promoted to [clerical] orders within a time required by law and should personally reside in the benefice; otherwise the grace of the said dispensation with respect to that benefice is completely without any influence. Given at

22. This is a kind of address for the "postman" to deliver the letter in the city of Constance to the petitioner, who obviously lived in the convent of the Schottenkloster (schotzen). This interesting information came from neither the supplication nor the original letter's text, but must have been added by the local episcopal administration.

Mantua by the seal of the office of the Penitentiary on the 27th of September, in the 2nd year of the pontificate of Lord Pope Pius II.

2.2. An *Ubi pater* Dispensation

Our second example concerning illegitimacy contains many interesting details. First of all, this case is very late—from August 1537—considering that the supplicant came from the Diocese of Bremen, Germany, which at that time should already have been thoroughly reformed. Second, this case demonstrates well how much—or how little—we sometimes can rely on the registrations in the Penitentiary records, and how careful one should be when interpreting the cases. Fortunately, we have two separate documents concerning this case—a copy of the petition in the Penitentiary registers and the original letter of grace in the Staatsarchiv Hamburg—which we can compare to one another and thus see in which details the scribes have made mistakes.

The supplicant mentioned in the original letter is Henricus Banscow, a cleric from the Diocese of Bremen. In the abbreviated copy of the supplication, the scribe erroneously wrote Bausel instead of Banscow, and instead of *Bremensis diocesis* he wrote *Remensis diocesis*. This is quite a remarkable error, for *Remensis diocesis* refers to the very important Archdiocese of Reims in France and has nothing to do with Bremen.

Henricus Banscow declared in his petition that he had earlier received a dispensation from his bishop or the pope to hold an ecclesiastical benefice despite being an illegitimate child of a priest and an unmarried woman; he now wanted to have the right to retain two benefices, one of which was the church in which his father held a benefice. Ludovicus Gomes, regent of the Penitentiary, on the 29th of August 1537 made a positive decision on Henricus' petition. The letter of grace of the Penitentiary was issued in the name of the Cardinal Penitentiary Antonius Pucci, who was cardinal of the church of Quattuor Coronati. As we can see, the letter is addressed to Henricus himself and not to the local bishop.

Such *ubi pater* dispensations were rare in the Penitentiary registers. Canon law forbade the illegitimate son of a priest to do service in the same church as his father; with a papal letter of the type presented here, this regulation could be overruled.

DOCUMENT 9. Henricus Banscow: Entry in the Penitentiary Register (Illustrations 9a–b):[23]

Above the text of the petition: Idem t vij[24]

Similis pro Henrico Bausel clerico Remensis [*sic!*] diocesis /[2]/ supplicatur etc. quatenus secum, cum quo aliter, ut asseritur, /[3]/ super defectu natalium, quem patitur de presbitero genitus /[4]/ et soluta, ad unum vel plura beneficia ecclesiastica /[5]/ obtinenda apostolica vel forsan ad primum beneficium /[6]/ sine cura ordinaria auctoritatibus dispensatum extitit, /[7]/ ut unum ex beneficiis huiusmodi vel aliud quodcumque, /[8]/ ad quod obtinendum apostolica auctoritate dispensari contigerit, /[9]/ qualitercumque qualificatum unum du[m] taxat in /[10]/ ecclesia etiam cathedrali, in qua pater suus fuit, est /[11]/ vel erit beneficiatus, etiam patre suo vivente, obtinere /[12]/ ac missas et alia divina officia in eadem ecclesia, /[13]/ etiam dicto patre suo presente, celebrare ut[25] illis /[14]/ cum per eum celebrantur interesse possit, sedes /[15]/ sedes [*sic!*] Apostolica dispen[sa]re misericorditer dignaretur; quatenus /[16]/ secum super premissis, dummodo in dicto beneficio /[17]/ patri suo non succedat succedat [*sic!*], ipse et idem pater suus /[18]/ in altaris ministerio insimul non ministrant, /[19]/ dispensare dignemini non obstantibus apostolicis necnon provincialibus /[20]/ et sinodalibus constitutionibus et ordinationibus necnon ecclesie, /[21]/ in qua forsan huiusmodi beneficium fuerit, etiam jura-

23. ASV, *Penitenzieria Ap., Reg. Matrim. et Div.*, vol. 94, fol. 601r–v. The supplication is connected with other similar petitions, and the dating of the case can be found together with the earlier case, *iiii. kal. septembris anno tertio Pauli Pape tertio* (29th of August 1537).

24. *Idem* refers to the proctor, in this case Cordellas, who took care of these petitions which were presented together to the Penitentiary. *t. vij*, in its turn, refers to the tax, seven *tournois*, the petitioner had to pay to the Penitentiary.

25. Should be: *ac*.

mento, /[22]/ confirmatione apostolica vel quavis firmitate alia roboratis /[601v]/ statutis et consuetudinibus, privilegiis quoque indultis /[2]/ et litteris apostolicis concessis, quorumcumque existant, ceterisque /[3]/ contrariis quibuscumque dignemini de gratia speciali. /[4]/ Fiat de speciali pro omnibus, L[udovicus Gomes], R[egens].

English translation:

In the same manner Henricus Banscow, cleric of the Diocese of Bremen—to whom, different from what is asserted, a dispensation from authoritative decrees has existed concerning defect of birth, which he suffers as the son of a priest and an unmarried woman, so that he may obtain one or several apostolic ecclesiastical benefices or may possibly obtain the first benefice without the ordinary duties of the care of souls—appeals that the Apostolic See mercifully deign to grant him dispensation so that he may be able to obtain one of this kind of benefice or another of whatever kind, for the sake of obtaining which he has come to be dispensed by the apostolic authority, [or] one of any manner of qualification, provided that it be in a church, even in the cathedral church where his father was, is, or will be beneficed, even while his father is still living, and so that he may be able to celebrate masses and other divine offices in the same church, even with his said father present, and so that he may be able to be present at them when his father celebrates them. Henricus appeals that you deign to grant him a dispensation concerning the afore-mentioned matters, provided that he does not succeed his father in the mentioned benefice [and that] he himself and his father do not minister at the same time in the ministry of the altar, [and he appeals that] you deign [to do this] by special grace, not allowing to get in the way apostolic and provincial and synodal constitutions and ordinations and [those] of the church in which such a benefice will possibly be, [or] even statutes and customs, [and] also privileges which have been granted and apostolic letters which have been sent—of whatever kind they may be—and whatever other contrary [statutes] which have been strengthened by an oath, apostolic confirmation, or whatever other source of strength. So be it for everybody by special mandate, L[udovicus Gomes], regent.

DOCUMENT 10. Henricus Banscow: Original Letter (Illustration 10)[26]

Antonius miseratione divina tituli Sanctorum Quattuor Coronatorum presbiter cardinalis, dilecto in Christo Henrico Banscow /2/ clerico Bremensis diocesis, salutem in Domino. Ex parte tua nobis fuit humiliter supplicatum quatenus tecum, cum quo alias, ut asseritur, super /3/ defectu natalium, quem pateris de presbitero genitus et soluta, ad unum vel plura beneficia ecclesiastica obtinenda apostolica vel /4/ forsan ad primum beneficium sine cura ordinaria auctoritatibus dispensatum extitit, ut unum ex beneficiis huiusmodi vel aliud quodcumque, /5/ ad quod obtinendum tecum apostolica auctoritate contigeris, qualitercunque qualificatum unum dumtaxat in ecclesia, etiam /6/ cathedrali in qua pater tuus fuit, est vel erit beneficiatus, etiam patre tuo vivente, obtinere ac missas et alia divina officia /7/ in eadem ecclesia, etiam dicto patre tuo presente, celebrare ac illis cum per eum celebrantur interesse possis, Sedes Apostolica dispen/8/sare misericorditer dignaretur. Nos itaque tuis in hac parte supplicationibus inclinati, auctoritate domini pape, cuius penitentiarie curam gerimus /9/ et de eius speciali mandato super hoc vive vocis oraculo nobis facto, tecum super premissis, dummodo in dicto beneficio /10/ patri tuo non succedas tuque et idem pater tuus in altaris ministerio insimul non ministretis, veris existentibus premissis, /11/ tenore presentium dispensamus, non obstantibus apostolicis ac provincialibus et synodalibus constitutionibus et ordinatio/12/nibus necnon ecclesie, in qua forsan huiusmodi beneficium fuerit, etiam juramento, confirmatione apostolica vel quavis firmitate /13/ alia roboratis statutis et consuetudinibus privilegiis quoque indultis et litteris apostolicis illi concessis, quorumcunque tenorum /14/ existant, ceterisque contrariis quibuscunque. Datum Rome apud Sanctumpetrum sub sigillo officii penitentiarie iiii kalendas septembris /15/ pontificatus domini Pauli pape III anno tertio.

In the left margin: bene.

26. Staatsarchiv Hamburg 710–711, Threse I, R. 71.

In the plica: A. de Villanova, Jul. Cardellus.
The red wax seal of the Penitentiary with hemp cord has survived partially.

English translation:

Antonius, by divine mercy Cardinal Priest of Sanctorum Quattuor Coronati, sends greeting in the Lord to the beloved in Christ Henricus Banscow, cleric of the Diocese of Bremen. You have appealed to us that the Apostolic See deign mercifully to grant dispensation to you—to whom a dispensation has already, as is asserted, been granted concerning defect of birth, which you endure as the son of a priest and an unmarried woman, so that you are able to obtain one or several ecclesiastical benefices by apostolic authority or possibly the first *sine cura* benefice by episcopal authority—so that you might be able to obtain one of such benefices, or another, of any kind for the obtaining of which you have come [to be dispensed] by the apostolic authority, one of any manner of qualification, in a single church, even in the cathedral church where your father was, is or will be beneficed, while your father is still living, and to celebrate masses and other divine offices in the same church, even with your mentioned father present, and to be present at them when your father celebrates them. Hence, having inclined toward your appeals in this respect, we, by the authority of the Lord Pope, who has entrusted the administration of the Penitentiary to us, and by his special mandate given to us in person on this account, mercifully grant you dispensation with the tenor of the present letter with regard to the aforementioned, provided that you do not succeed your father in the mentioned benefice, and you and your father do not minister at the same time as a priest at the altar, notwithstanding apostolic and provincial and synodal constitutions and ordinations [nor the statutes of] the church in which such benefice will possibly be, even if strengthened by an oath, apostolic confirmation or whatever statutes and customs confirmed by another authority, and also granted privileges and confirmed apostolic letters, whatever might exist, and whatever other contrary [statutes]. Given in Rome at Saint Peter's by the seal of the office of the Penitentiary on the 29th of August, in the 3rd year of the pontificate of Lord Pope Paul III.

3. Letters of Confession

As already explained in the first part of the book, letters of confession were of strictly personal importance for the petitioner only, and therefore their chance of survival was rather low. Thus the confessional letter preserved in the Stadtarchiv Mainz, Germany, is an *avis rara*. Only through original letters can one really study these matters, for the very short entries in the Penitentiary registers do not offer very much information on the supplicants or on the circumstances surrounding the petitions.

Furthermore, this document is the only testimony of the petition in question, for it was not recorded in the registers of the Penitentiary. Indeed, petitions for confession letters are the most inadequately registered instances among the petitions presented to the Penitentiary. This must be because the letters of confession did not have any legal consequences, and thus their registration did not play an important role.

According to our example, the Cardinal Penitentiary Philippus Calandrini conceded on the 11th of December 1472 to a priest called Henricus Sartoris (the latinized form of German name Heinrich Schneider = Henry Taylor) from Mainz, together with his brothers and sisters, a five-year privilege allowing them to choose for themselves a confessor. He also granted the chosen confessor the right to absolve them from all sins except those for which the Holy See had to be consulted, and from the vow of pilgrimage, except to Jerusalem, Rome, or Santiago de Compostela.

DOCUMENT 11. Henricus Sartoris: Privilege for Confession (Illustration 11)[27]

Philippus miseratione divina episcopus Portuensis, dilectis in Christo Henrico Sartoris presbitero et eius fratribus /²/ et sororibus Maguntinensis diocesis, salutem in Domino. Ut animabus vestris salubrius consulatur, auctoritate domini pape, /³/ cuius penitentiarie curam gerimus, devotioni vestre concedimus quatenus liceat vobis ydoneum et discretum /⁴/ presbiterum in confessorem eligere, qui super peccatis, que sibi confitebimini, nisi talia sint propter que /⁵/ merito sit sedes apostolica consulenda, vobis auctoritate predic-

27. Stadtarchiv Mainz, Urkunden Altmünster 11.11.1472.

ta provideat de absolutionis debite /6/ beneficio et penitentia salutari hinc ad quinquennium quotiens fuerit oportunum, vota vero /7/ peregrinationis et abstinentie, si qua emisistis que commode servare non potestis, ultramarino, /8/ beatorum Petri et Pauli atque Jacobi apostolorum votis dumtaxat exceptis, commutet vobis hac vice /9/ idem confessor in alia opera pietatis. Datum Rome apud Sanctumpetrum sub sigillo officii /10/ penitentiarie iii idus novembris pontificatus domini Sixti pape IIII anno secundo.

Under the plica: P. de Ursis;[28] Ja. de Cremonen.;[29] Clous
In the plica: Jo. Rosa[30]
On the *verso:* A. Piscatoris[31]

English translation:

Philippus, by divine mercy bishop of Porto [Santa Rufina], [sends] greeting in the Lord to the beloved in Christ priest Henry Sartoris and his brothers and sisters in the Diocese of Mainz. In order that your souls be most advantageously counselled, by the authority of the Lord Pope, who has entrusted the administration of the Penitentiary to us, we grant to your devotion that you be able to elect a suitable and distinguished priest as a confessor, who by the aforementioned authority will provide you with the due service of absolution and salutary penance from now on for five years as often as it should be necessary with regard to those sins which you will confess to him, unless they are such that the Apostolic See must be justly consulted; the same confessor may even commute for you to other works of piety the vows of pilgrimage and abstinence if you have made any which you are not able to observe appropriately, save the pledges [to the shrines] on the other side of the sea [= Jerusalem], of the blessed apostles Peter and Paul, as well as of James. Given in Rome at Saint Peter's by the seal of the office of the Penitentiary on the 11th of November, in the 2nd year of the pontificate of Lord Pope Sixtus IV.

28. P. de Ursis is the name of the person who acted as *distributor* in this case.

29. Jacobus de Cremona is the name of the person who acted as *computator* in this case.

30. Johannes Rosa is the name of the scribe who composed the letter.

31. A. Piscatoris was the proctor in this case. Concerning his activity with German petitioners during the pontificate of Pius II (1458–1464), see RPG IV, n. 381.

4. Leaving a Monastery

For religious persons—nuns and monks—in the Middle Ages, entry into a monastery or convent after having pronounced the formal *professio*—the vow of poverty, chastity, and obedience—was a definitive lifetime decision. Canon law rules did not allow monks or nuns to leave their order or religious house without the permission of the abbot or prior, not even to change to another house of the same order. Nevertheless, in many cases nuns and monks did want to leave their *ovile,* or sheepfold, as the oft-used Latin expression goes.

As explained in the first part of this book, changing from one monastery to another was possible with the permission of the pope. Thus we find among the entries in the Penitentiary registers many requests for a license for what is known in the canonical *terminus technicus* as a *transitus*—changing from one monastery or monastic order to another.

We want to present here a case concerning a license to change from one monastery to another. There are two surviving documents in this case: in addition to the entry in the Penitentiary records, we also have for this case a very well preserved example of an original letter issued by the Penitentiary, currently kept in the Staatsarchiv Thurgau, Switzerland.

The person in question in this case is Barbara de Rischach, an Augustinian nun in the monastery of St. Katharinental near Diessenhofen, Switzerland, and a member of a noble family in southern Germany (Truchsessen von Waldburg). According to the surviving documentation, she had asked her superior for permission to move to another nunnery, but her request was rejected. She therefore turned to the authority of Pope Sixtus IV.[32]

On the 8th of February 1482 Julianus, Bishop of Bertinoro, decided in favor of the supplicant, granting her, as she had requested, a license to transfer to another monastery. On the same day, the Peni-

32. On the case of Barbara de Rischach, see M. Svec, "Apostasie und Transitus in der Registerüberlieferung und *in partibus,*" in K. Salonen, C. Krötzl, eds., *The Roman Curia, the Apostolic Penitentiary and the Partes in the Later Middle Ages* (Acta Instituti Romani Finlandiae 28; Rome, 2003), 183–200.

tentiary addressed a letter in the name of the Cardinal Penitentiary, Julianus, bishop of Sabina, to the bishop of Constance, who at that time was Otto von Sonneberg. In this letter, the Cardinal Penitentiary asked the bishop to check her reasons for changing monastery, and if her argumentation was valid to decide in her favor. Thanks to the original letter, which on the reverse contains some remarks probably written by the prior, we know that Barbara finally got permission to transfer into the convent of Schönensteinbach in Alsatia, France.

DOCUMENT 12. Barbara Rischach: Dispensation to Transfer to Another Monastery (Illustration 12)[33]

In the left margin: Rome vi idus februarii[34]
In the right margin: Constantien. dioc.

Soror Barbara de Rischach monialis professa monasterii /2/ in Dissenhoven ordinis sancti Augustini sub cura et regimine ordinis fratrum /3/ predicatorum degentium Constantiensis diocesis, quod ipsa cum sui animi /4/ quiete non possit in dicto monasterio et ordine remanere, quatenus sibi trans/5/ferendi se ad aliquem alium ordinem paris vel arctioris observantie /6/ regularis concedere mandare dignemini de gratia speciali et expresso. Fiat /7/ de speciali et expresso, Jul[ianus] episcopus Brictonoriensis, Regens.

English translation:

Sister Barbara of Rischach, professed nun of the Augustinian monastery in Diessenhofen, which is under the care and governance of the Dominicans living in the Diocese of Constance, since she herself is not able to remain in said monastery and order with her soul at peace, [beseeches] that you deign by special and expressed grace to order that she be allowed to transfer herself to another order of equal or stricter observance of the Rule. So be it by special and expressed mandate, Julianus, bishop of Bertinoro, regent.

33. ASV, *Penitenzieria Ap., Reg. Matrim. et Div.*, vol. 31, fol. 162v. A summary of this case is published in RPG VI, n. 3241.

34. Rome, 8th of February 1482.

DOCUMENT 13. Barbara Rischach: Original Letter Granting Permission (Illustration 13)[35]

Venerabili in Christo patri Dei gratia episcopo Constanciensi vel eius vicario in spiritualibus, Julianus miseratione divina episcopus Sabinensis, salutem et /[2]/ sinceram in Domino caritatem. Cum, sicut exhibita nobis ex parte sororis Barbere de Rischach monialis professe monasterii in Diessenhoven /[3]/ ordinis Sancti Augustini sub cura et regimine fratrum predicatorum degentium vestre diocesis petitio continebat, ipsa propter certas et legiti/[4]/mas causas non possit cum sui quiete animi et sana conscientia in dictis monasterio et ordine remanere, trasferendi se ad aliquem alium /[5]/ ordinem paris vel arcioris observantie regularis indulgeri sibi licentiam per sedem apostolicam humiliter supplicari fecit, salutem /[6]/ intendens propriam efficaciter procurare. Nos igitur, qui sui et singulorum animarum salutem ferventi desiderio affectamus, anime sue saluti /[7]/ providere volentes, auctoritate domini pape, cuius penitentiarie curam gerimus et de eius speciali et expresso mandato super hoc vive vocis oraculo /[8]/ nobis facto, circumspectioni vestre comittimus quatenus, si per diligentem inquisitionem repereritis causas, quas dicta soror Barbera /[9]/ nobis duxerit alegandas et propter quas ad id petendum movetur, fore tales, quod merito sit sibi talis licentia concedenda, super /[10]/ quibus vestram conscientiam oneramus, ut sui superioris super hoc per se vel alium licentia petita etiam non obtenta ad aliquem /[11]/ alium ordinem, dummodo in eo vigeat par vel artior observantia regularis, valeat hac vice se trasferre et in eo professione facta /[12]/ in dictis primo monasterio et ordine non obstante gratum Domino reddere famulatum, licentiam concedatis eidem ipsam postquam in monasterio et /[13]/ ordine, ad quod se duxerit trasferendam, professa fuerit, a predictis primi monasteri et ordinis observantiis absolventes constitutio/[14]/nibus apostolicis ac statutis ordinationibus et privilegiis ipsius ordinis seu eorum alteri a sede

35. Staatsarchiv Thurgau, Frauenfeld, 7.44.9 B. We thank Milena Svec-Götschi for letting us use the documentation of this case.

predicta concessis non obstantibus /15/ quibuscumque. Datum Rome apud Sanctumpetrum sub sigillo officii penitentiarie vi idibus februarii pontificatus domini Sixti /16/ pape IIII anno undecimo.

In the upper margin: Videat eam reverendus dominus regens.
In the left margin at the height of the fifth line: Visa per me
In the right margin at the height of the fifth line: Julianum episcopum Brictonoriensem regentem
In the plica: pro B. de Bubalis; A. de Calandrinis[36]
The seal of the Penitentiary in red wax and hemp cord

English translation:

Julianus, by divine mercy bishop of Sabina [sends] greeting and sincere love in the Lord to the father venerable in Christ, the bishop of Constance by the grace of God, or to his vicar in spiritual affairs. Since—as the petition made to us by Sister Barbara of Rischach, a professed nun of the Augustinian monastery in Diessenhofen which is under the care of the Dominicans living in your diocese, contained—she is not able to remain in said monastery and order with sound conscience and her soul at peace because of certain and legitimate reasons, intending efficaciously to look after her own well-being she humbly appealed to the Apostolic See to be granted a license to transfer to some other order of an equal or stricter observance of the Rule. We, therefore, who strive after the salvation of her and every single soul with ardent desire, wanting to provide for the salvation of her soul, by the authority of the Lord Pope, who has entrusted the administration of the Penitentiary to us, and by his special and expressed mandate given to us in person on this account, submit to your consideration that, if through a careful examination you discover that the reasons which the said Sister Barbara thought ought to be recounted to us and on account of which she is being moved to make an appeal, will be such that such a license is deservedly to be granted to her—concerning which we burden your conscience you may grant her this license so that, even though she or another petitioned [but] did not also receive a license to this effect from her superior, she may be able to transfer herself in this way to some other order, provided that an equal or stricter observance of the Rule flourishes there, and so that, after she has made her vows there in words without hindrance of the first monastery and or-

36. A. de Calandrinis is the name of the scribe who composed the letter.

der, she may be able to render grateful service to the Lord [We also submit to your consideration that,] after she has professed in the monastery and order to which she thought she ought to be transferred, you absolve her from the aforementioned observances of the first monastery and order without hindrance *(non obstante)* of apostolic constitutions and the statutes, ordinations, and privileges of this same [first] order or whatever [statues, ordinations, and privileges] have been granted by the aforementioned See to the second of them. Given in Rome at Saint Peter's by the seal of the office of the Penitentiary, on the 8th of February in the 11th year of the pontificate of Lord Pope Sixtus IV.

5. Violence and Murder

Violence and murder are very common matters in the Penitentiary records, among both the *de diversis formis* and the *de declaratoriis* cases. In the *de declaratoriis* category, petitioners turned to the Penitentiary to ask for a letter of declaration attesting that they were not guilty of murder even though they had participated in events that had lead to someone's death. The petitioners, often priests, needed these declarations, as without them they could not continue in their ecclesiastical careers, for canon law did not allow persons guilty of murder to act as priests, and especially not as confessors. In *de diversis formis* cases, on the other hand, the supplicants—often laymen—usually admitted to being guilty of murder and asked for absolution from their sin. As murder cases are more common among the *de declaratoriis* petitions than among the *de diversis formis* cases, we have chosen as an example a declaratory case. This example, of which we have two documents (the petition in the Penitentiary register, and the original letter of declaration, now preserved in the Swedish National Archives), nicely shows how detailed the *narratio* part of the petition was, and also how minutely the details in the supplication were copied in the letter issued by the Penitentiary.

In our example, a Swedish priest, Olavus Petri (in Swedish, Olof Pederson), dean of the Diocese of Skara, applied for a declaratory letter that would prove his innocence in a case involving death. As usual with declaratory letters, this petition is much longer and more detailed than the supplications normally carried to the Penitentiary for an absolution or a dispensation. With this detailed petition the supplicant tried to explain as minutely as possible all details which had led to the other person's death. In addition, he mentions all those details (required by canon law rules) which could prove that he did not wish to harm the other person, and that he was very sorry for what had happened—i.e., the facts required to be declared not guilty.

The case of Olavus is somewhat different from typical declaratory cases, in which the supplicant had usually, through his own violent behavior, caused someone else's death. But since canon law considered to be guilty of murder those persons who happened to be present when manslaughter had taken place, or persons who were in some way connected with the facts leading to the death, these persons also often sought declaratory letters proving their innocence—just as Olavus did.

Olavus, who in the role of dean of the Diocese of Skara was also bishop's official *(officialis sedis episcopalis),*[37] had ordered his men to capture a layman called Petrus Simonis (in Swedish, Peter Simonsson), who had earlier offended another layman. As the offended layman was a peasant of Dean Olavus, Olavus wanted to bring Petrus before his court of law to punish him. When the dean's men went to capture Petrus, he would not surrender himself, and so there was a fight between the men, in which both he and one of the dean's men were wounded. Petrus was then captured by Olavus' men and thrown into the ecclesiastical prison. He was interrogated and judged the following day, and after humbling himself he was sent home. After a few days, however, Petrus regrettably died of the wounds he had received in the course of his capture. Consequently, Olavus was considered guilty of his death, for it was he who had ordered the

37. From 1452 on, it was common for the dean of Skara to act as the *officialis sedis episcopalis;* this meant that the dean was the bishop's substitute in juridical matters (both *foro externo* and *foro interno*). Since in this case the dean seems to act as the prime mover in a juridical case, Olavus Petri was probably acting in this office. See Y. Brilioth, *Svenska kyrkans historia II—Senare medeltiden* (Stockholm, 1941), 412.

men to capture Petrus, which action resulted in his wounds. As Olavus had had no intention of harming Petrus in sending his men to capture him, and it had been Petrus himself who had initiated the violence, Olavus asked the Penitentiary for a declaratory letter stating that he was in no way guilty of the death of Petrus, which he fully regretted.

The Penitentiary granted him such a declaratory letter, but ordered the *ordinarius*, in this case Brynolf Gerlaksson, bishop of Skara, to make sure that Olavus had not given advice, help, approval, or exhortation in these events, and was not guilty of the death of Petrus in any other way. If he found that Olavus was not guilty, he could provide Olavus with the official declaratory letter.

DOCUMENT 14. Olavus Petri: Petition to the Penitentiary (Illustrations 14a–b)[38]

In the left margin of fol. 172v: Rome xvj kalendas marcii[39]
In the right margin of fol. 172v: Scaren.

Alavus Petri presbiter Scarensis ecclesie decanus, quod cum alias /[2]/ quondam Petrus Simonis laycus, dum adhuc viveret, quendam /[3]/ colonum seu prediorum suorum inquilinum sepe invaderet seu persequeretur, /[4]/ ipse exponens volens ipsorum tam Petri invasorum quam coloni sui /[5]/ indempnitati hincinde subvenire quosdam famulos duntaxat /[6]/ ad capiendum dictum Petrum invasorem et, ut eum captum /[7]/ ad se caute duxerunt, eis committendo transmisit; qui famuli /[173r]/ cum tarde et in noctis crepusculo dictum Petrum declinantem /[2]/ et vociferantem ex hoc magis quod pervisum[40] esse conside/[3]/rassent et ipsum tunc insecuti fuerunt quos cum dictus Petrus /[4]/ sensisset insequentes eum, arcum eius, quem et tunc secum et in /[5]/ suis manibus ferebat, tetendit et telum impositum ex eo

38. ASV, *Penitenzieria Ap., Reg. Matrim. et Div.*, vol. 33, fol. 172v–173r.
39. Rome, 14th of February 1484.
40. Should be: *previsum*.

emisit, /[6]/ cum quo quendam ex famulis predictis armis tamen protectum /[7]/ sagitavit, illo ob hoc illeso remanente; qui tunc famulus volens /[8]/ similiter iniuriam propulsare et ipse arcu suo, quem similiter in suis /[9]/ ferebat manibus, extenso et per eum ex illo telo superposito et /[10]/ emisso dictum Petrum invasorem et in illius pectore vulneravit. /[11]/ Qui potuis[41] cum arcu, quem ad huc in suis manibus tenebat, /[12]/ eundem famulum, qui eum ut prefertur sagitavit tetigitque, et in /[13]/ illius capite percussit et vulneravit; attamen et dictus Petrus /[14]/ invasor postea victus et captus in carcerem ea nocte est /[15]/ ductus. Qui et altera sequente die se humiliando et de ulteriori /[16]/ molestia exponenti ac suis et famulis predictis et per eum /[17]/ amplius et in futurum non inferenda promissione facta et a carce/[18]/ribus liber est dimissus; qui tamen paucis postea diebus super/[19]/veniens diem vite sue clausit extremum. Cum autem, pater sancte, /[20]/ dictus exponens in morte dicti Petri absque[42] ut premittitur /[21]/ culpabilis non fuerit, ymo de ipsius morte subsecuta ab /[22]/ intimis doluerit et doleat impresenciarum, cupiatque dictus /[23]/ exponens ex magno devotionis fervore in omnibus etiam /[24]/ sacris et presbiteratus ordinibus suis licite ministrare, a nonnullis tamen /[25]/ ipsius exponentis emulis asseritur ipsum propter premissa /[26]/ homicidii reatum etc. incurrisse et propterea in omnibus suis etiam /[27]/ presbiteratus ordinibus ministrare non posse. Ad ora igitur talium etc. /[28]/ et emulorum obstruenda, supplicatur eidem sanctitati vestre pro parte dicti exponentis, /[29]/ quatenus ipsum occasione premissorum nullum homicidii reatum incurrisse /[30]/ nullamque irregularitatis maculam seu inhabilitatis notam con/[31]/traxisse sed predictis non obstantibus in dictis suis etiam sacris et /[32]/ presbiteratus ordinibus libere et licite ministrari posse misericorditer declarari /[33]/ mandare dignemini de gratia speciali. Fiat ut infra, Jul[ianus] episcopus Ber/[34]/thonoriensis, Regens. Committatur ordinario, et si vocatis vocandis /[35]/ sibi constiterit quod exponens consilio, auxilio, favore, ad[h]ortatione aut /[36]/ aliter quam ut premittitur in morte dicti Petri culpabilis /[37]/ non fuerit et de aliis expositis, declaret ut /[38]/ petitur.

41. Should be: *Petrus.*

42. Should be: *alius quam.*

English translation:

Dean Olavus Petri, priest of the church of Skara, [explains] that when on various occasions the late Petrus Simonis, a layman, while he was still alive, often assailed or persecuted a certain villein or lodger of his manor, the petitioner himself wanted to bring a judicial remedy to the immunity of both Petrus the assailant and his villein from this point forward. He [consequently] dispatched certain servants, ordering them merely to capture said Petrus the assailant and to bring the captive cautiously to him. When these servants had perceived that the said Petrus was fleeing late and in the darkness of the night and was crying out greatly as a result of the situation which he discerned, they had then followed him. After the said Petrus had sensed them following him, he aimed his bow, which he was carrying with him at that time in his hands, and released from it a cocked arrow with which he shot one of the aforementioned servants who was, however, protected by armor, and who remained unharmed by this. Next this servant wanted similarly to inflict injury. Carrying a bow in his hands in the same way as Petrus, with aimed bow he cocked and released an arrow from it and wounded said Petrus the assailant in his chest. With the bow which he was holding in his hands to this point, Petrus struck and wounded in the head that same servant who had, as is recounted, shot at and hit him; but nevertheless said Petrus the assailant was later in the same night overcome and captured and led to prison. On the second day after these events, both humbling himself and having promised not to inflict any further and future harm to the petitioner, his men, and the aforementioned servants, he was set free from the prison; however, coming up on a few days later, he closed out the last day of his life. However, some enemies of the mentioned petitioner claim that he has incurred guilt, etc. because of the abovementioned homicide, and for this reason is not able to minister in all his orders, even the priestly orders; but since, o holy father, the mentioned petitioner was not guilty in the death of the mentioned Petrus otherwise than is mentioned above—nay, he deeply grieved his subsequent death, and continues to grieve—and [since] the mentioned petitioner desires, out of great zeal of devotion, to minister lawfully in all his orders, even the sacred and priestly orders, therefore, in order to stop the mouths of rivals and such people, etc., the mentioned petitioner beseeches that your holiness mercifully deign to order to be declared by special grace that he has incurred no guilt of homicide, defect of irregularity, or mark of disability, but indeed that despite the aforementioned he is able to minister freely and lawfully in his mentioned orders, even the sacred and priestly. So be it as below, Julianus, bishop of Bertinoro, Regent. Let this be entrusted to the ordinary and if, having convened all who were to be convened, he concludes that the petitioner was not guilty through counsel, aid, approval, exhortation, or otherwise than is mentioned above in the death of the mentioned Petrus and concerning the rest which is explained, let him declare as is sought.

DOCUMENT 15. Olavus Petri: Original Letter from the Penitentiary (Illustration 15)[43]

Venerabili in Christo patri . . . dei gratia episcopo Scarensi vel eius vicario in spiritualibus, Julianus miseratione divina episcopus Ostiensis, salutem et sinceram in Domino caritatem. Ex /[2]/ parte Olavi Petri presbiteri decani ecclesie Scarensis nobis oblata petitio continebat quod cum alius quondam Petrus Symonis laicus, dum viveret in humanis, colonum /[3]/ quendam seu prediorum suorum inquilinum sepe invaderet seu persequeretur, ipse exponens volens ipsorum tam Petri invasoris quam coloni sui hinc inde indempnitati /[4]/ subvenire quosdam famulos duntaxat ad capiendum dictum Petrum invasorem, et ut eum captum ad se ducerent, eis committendo transmisit; qui famuli cum /[5]/ tarde in noctis crepusculo dictum Petrum declinantem et vociferantem ex hoc magis quod previsum esse considerantes ipsum tunc insecuti fuerunt; quos cum dictus /[6]/ Petrus sensisset insequentes eum, arcum eius, quem et tunc secum et in suis manibus ferebat, tetendit et telum impositum ex eo emisit et quendam /[7]/ ex famulis predictis armis tamen protectum sagittavit, illo ob hoc illeso remanente; qui tunc famulus volens similiter iniuriam propulsare et ipse arcu suo, quem /[8]/ similiter in suis tenebat manibus, extenso et per eum ex illo telo superposito et emisso dictum Petrum invasorem et in illius pectore vulneravit; qui Petrus /[9]/ cum arcu, quem ad huc in suis manibus tenebat, eundem famulum, qui eum ut prefertur sagittavit tetigitque, et in illius capite percussit et vulneravit; attamen /[10]/ et dictus Petrus invasor postea victus et captus in carcerem ea nocte ductus est. Qui et altera sequente die se humiliando et de ulteriori molestia expo/[11]/nenti ac suis et famulis predictis et per eum amplius et

43. Stockholm, Riksarkivet, Or. Perg., 14.2.1484.

in futurum non inferenda promissione facta et e[44] carceribus liber dimissus est; qui tamen paucis /[12]/ post diebus supervivens, sicut Domino placuit, diem suum clausit extremum. Cum autem, sicut eadem subiungebat petitio, dictus exponens alius quam ut pre/[13]/mittitur in morte dicti Petri culpabilis non fuerit, immo de eius morte ab intimis doluerit prout dolet de presenti, cupiatque ex magno devotionis fervore /[14]/ in omnibus suis etiam presbiteratus ordinibus ministrare et altissimo Domino perpetuo famulari, a nonnullis tamen simplicibus et iurisignaris ac ipsius exponen/[15]/tis forsan emulis asseritur exponentem ipsum propter premissa homicidii reatum incurrisse et irregularitatis maculam sive inhabilitatis notam con/[16]/traxisse et propterea in dictis suis ordinibus licite ministrare non posse. Ad ora igitur talium et aliorum sibi super hoc in futurum forsan obloqui volen/[17]/tium emulorum obstruenda, supplicari fecit humiliter dictus exponens sibi super hiis per sedem apostolicam misericorditer provideri. Nos igitur, auctoritate domini pape, /[18]/ cuius penitentiarie curam gerimus, circumspectioni vestre committimus quatenus, si vocatis vocandis vobis constiterit quod exponens consilio, auxilio, favore, /[19]/ adhortatione aut alius quam ut premittitur in morte dicti Petri culpabilis non fuerit et de aliis expositis, super quibus vestram conscientiam oneramus, /[20]/ declaretis exponentem ipsum premissorum occasione nullum homicidii reatum incurrisse nullamque irregularitatis maculam sive inhabilitatis notam /[21]/ contraxisse sed premissis non obstantibus in dictis suis ordinibus libere et licite alio sibi non obstante canonico ministrare posse. Datum Rome /[22]/ apud Sanctumpetrum sub sigillo officii penitentiarie xvi kalendas martii pontificatus domini Sixti pape IIII anno tertiodecimo.

In the upper margin: Videat eam Dominus A[ntonius] de Grassis
In the left margin: 1483
In the left margin at the level of the fifth line: Visa per me
In the right margin at the level of the fifth line: A. de Grassis Auditorem
Under the *plica:* F. Ro- sex tur. -sa;[45] Cundelmario[46]

44. Should be: *a.*

45. F. Rosa is the name of the person who acted as *referendarius-taxator* in this case, and the tax was 6 *tournois.*

46. Cundelmario is the name of the person who acted as *computator* in this case.

In the *plica:* M. de Magistris[47]
On the *verso:* Jo. de Medina;[48] A. Ziremberger[49]
The seal is missing.

English translation:

Julianus, by divine mercy bishop of Ostia, [sends] greeting and sincere love in the Lord to the venerable in Christ father . . . , by the grace of God bishop of Skara, or to his vicar in spiritual affairs. A petition brought to us on behalf of priest Olavus Petri, dean of the church of Skara, contained that when on various occasions the late Petrus Simonis, a layman, while he was still alive, often assailed or persecuted a certain villein or lodger of his manor, the petitioner himself wanted to bring a judicial remedy to the immunity of both Petrus the assailant and his villein from this point forward. He [consequently] dispatched certain servants, ordering them merely to capture said Petrus the assailant and to bring the captive cautiously to him. When these servants had perceived that the said Petrus was fleeing late in the darkness of the night and was crying out greatly as a result of the situation which he discerned, they had then followed him. After the mentioned Petrus had sensed them following him, he aimed his bow, which he was carrying with him at that time in his hands, and released from it a cocked arrow with which he shot one of the aforementioned servants who was, however, protected by arms, and who remained unharmed by this. Next this servant wanted similarly to inflict injury. Holding a bow in his hands in the same way as Petrus, with aimed bow he cocked and released an arrow from it and wounded said Petrus the assailant in his chest. With the bow which he was holding in his hands to this point, Petrus struck and wounded in the head that same servant who had, as is recounted, shot at and hit him; but nevertheless said Petrus the assailant was later in the same night overcome and captured and led to prison. On the second day after these events, both humbling himself and having promised not to inflict any further and future harm to the petitioner, his men, and the aforementioned servants, he was set free from the prison; however, though surviving for a few days afterwards, as it pleased the Lord, he closed out the last day of his life. However, some

47. M. de Magistris is the name of the scribe who composed the letter.
48. Johannes de Medina, a cleric from the Diocese of Salamanca in Spain, was a well-known Penitentiary proctor. See E. Göller, *Pönitentiarie* II/2, 81.
49. Andreas Ziremberger was also a well-known Penitentiary proctor. Regarding him, see also ASV, *Penitenzieria Ap., Reg. Matrim. et Div.*, vol. 35, fol. 249v, as well as vol. 37, fol. 187v.

people, who are simple and ignorant of law, and perhaps enemies of the petitioner himself, claim that the petitioner himself has incurred guilt because of the abovementioned homicide and has contracted a defect of irregularity or mark of disability, and for this reason is not able to minister lawfully in his mentioned orders; but since, however, as appears in the petition, the mentioned petitioner was not guilty in the death of the mentioned Petrus otherwise than is mentioned above—nay, he deeply grieved his death, as he continues to grieve—and [since] he desires out of great zeal of devotion to minister in all his orders, even the priestly ones, and to serve perpetually the highest Lord, therefore, in order to obstruct the mouths of such people and other enemies who perhaps in future might wish to speak against him on this account, the mentioned petitioner humbly beseeches that the Apostolic See mercifully provide him [grace] concerning these. We therefore, by the authority of the Lord Pope, who has entrusted the administration of the Penitentiary to us, submit to your consideration that if, having convened all who were to be convened, you are certain that the petitioner was not guilty in the death of the mentioned Petrus through counsel, aid, approval, exhortation or otherwise than is mentioned above, and concerning the rest which is explained—concerning which we burden your conscience—you [should] declare that the petitioner himself has incurred no guilt of homicide because of the aforementioned and has not contracted any defect of irregularity or disability, but that despite the aforementioned he is able to minister freely and lawfully in his mentioned orders without any other canonical hindrance to himself. Given in Rome at St. Peter's by the seal of the office of the Penitentiary on the 14th of February, in the 13th year of the pontificate of Lord Pope Sixtus IV.

6. Defect of Age

In the first part of this book, we explained that the church did not allow men of too young an age to enter into an ecclesiastical career, and therefore stipulated in the fifteenth century an age limit for each of the ecclesiastical offices; for example, candidates younger than 25 years of age could not be ordained to the priesthood. This rule could be bypassed, however, if the underaged candidate was otherwise considered suitable and could obtain a dispensation from the Penitentiary.

Such dispensations were quite commonly handled by the officials of the Penitentiary, and in what follows we present a case of this type. Unfortunately, we can offer readers only one document concerning this case: the text of the letter of the Penitentiary—currently kept in the chapter archives of the Church of San Lorenzo in Chiavenna, Italy—because registration of petitions in the registers of the Penitentiary during the pontificate of Nicholas V was not complete.

This case concerns a young Italian person, the deacon Johannes de Castro Novo (in Italian, Giovanni Castelnuovo), son of Guglielmo, from the Diocese of Como in northern Italy, who wanted to be ordained to the priesthood despite being a minor. The Penitentiary granted him the requested grace, and a letter of grace was issued in the name of the Cardinal Penitentiary Domenico Capranica on the 13th of February 1454. As was common practice in these cases, the letter of grace is addressed directly to Johannes himself.

This case is, however, somewhat peculiar, for instead of asking for a dispensation in order to be ordained at the age of 24, as was the common practice, Johannes wanted to become a priest at the age of 23. Unlike the more common dispensations for 24-year-old candidates, in this case the Penitentiary could not rely on its normal powers; but it was allowed to grant Johannes this grace through special authority which it had been directly given by the popes: *Fiat de speciali et expresso.*[50]

The reason this letter of dispensation has survived until now is probably the fact that Johannes himself later became the archpriest of the Church of San Lorenzo in Chiavenna; his dispensation was conserved in the archives of that church.

50. Concerning the case and the documents, see P. Ostinelli, *Penitenzieria Apostolica,* 88–90.

DOCUMENT 16. Johannes de Castro Novo: Letter of Dispensation from the Penitentiary (Illustration 16)[51]

Dominicus miseratione divina tituli sancte crucis in Jerusalem presbiter cardinalis, dilecto in Christo Johanni Guillermi de Castro /[2]/ novo dyacono Cumane diocesis ac canonico prebendato ecclesie sancti Laurentii de Clavena dicte diocesis, salutem in Domino. /[3]/ Ut erga sedem apostolicam eo amplius crescat tue devotionis affectus quo eam benigniorem invenias tibi faciendo gra/[4]/tiam specialem, porrectis nobis pro parte tua supplicationibus, quantum cum Deo possumus, benignius annuen/[5]/tes, auctoritate domini pape, cuius penitentiarie curam gerimus et de eius speciali et expresso mandato super hoc vive vocis oraculo /[6]/ nobis facto, super defectu etatis tue, quem pateris qui ut asseris in vigesimotertio etatis tue anno constitutus existis, /[7]/ ut eo ac Lugdunen et Lateranen conciliorum et quibusvis aliis constitutionibus contrariis non obstantibus pos/[8]/sis ad presbiteratus ordinem libere promoveri et in eo et aliis tuis ordinibus libere et licite ministrare valeas alio tibi non /[9]/ obstante canonico, tecum tenore presentium misericorditer dispensamus. Datum Rome apud Sanctumpetrum sub sigillo officii /[10]/ penitentiarie idibus februarii pontificatus domini Nicolai pape V anno septimo.

In the upper margin: Videat eam Reverendus dominus Cardinalis
In the left margin at the level of the fifth line: Visa per me
In the right margin at the level of the fifth line: Card. S. + J.[52]
Under the *plica:* De Bucchoni duodecim tur. is;[53] Fulco[54]

51. Archivio Capitolare Laurenziano, Chiavenna, Pergamene 784. We wish to thank Paolo Ostinelli for pointing out this document to us.

52. Domenico Capranica, Cardinal of Sancte Crucis in Jerusalem.

53. De Bucchoniis is the name of the person who acted as *referendarius-taxator* in this case, and the tax was 12 *tournois.*

54. Fulco is the name of the person who in this case acted as the *computator* of the Penitentiary.

English translation:

Dominicus, by divine mercy Cardinal Priest of the Church of Sancte Crucis in Jerusalem, [sends] greeting in the Lord to the beloved in Christ Johannes Guillermi de Castro Novo, deacon of the Diocese of Como and prebendary canon of the Church of Sancti Laurentii de Chiavenna. In order that the fondness of your devotion toward the Apostolic See might increase the more you find her generous in giving special grace to you, consenting benevolently to the appeals submitted to us on your behalf we, as much as before God we are able, by the authority of the Lord Pope, who has entrusted the administration of the Penitentiary to us, and by his particular and express mandate given to us by his own mouth, mercifully grant dispensation with the tenor of this present letter regarding the defect of your age which you suffer, being, as you assert, in your 23rd year, so that despite the defect and the councils of Lyon and Lateran and whatever other contrary constitutions, you can be promoted freely to priestly order, and so that you will be able to minister in that order and any other orders freely and lawfully without any other canonical hindrance to you. Given in Rome at St. Peter's by the seal of the office of the Penitentiary on the 13th of February, in the 7th year of the pontificate of Lord Pope Nicolas V.

7. *Cum ex eo* of Pope Boniface VIII and Privileges for Priests to Study at the University

The Penitentiary records contain some petitions from priests who wanted to study. Priests were not allowed to study at (foreign) universities without obtaining a special permit. According to canon law, a parish priest with the cure of souls for his parishioners had to be present in his parish; he could not just receive the income and reside elsewhere. If a priest did not obey this rule, he was in danger of losing his benefice.

However, canon law offered the possibility for parish priests to be absent from their parishes if they had good reason for it. According to the *Cum ex eo* constitution of Pope Boniface VIII, studying at a foreign university was considered one of the valid reasons not to reside in one's parish, and thus it was possible to gain a dispensation from the residence obligation. Consequently, with the help of this constitution, a young priest could get income from a benefice without being bound to the residence obligation. With the income he was supposed to hire a substitute, and what remained he could use as a "scholarship" for his studies.

Even though it was not the principal task of the Penitentiary to grant these licenses—normally it was the responsibility of the local bishops to provide the priests of their dioceses with these permits—some petitioners turned to the Penitentiary with this kind of request.

We have here one example of such a case, in which a certain Petrus Gruerii from the Diocese of Châlon-sur-Saône in France asks for a dispensation that he not be required to be promoted to holy orders within three years (although *Cum ex eo* allows seven years) of receiving his benefice. Petrus is required to take the subdiaconate, because the canon *Cum ex eo* requires he do so within a year. Second, he asks to be permitted to hold his benefice and to postpone seeking further promotion (to deacon and priesthood) for three years.

That Petrus had turned to the Penitentiary in this matter, and not to his own bishop, was probably due to the fact that he was a *familiaris* of the Cardinal Penitentiary, Philippus Calandrini; thus he was probably in Rome at the time of making the petition and consequently had easier access to such a dispensation through the Penitentiary. An interesting matter which can be seen in this context is that the Penitentiary sometimes granted graces for free. As Petrus Gruerii claims to be an associate of the head of the office, the Penitentiary granted him the letter without payment *(gratis)*, as we may read under the entry.

There are two documents left from the case of Petrus: a copy of his supplication and a copy of the letter of grace granted by the Penitentiary. Both copies are to be found in the same Penitentiary register.

DOCUMENT 17. Petrus Gruerii: Entry in the Penitentiary Registers (Illustration 17)[55]

In the left margin: Rome kalendis marcii[56]
In the right margin: Cabilonen.

Petrus Gruerii clericus Cabilonensis rector parrochialis ecclesie /²/ de Augeyo Eduensis diocesis, devote creature vestre Phi[lippi] episcopi /³/ Portuensis maioris penitentiari vestri familiaris continuus commensalis, quatenus /⁴/ sibi specialem gratiam facientem, ut non obstante dicta parrochiali ecclesia, quam /⁵/ obtinet, exinde in serviciis prefati episcopi Portuensis in Romana curia /⁶/ vel extra autem aliquo studio generali ad aliquem ex sacris /⁷/ ordinibus hinc ad triennium se promoveri facere minime teneatur /⁸/ dispensari, nec id a quoquam cohartari valeat, quominus ipsius ecclesie /⁹/ fructus etc. percipere valeat generalis concilii felicis recordationis Bonifatii pape /¹⁰/ VIII et qualibet alia constitutione contraria non obstante ceteriisque contrariis /¹¹/ quibuscumque. Fiat de speciali et expresso, Phi[lippus] episcopus Portuensis.

English translation:

Petrus Gruerius, cleric of Châlon-sur-Saône, rector of the parochial church of Augeyo of the Diocese of Autun, continued commensal [and] familiar of Your Devoted Creation Philippus, bishop of Porto [Santa Rufina], Cardinal Penitentiary, [appeals] for a special favor to be dispensed so that, despite the mentioned parochial church which he holds, [from which he is departing] into the service of the aforementioned bishop of Porto [Santa Rufina] in the Roman Curia, or outside in some *studium generale*, he is not obliged to be promoted to any of the holy orders for three years hence, nor can he be held to it unwillingly by anyone, [and nothing can prevent him] from receiving his income from that church etc. notwithstanding [the decision] of the general council of Pope Boniface VIII, of happy remembrance, and despite any other contrary constitutions and whatever other contrary [statutes]. So be it by special and expressed mandate, Phi[lippus] bishop of Porto [Santa Rufina].

55. ASV, *Penitenzieria Ap., Reg. Matrim. et Div.*, vol. 20, fol. 204v.
56. Rome, 1st of March 1472.

DOCUMENT 18. Petrus Gruerii: Letter in the Penitentiary Registers (Illustration 18)[57]

In the left margin: Rome kalendis marcii[58]
In the right margin: Cabilonen.

Philippus miseratione divina episcopus Portuensis, dilecto in Christo Petro Gruerii /[2]/ clerico Cabilonensi rectori parrochialis ecclesie de Curgeyo Eduensis diocesis /[3]/ ac familiari nostro, salutem in Domino. Grata familiaritatis obsequia, que /[4]/ nobis hactenus impendisti et adhuc sollicitis studiis impendere /[5]/ non desistis necnon vite ac morum honestas aliaque laudabilia /[6]/ probitatis et virtutum merita, quibus personam tuam tam fa/[7]/miliari experiencia quam etiam fidedignorum testimonio iuvari /[8]/ percepimus, nos inducunt, ut personam tuam specialis prerogativa /[9]/ favoris et gratie prosequamur. Hinc est quod nos tuis in /[10]/ hac parte supplicationibus inclinati, auctoritate domini pape, cuius penitentiarie /[11]/ curam gerimus et de eius speciali et expresso mandato /[12]/ super hoc vive vocis oraculo nobis facto, tenore presencium /[13]/ misericorditer dispensamus tecum, ut ratione parrochialis ecclesie predicte, quam /[14]/ ut asseris rite obtines, dum tamen fueris in serviciis nostris /[15]/ in Romana Curia vel extra et infra unum mensem /[16]/ ad subdiaconatus ordinem sis promotus, hinc ad triennium /[17]/ ad diaconatus et presbyteratus ordines te promoveri facere minime /[18]/ tenearis, nec ad id a quoquam invitus valeas coartari, et /[19]/ pro eo, quod te promoveri non feceris ad diaconatus et presbiteratus /[20]/ ordines, nichil possit tibi obsistere, quominus ipsius ecclesie /[21]/ fructus facias interim tuos generalis consilii domini Bonifacii /[22]/ pape VIII et qualibet alia constitutione contraria non obstante, /[23]/ proviso tamen quod dicta ecclesia interim debitis non fraudetur /[24]/ obsequiis et animarum cura in ea nullatenus negligatur. /[25]/ Datum Rome apud Sanctumpetrum sub sigillo /[26]/ officii penitentiarie kalendis marcii pontificatus domini Sixti pape IIII /[27]/ anno primo.

57. ASV, *Penitenzieria Ap., Reg. Matrim. et Div.*, vol. 20, fol. 190r.
58. Rome, 1st of March 1472.

In the upper margin: Videat eam reverendissimus dominus Cardinalis
In the left margin at the level of the ninth line: Visa per me
In the right margin at the level of the ninth line: Phi[lippum] episcopum Portuensem
Below the letter on the left side: B. Anconita duodecem tur. nus;[59] P. de Ursis[60]
Below the letter on the right side: A. de Benenatis
In the left margin below the text: Gratis pro familiari reverendissimi // domini Cardinalis

English translation:

Philippus, by divine mercy bishop of Porto [Santa Rufina], [sends] greeting in the Lord to the beloved in Christ Petrus Gruerius, cleric of Châlon-sur-Saône, rector of the parochial church of Curgeyo of the Diocese of Autun and our familiar. The pleasing compliance of familiarity which you have shown us and up until now with anxious devotion have not ceased to show, and certainly the honesty of life and manners and other laudable merits of uprightness and virtues which we have both through personal experience and through the testimony of trustworthy persons perceived to support your person, have guided us to honor your person with the prerogative of special favor and grace. Hence having inclined toward your appeals in this regard, we, by the authority of the Lord Pope, who has entrusted the administration of the Penitentiary to us, and by his special and expressed mandate given to us in person on this account, mercifully grant you dispensation with the tenor of the present letter, so that with respect to the aforementioned parochial church, which, as you assert, you hold rightly, as long as you shall be in our service in the Roman Curia or outside, and have been promoted to the order of subdeacon within one month, you are not obliged to be promoted to the orders of deacon and priest for three years hence, nor can you be held to it unwillingly by anyone, and nothing can prevent you, for not having had yourself promoted to the orders of deacon and priest, from receiving your income from that church, notwithstanding [the decision] of the general council of Lord Pope Boniface VIII and in spite of whatever other contrary constitution, provided, however, that the mentioned church is not in the meanwhile defrauded from due divine service and that the care of

59. B. Anconitanus was the name of the person who acted as *referendarius-taxator* in this case, and the tax was 12 *tournois.*

60. P. de Ursis was the name of the person who in this case acted as the *computator* of the Penitentiary.

souls is not in any way neglected in it. Given in Rome at Saint Peter's by the seal of the office of the Penitentiary on the 1st of March, in the 1st year of the pontificate of Lord Pope Sixtus IV.

8. Procession

The last example that is classified as a *de diversis formis* case in the Penitentiary registers is quite an atypical case for the Penitentiary, since this kind of case did not normally belong to the powers of the office. It is likely that the supplicants used the decision of the Penitentiary as a second instance sentence for their benefit against possible local adversaries.

The supplicants, the friars of the house of St. Anthony in Cologne, requested a permit to hold annually (on the sixth Sunday after Easter, the *Domenica "Exaudi"*) a big procession in which they could carry the Eucharistic Host, as well as images of St. Anthony, through the parish of St. Peter, as well as through some other parishes, such as St. Martin (= Groß St. Martin), St. Columba, St. Bridget, and others. They stated that they wanted to perform the procession every year, but were not sure whether they were allowed to do so without a papal permit, because they intended to extend their procession outside the boundaries of their own parish and to pass through several neighboring parishes. Thus they turned to the Penitentiary to ask for such a permit, which was granted to the brothers by the regent of the Penitentiary Mercurius de Vipera on the 6th of April 1512.

What is striking about this decision of the Penitentiary is that the office referred the case to the local church authorities, to whom the letter of the Penitentiary, issued in the name of the Cardinal Penitentiary Leonardus Grossus de Ruvere (= della Rovere), is also addressed ("to the archbishop of Cologne, or his general vicar, as well as to the provost *(praepositus)* of the parish of St. Cunibert and the dean of the parish of St. George"). These commissioners were expected to ensure that no one opposed this permit, and if someone did oppose it, the commissioners had the power to excommunicate him and even to call in the secular arm to enforce the mandate. This kind of phrasing is not common in Penitentiary documents, and probably refers to the fact that the house of St. Anthony was using the Penitentiary decision as a defense against its adversaries.

There are two remaining documents concerning this petition: the copy of the petition registered in the registers of the Penitentiary, and the letter of the Penitentiary, which is currently kept in the collections of the town archives of Cologne.

DOCUMENT 19. Friary of St. Anthony in Cologne: Privilege in the Penitentiary Register (Illustrations 19a–b)[61]

In the left margin of fol. 235r at the height of the first line: Licentia faciendi processionem
In the left margin of fol. 235r: .viii idus aprilis[62]
In the right margin of fol. 235r: Colonien.
Above the petition text of fol. 235r: Villareal t. xviiii.[63]

Wentzclaus Vluer de Arhelgen preceptor et fratres domus /²/ sancti Antonii Coloniensis exponunt quod ipsi, qui a nonnullis /³/ temporibus citra quandam processionem in die dominica, in qua /⁴/ sancta mater ecclesia in introitu misse decantat /⁵/ Exaudi, cum deportatione corporis Domini nostri Jhesu Christi /⁶/ ac imaginis beati Antonii honorifice et cum decanta/⁷/tionibus et reverentia debitis per parrochiam sancti /⁸/ Petri civitatis Coloniensis, in qua domus eorum situata /⁹/ existit, ad quam magna populi multitudo cum magna devotione /¹⁰/ confluit, facere consueverunt, cuperent ob singularem /¹¹/ devotionis devotionis [*sic!*] affectum processionem huiusmodi continuendo /¹²/ et augendo illam tam per predictam quam sanctorum Martini, Co/¹³/lombe et Brigide ac alias parrochias dicte civitatis /¹⁴/ honorifice ac cum decantationibus et reverencia predictis /¹⁵/ ad laudem et gloriam omnipotentis Dei et eiusdem beati An/¹⁶/tonii iuxta huiusmodi laudabilem consuetudinem eorum fac-

61. ASV, *Penitenzieria Ap., Reg. Martim. et Div.*, vol. 57, fol. 235r–v.

62. 6th of April 1512.

63. A. de Villareal was the proctor who took care of this case, and 19 *tournois* is the amount of tax.

ere. /[17]/ Dubitant tamen id facere posse sede apostolica super hoc in/[18]/consulta, supplicatur etc. quatenus eis et pro tempore existentibus /[19]/ domus huiusmodi preceptori et fratribus, ut in die dominica /[20]/ predicta processionem huiusmodi per dictas ac quascumque alias /[21]/ parrochias dicte civitatis facere et corpus Domini nostri Jhesu /[22]/ Christi ac imaginem beati Antonii huiusmodi cum decant[at]ionibus, /[23]/ reverencia et solemnitatibus in similibus fieri solitis et /[24]/ debitis in eadem deferre libere et licite possint et valeant /[25]/ ac pro tempore existentes preceptor et fratres predicti perpetuis /[26]/ futuris temporibus possint et valeant, indulgere plenamque /[27]/ et liberam licentiam concedere et etiam facultatem, non /[28]/ obstantibus constitutionibus et ordinationibus apostolicis ac /[29]/ statutis tam provincialibus quam synodalibus ceterisque etc. /[30]/ Et insuper iudicem seu iudices, qui eisdem in premissis efficacis /[31]/ defensionis presidio assisten.[64] non permittant eos contra /[32]/ premissorum tenorem per archiepiscopum Coloniensem vel /[33]/ eius vicarium seu officiales aut quoscumque alios /[34]/ iudices tam ecclesiasticos quam seculares vel personas alias /[235v]/ cuiuscumque dignitatis, status, gradus, ordinis vel conditionis /[2]/ existentes, in personis vel bonis eorum tacite vel expresse, directe /[3]/ vel indirecte, quovis quesito colore vel ingenio mollestari [*sic!*], /[4]/ perturbari seu inquietari, contradictores etc. invocato etc. /[5]/ Fiat de speciali, M[ercurius de Vipera], R[egens].

/[6]/ Et committatur assistenda predicta officiali Coloniensi ac /[7]/ preposito sancti Cuniberti et decano sancti Georgii /[8]/ collegiatarum ecclesiarum Coloniensis. Fiat, M.

English translation:

Preceptor Wenceslaus Vluer of All Saints and the brothers of the house of St. Anthony in Cologne explain that they themselves, who have been accustomed to perform for some time a certain procession on the Sunday on which the Holy Mother Church sings *Exaudi* in the introit of the Mass, bearing the body of our Lord Jesus Christ with respect, due chants, and reverence together with the image of St. Anthony through the parish of St. Peter in the city of Cologne, in which their house is located, to which a great crowd assembles with great devotion, desire to perform such a procession out of remarkable

64. Should be: *assistere.*

feeling of devotion, continuing and increasing it through both the aforementioned [parish] as well as the parishes of St. Martin, St. Columba, St. Bridget, and others of the mentioned city, with respect, the aforementioned chants, and reverence, for the praise and glory of omnipotent God and the same St. Anthony, according to their praiseworthy custom of this kind. However, since they doubt that they would be able to do this without consulting the Apostolic See on this, they appeal etc. that [you deign] to grant indulgence and confirm a full and free license and power to them, and to the preceptor and the brothers living in this house at any time, so that they have the power and are able to perform the procession of this kind on the aforementioned Sunday through the mentioned and some other parishes of the mentioned city, and to carry in it freely and lawfully the body of our Lord Jesus Christ and such an image of St. Anthony, together with the chants, reverence, and solemnities which are customary and due in similar processions, and that the preceptor and aforementioned brothers living there at any time are able and have the power [to do so] for eternal future time despite constitutions, apostolic regulations, and both provincial and synodal statutes and others etc., and moreover [that you order] a judge or judges who, assisting efficaciously in defending the aforementioned privileges, will not permit the archbishop of Cologne, or his vicar or officials or whatever other judges, either ecclesiastical or secular, or other persons, be they of whatever rank, status, position, order or condition, to trouble, interfere with, or in any way disturb them against the tenor of the aforementioned, against their person or goods, secretly or expressly, directly or indirectly, by any devised pretext or deceit, objectors etc., calling for etc. So be it by special mandate, Mercurius de Vipera, regent.

The order to assist is sent to the official of Cologne, and to the provost of the St. Cunibert and the dean of St. George, both collegiate churches of Cologne. So be it, M.

DOCUMENT 20. Friary of St. Anthony in Cologne: Original Privilege (Illustrations 20a–b)[65]

Leonardus miseratione divina tituli sancte Susanne presbyter cardinalis, dilectis in Christo Ventzelao Vluer de Arhelgen preceptori /[2]/

65. Stadtarchiv Köln, HUA 1 (Haupturkundenarchiv 1), 3/15696. We wish to thank Dr. Joachim Deeters of Stadtarchiv Köln for his kind help in getting the photo.

et fratribus domus sancti Antonii Coloniensis, salutem in Domino. Meruit vestre devotionis et religionis zelus necnon sincera fervensque devotio, quibus /[3]/ Romanam ecclesiam et sedem apostolicam prosequimini ut votis vestris, illis presertim per que vestra et aliorum christifidelium devotio necnon divini cultus augmentum /[4]/ et sanctorum Dei honorificentia augeantur, libenter annuamus illaque vobis salubriter concedamus, per que animarum vestrarum salutem Deo propitio salubriter /[5]/ consequi valeatis. Sane pro parte vestra nobis oblata petitio continebat quod vos, qui ut asseritis annuatim in die domenica, in qua sancta mater /[6]/ ecclesia in introitu misse decantat "Exaudi," quandam processionem cum deportatione sacrosancti corporis Domini nostri Jesu Christi ac imaginis beati Antonii /[7]/ honorifice et cum decantationibus ac reverentia debitis per parrochiam sancti Petri civitatis Coloniensis, in qua domus vestra situata existit, ad /[8]/ quam magna populi multitudo cum maxima devotione confluit, facere consuevistis, cuperetis ob singularem devotionis affectum processionem huiusmodi /[9]/ continuando et augendo illam tam per predictam quam sanctorum apostolorum necnon Martini, Columbe et Brigide ac alias parrochias dicte civitatis honorifice /[10]/ et cum decantationibus et reverentia predictis ad laudem et gloriam omnipotentis Dei et eiusdem beati Antonii iuxta huiusmodi laudabilem consuetudinem /[11]/ vestram facere. Dubitatis tamen id licite facere posse sede apostolici super hoc inconsulta, super quibus supplicari fecistis humiliter vobis et successoribus vestris /[12]/ per eiusdem sedis clementiam misericorditer provideri. Nos igitur attendentes, quod in his que ad divini cultus et christifidelium devotionis augmentum tendunt, /[13]/ favorabiles esse debemus atque benigni vestroque pio et laudabili desiderio in hac parte favorabiliter annuentes, auctoritate domini pape, cuius penitentiarie curam gerimus /[14]/ et de eius speciali mandato super hoc vive vocis oraculo nobis facto, vobis et pro tempore existenti domus huiusmodi preceptori et fratribus, ut in /[15]/ die domenica predicta processionem huiusmodi per dictas ad quascumque alias parrochias dicte civitatis facere et corpus Domini nostri Jesu Christi ac imaginem /[16]/ beati Antonii huiusmodi cum decantationibus, reverentia et sollemnitatibus in similibus fieri solitis et debitis in eadem deferre libere et licite possitis ac /17/ valeatis et pro tempore existentes preceptor et fratres predicti perpetuis futuris temporibus possint et valeant, tenore presentium indulgemus ac plenam /18/ et liberam licentiam concedimus et facultatem, non obstantibus constitutionibus et ordinationibus apostolicis ac statutis tam provincialibus quam sinodalibus /19/ ceterisque contrariis quibuscumque. Et nichilominus discretis viris officiali venerabilis in Christo patris Dei gratia archiepiscopi Coloniensis /20/ in spiritualibus generali ac preposito sancti Cuniberti et decano sancti Georgii collegiatarum ecclesiarum Coloniensium et eorum cuilibet, eadem auctoritate /21/ et mandato predictis, committimus et mandamus quatenus vobis in premissis efficaciter defensionis presidio assistentes non permittant vos /22/ contra tenorem presentium per eundem archiepiscopum vel eius vicarium seu officiales aut quoscunque alios iudices tam ecclesiasticos quam seculares vel alias personas, /23/ cuiuscunque dignitatis, status, gradus, ordinis vel conditionis existant, in personis, bonis et rebus vestris tacite vel expresse directe vel indirecte /24/ quovis quesito colore vel ingenio molestari, perturbari seu quomodolibet inquietari, contradictores quoslibet et rebelles per censuras ecclesiasticas et /25/ alia oportuna iuris remedia compescendo, invocato etiam ad hoc si opus fuerit auxilio brachii secularis. Datum Rome apud Sanctum Petrum /26/ sub sigillo officii penitentiarie viii idus aprilis pontificatus domini Julii pape II anno nono.

In the left margin at the level of the second line: Bene

Above the plica on the left: p

Above the plica: D. Pulcurici; Jo. Ja. de Bonisauguriis[66]

On the *verso* (Illustration 20b): A. de Villareal;[67] F. de Gomiel, Jo. de Cingulo.

Bulla super deportacione venerabilis sacramenti ac imaginis sancti Anthonii per diversas parochias Dominica Exaudi

The seal of the Penitentiary in red wax with hemp cord almost entirely preserved.

66. Johannes Jacobus Bonisauguriis is the name of the scribe who composed the letter of the Penitentiary.

67. A. de Villareal was the proctor who took care of this case.

English translation:

Leonardus, by divine mercy Cardinal Priest of Sancta Susanna, [sends] greeting in the Lord to the beloved in Christ preceptor Ventzeslaus Vluer of Arhelgen and the brothers of the house of St. Anthony in Cologne. The zeal of your devotion and piety, and certainly your sincere and fervent devotion with which you attend to the Roman Church and the Apostolic See, merit that we freely assent especially to those of your prayers through which your devotion, and the devotion of other Christians, and certainly the increase of divine worship and respect of the saints of God, are increased, and [that] we grant salubriously to you those things through which you are able to pursue salubriously the well-being of your souls with God's favor. The petition which has been brought to us on your behalf contained that you, as you claim, have had a yearly custom to perform, on the Sunday in which the Holy Mother Church sings *Exaudi* in the introit of the Mass, a certain procession bearing the sacrosanct body of our Lord Jesus Christ honorably with due chants and reverence, together with the image of St. Anthony through the parish of St. Peter in the city of Cologne, in which your house is located, to which a great crowd assembles with very great devotion, and that you desire to perform such procession out of remarkable feeling of devotion, continuing and increasing it through both the aforementioned [parish] as well as the parishes of St. Martin, St. Columba, St. Bridget, and others of the mentioned city, [and you desire to perform it] honorably with the aforementioned chants and reverence, to the praise and glory of the omnipotent God and the same St. Anthony, according to your praiseworthy custom of this kind. Nevertheless, you doubt that you can do this lawfully without consulting the Apostolic See on this matter, concerning which you have humbly appealed that [your desire] be mercifully provided for you and your successors through the clemency of the same See. Therefore, mindful of that which in these matters aims toward an increase in divine worship and devotion of Christians, we ought to be favorable, and nodding favorably to your pious and laudable desire in this, by the authority of the Lord Pope, who has entrusted the administration of the Penitentiary to us, and by his special mandate given to us in person on this account, we grant indulgence by the tenor of the present letter, and confirm a full and free license and ability to you and to the preceptor and brothers of this house living there at any time, so that on the aforementioned Sunday you are freely and lawfully able and have the power to perform such a procession through the mentioned and whatever other parishes of the mentioned city, and to carry in it the body of our Lord Jesus Christ and such an image of St. Anthony, together with chants, reverence, and solemnities which are customary and due in similar processions, and that the aforementioned preceptor and brothers living there at any time are able and have the power [to do so] for eternal future times, despite constitutions, apostolic regulations, and both provincial and synodal statutes, and whatever other contrary [statutes] etc. Nevertheless, to the distinguished men—the general official in spiritual affairs of the venerable in Christ, by divine grace, archbishop of Cologne, the provost of St. Cunibert, and the dean of St. George, both collegiate churches in Cologne, and to whomever of their attendants—by the same aforementioned authority and mandate, we submit and order that, assisting you efficaciously in defending the aforementioned privileges, they not allow that the same archbishop or his vicar or officials or whatever other judges, either ecclesiastical or secular, or other persons, be they of whatever rank, status, position, order or condition, trouble, interfere with, or in any way disturb you against the tenor of the present letter, against your person, goods or affairs, secretly or expressly, directly or indirectly, by any devised pretext or deceit; restraining any objectors and rebels by ecclesiastical censures and other suitable remedies of law, and even calling the secular arm for help if need be. Given in Rome at St. Peter's by the seal of the office of the Penitentiary on the 6th of April, in the 9th year of the pontificate of Lord Pope Julius II.

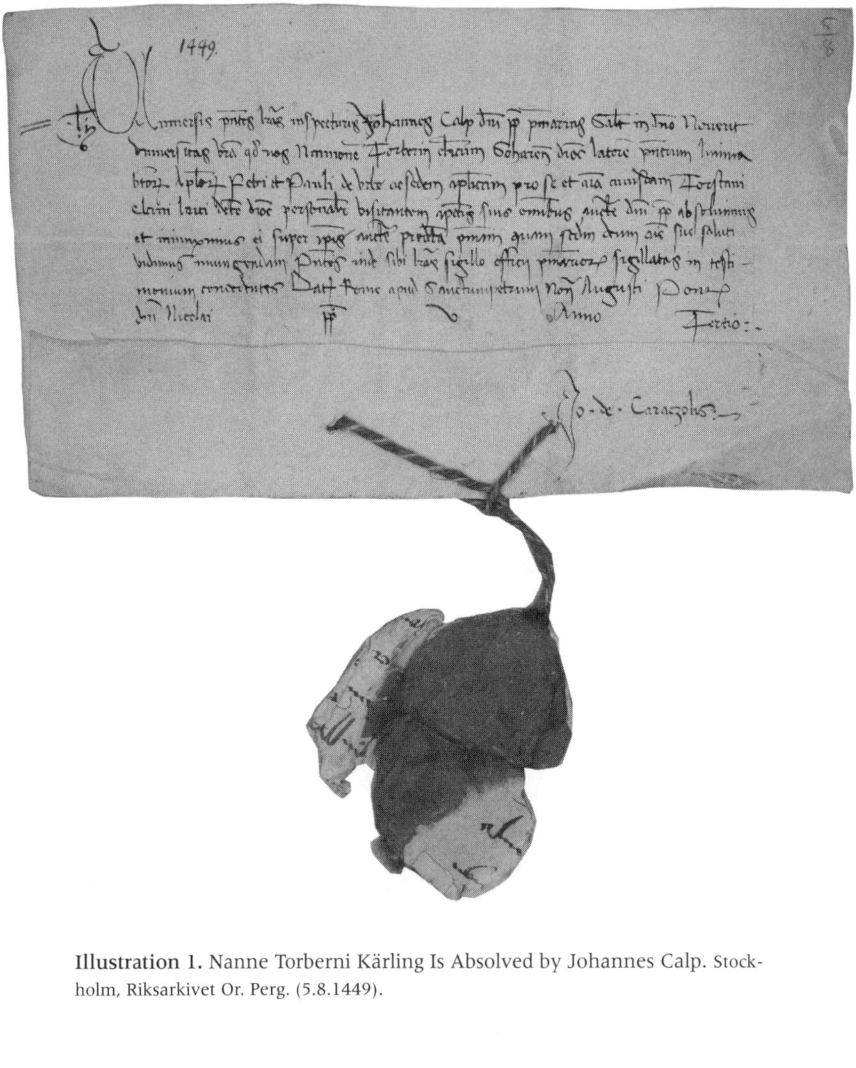

Illustration 1. Nanne Torberni Kärling Is Absolved by Johannes Calp. Stockholm, Riksarkivet Or. Perg. (5.8.1449).

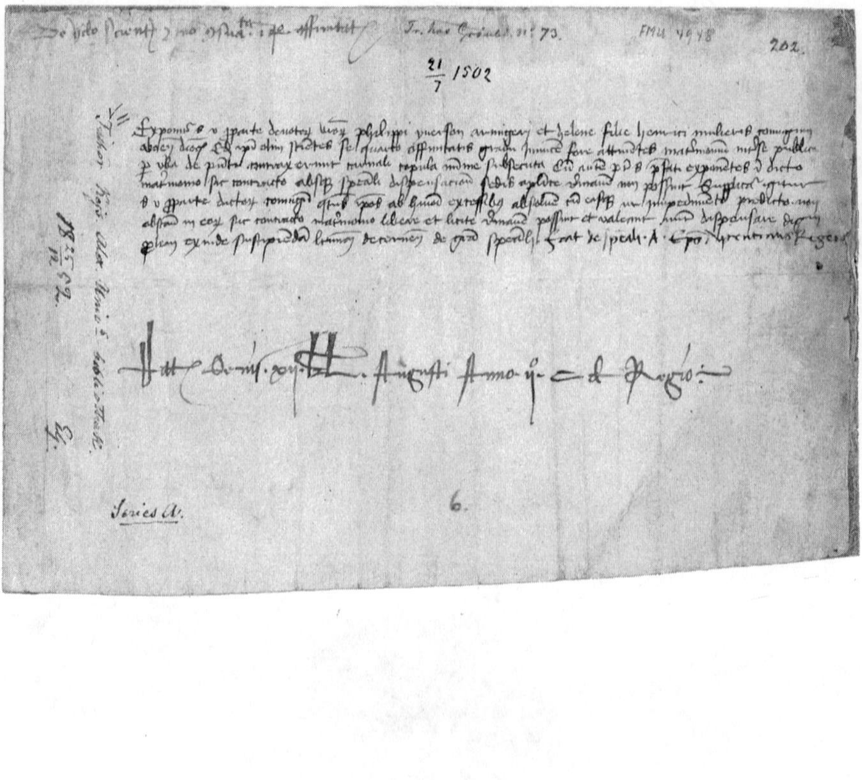

Illustration 2. Philippus Yverson and Helena Henrici: Original Supplication. National Library of Finland, Scheelska samlingen (21.7.1460).

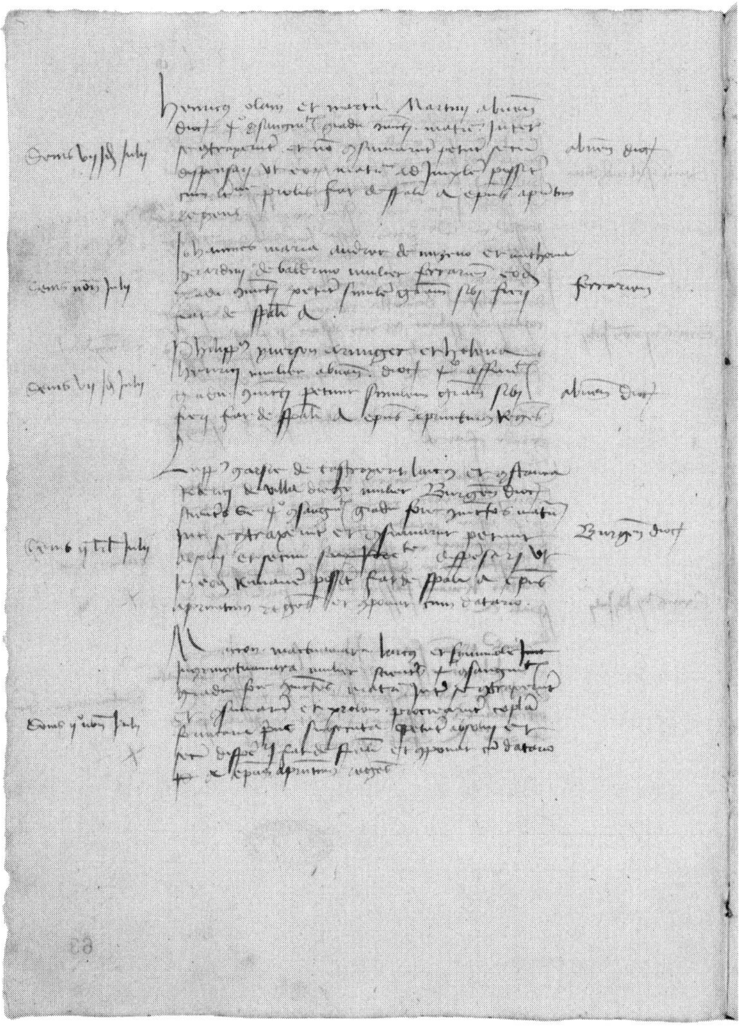

Illustration 3. Philippus Yverson and Helena Henrici: Enregistered Summary. Archivio Segreto Vaticano, Penitenzieria Apostolica, Registra matrimonialium et diversorum, vol. 8, fol. 63v.

Illustration 4. Johannes Vitalis: Dispensation in the Penitentiary Register.
Bonn, University Library, Handschriften Abteilung, S327.

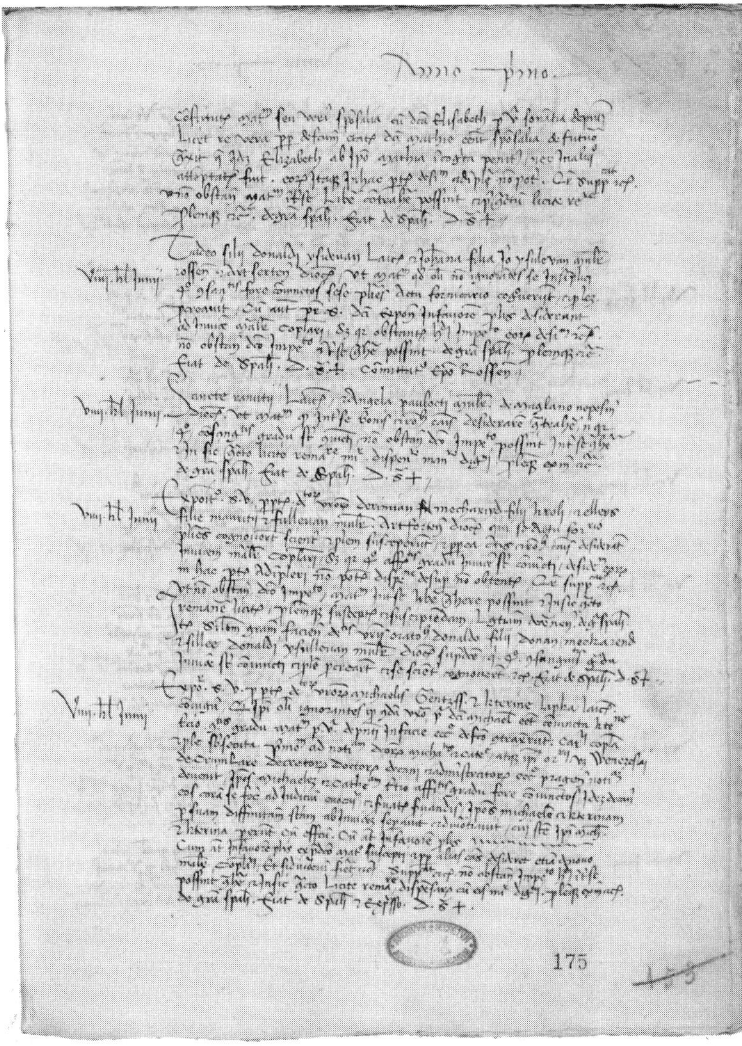

Illustration 5. Michael Genczss and Katerina Lapka: Petition in Registers.
Archivio Segreto Vaticano, Registra matrimonialium et diversorum, vol. 6, fol. 175r.

Illustration 6. Michael Genczss and Katerina Lapka: Letter in Prague Archives. Prague (Praha), Archiv prazske metropolitni kapituly, Cod. VI-5, fol. 62v.

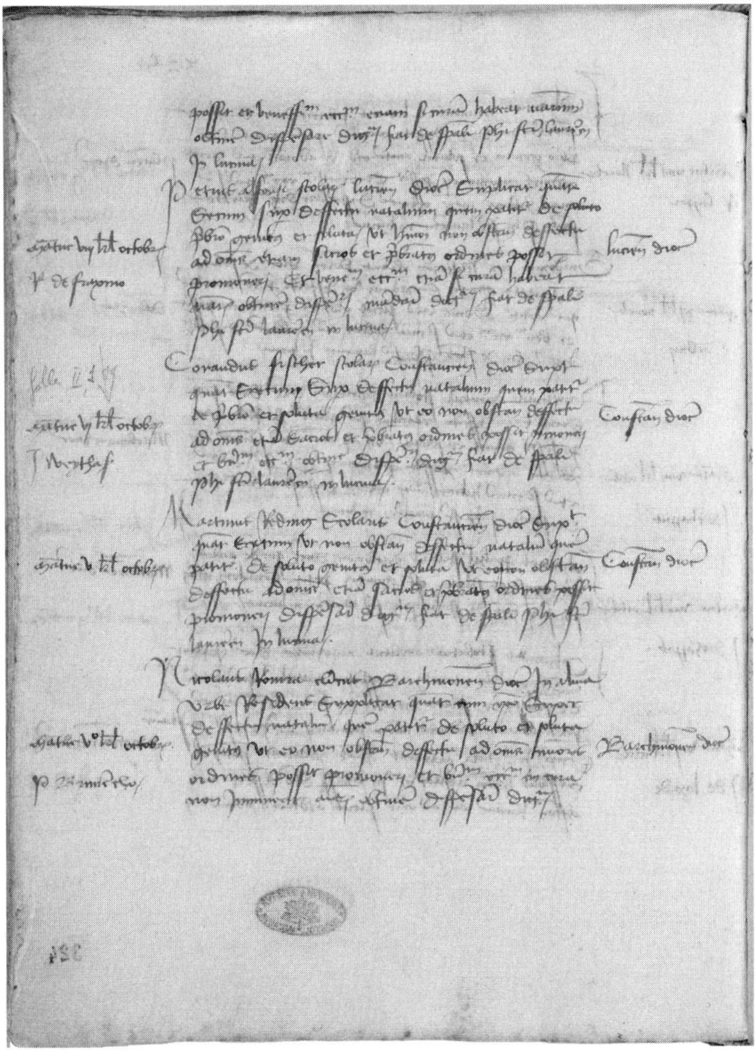

Illustration 7. Conrad Fischer: Entry in the Penitentiary Register. Archivio Segreto Vaticano, Registra matrimonialium et diversorum, vol. 7, fol. 324v.

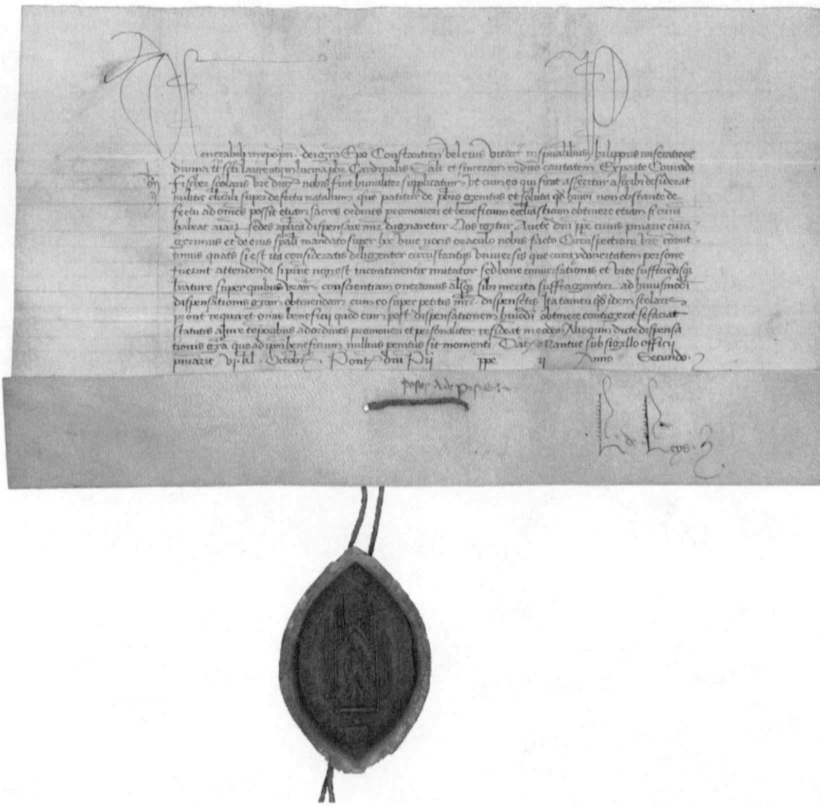

Illustration 8. Conrad Fischer: Original Letter. Karlsruhe, Generallandesarchiv, B IV 1650 (26.9.1459).

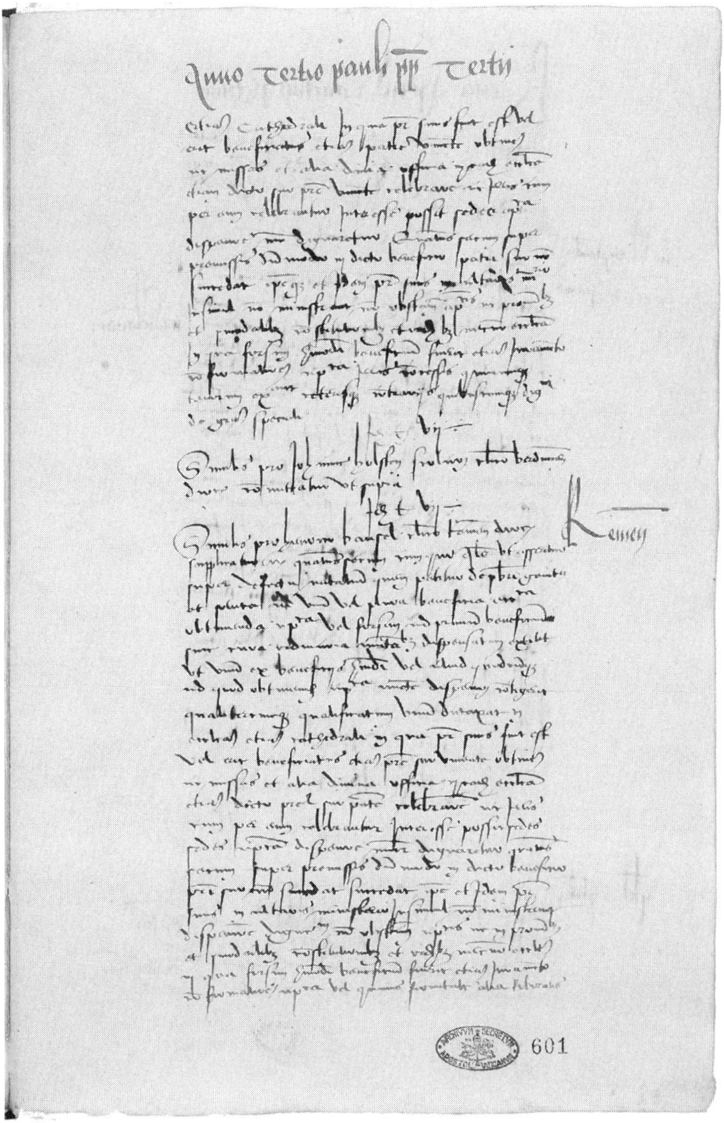

Illustration 9a. Henricus Banscow: Entry in the Penitentiary Register. Archivio Segreto Vaticano, Registra matrimonialium et diversorum, vol. 94, fol. 601r.

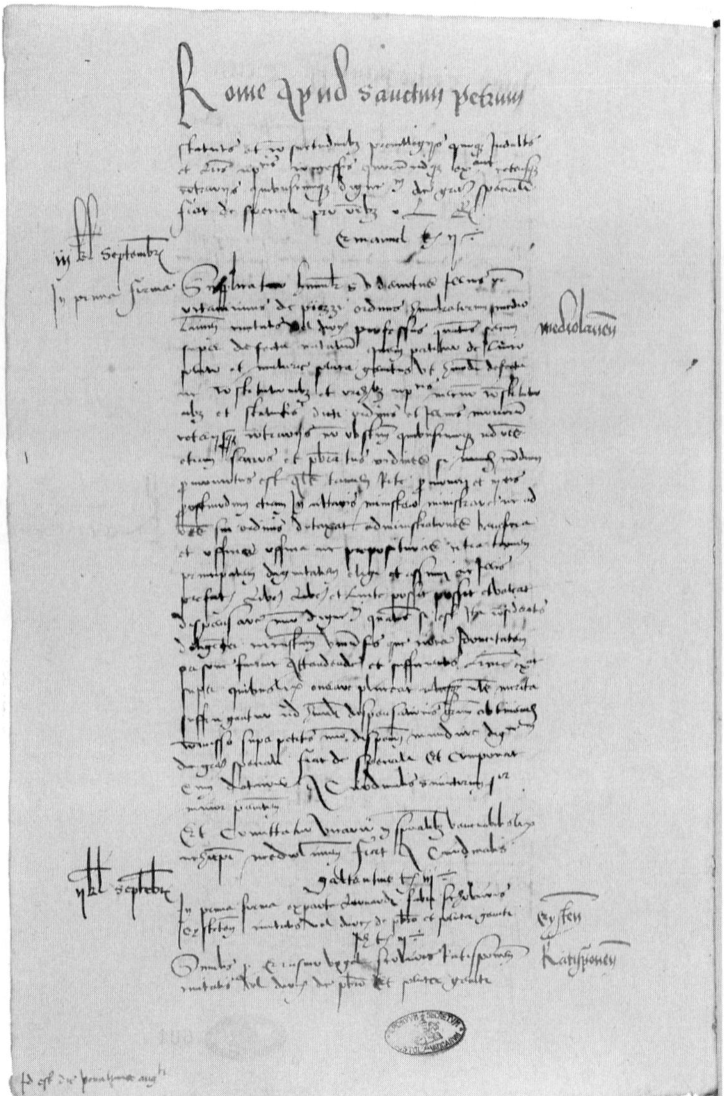

Rome apud sanctum petrum

Mediolanen

Ratisponen

Illustration 9b. Henricus Banscow: Entry in the Penitentiary Register (cont.).
Archivio Segreto Vaticano, Registra matrimonialium et diversorum, vol. 94, fol. 601v.

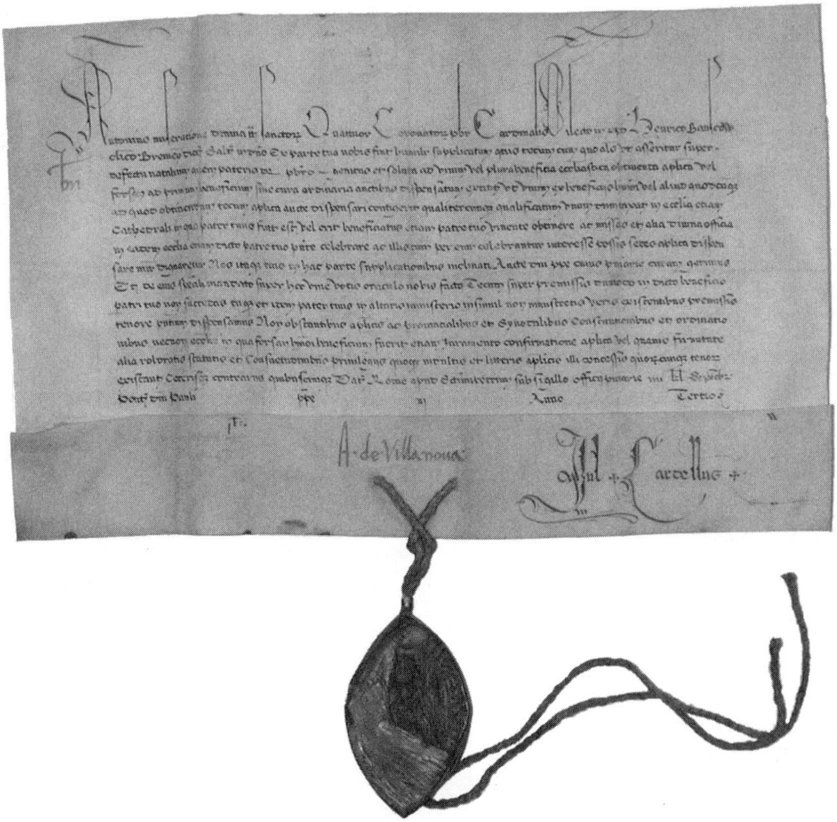

Illustration 10. Henricus Banscow: Original Letter. Hamburg, Staatsarchiv 710-1.

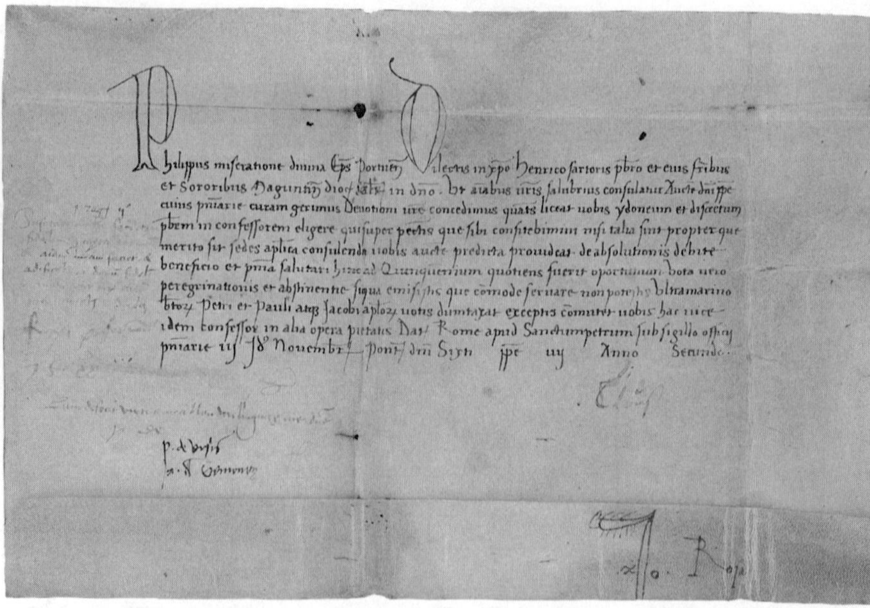

Illustration 11. Henricus Sartoris: Privilege for Confession. Mainz, Stadtarchiv, Urkunden Altmünster 11.11.1472.

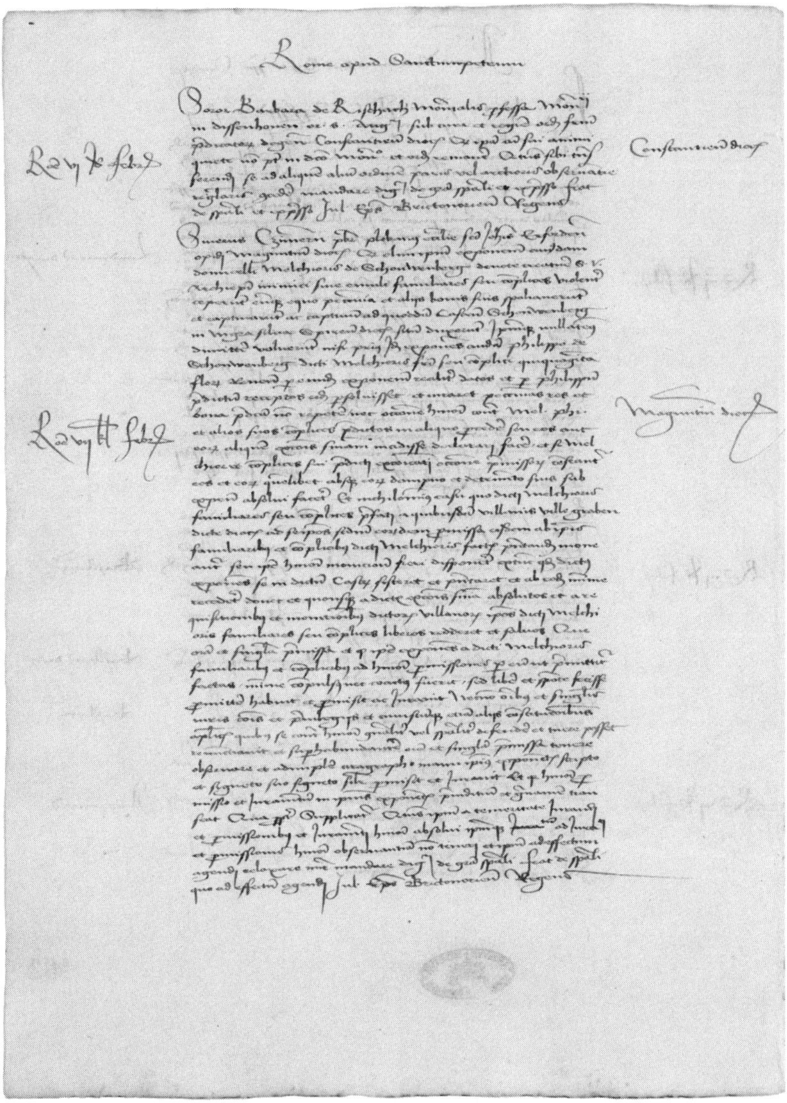

Illustration 12. Barbara Rischach: Dispensation to Transfer to Another Monastery. Archivio Segreto Vaticano, Registra matrimonialium et diversorum, vol. 31, fol. 162v.

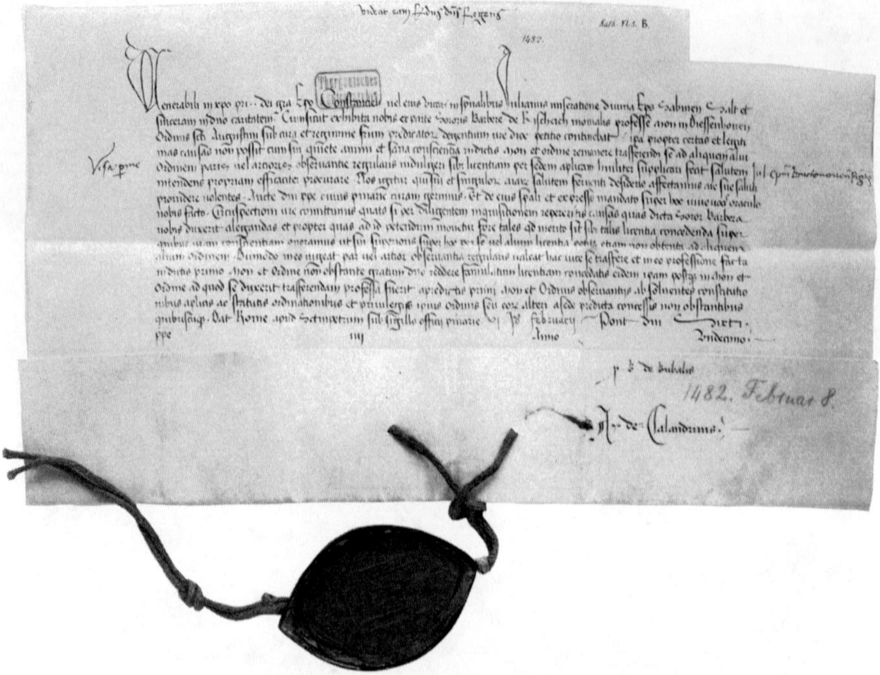

Illustration 13. Barbara Rischach: Original Letter Granting Permission. Frauenfeld, Staatsarchiv Thurgau 7.44.9 B.

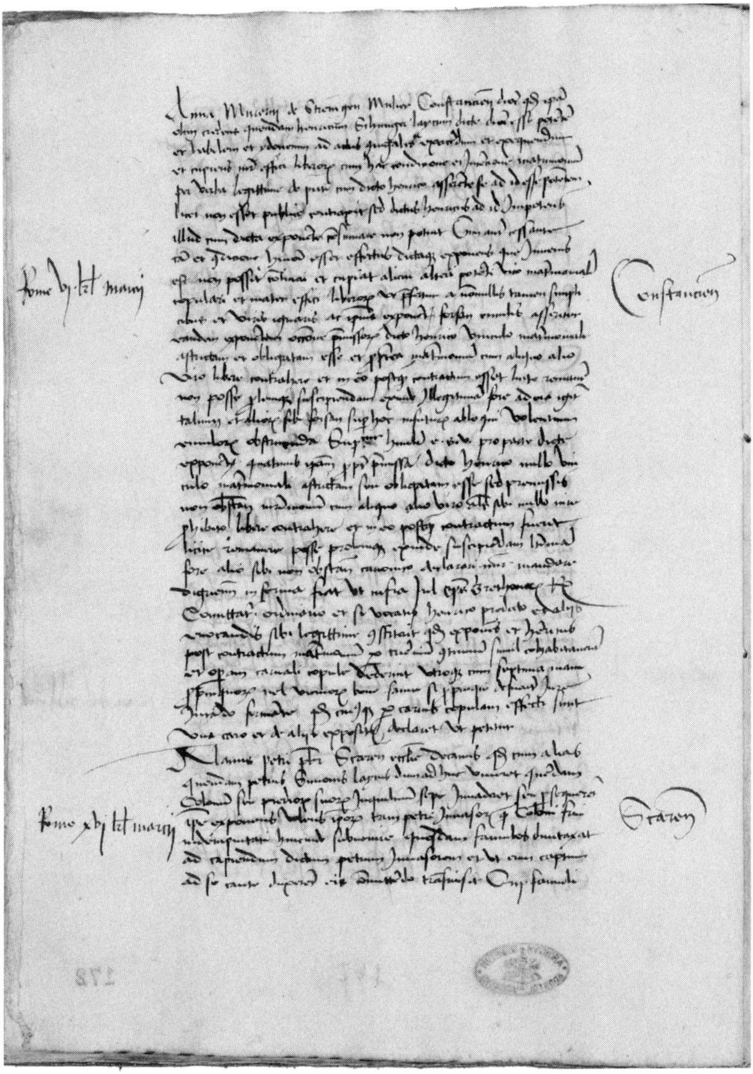

Illustration 14a. Olavus Petri: Petition to the Penitentiary. Archivio Segreto Vaticano, Registra matrimonialium et diversorum, vol. 33, fol. 172v.

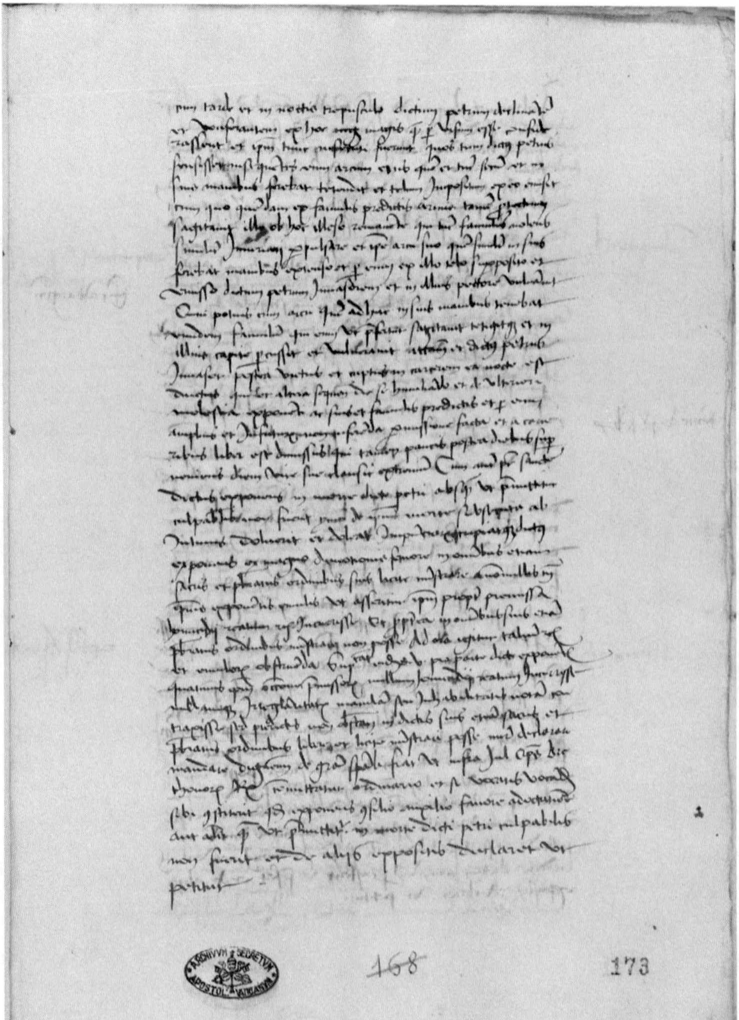

Illustration 14b. Olavus Petri: Petition to the Penitentiary (cont.). Archivio Segreto Vaticano, Registra matrimonialium et diversorum, vol. 33, fol. 173r.

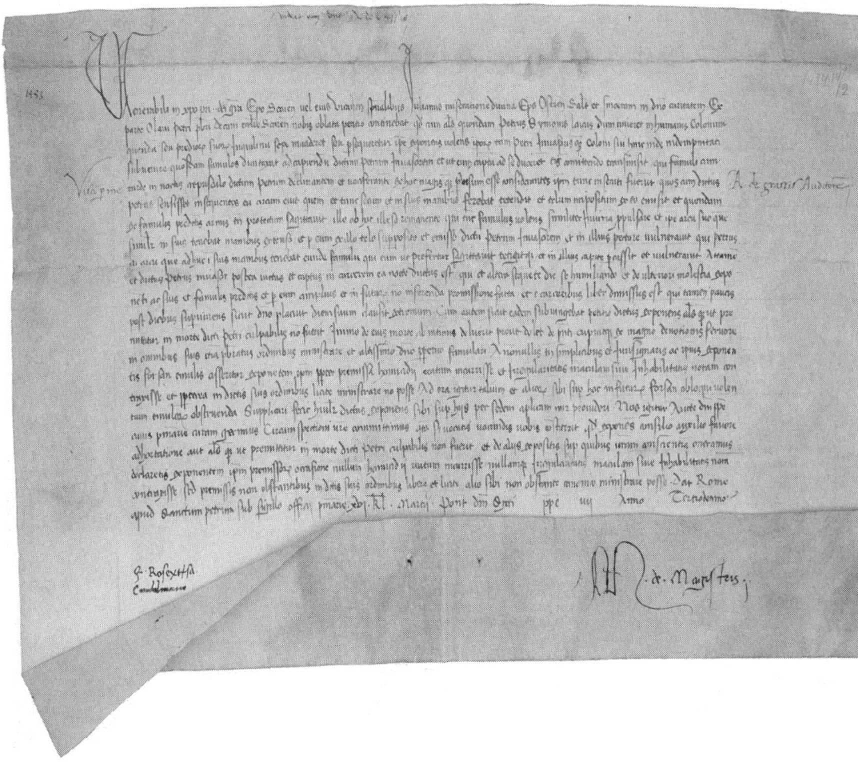

Illustration 15. Olavus Petri: Original Letter from the Penitentiary. Stockholm, Riksarkivet, Or. Perg., 14.2.1484.

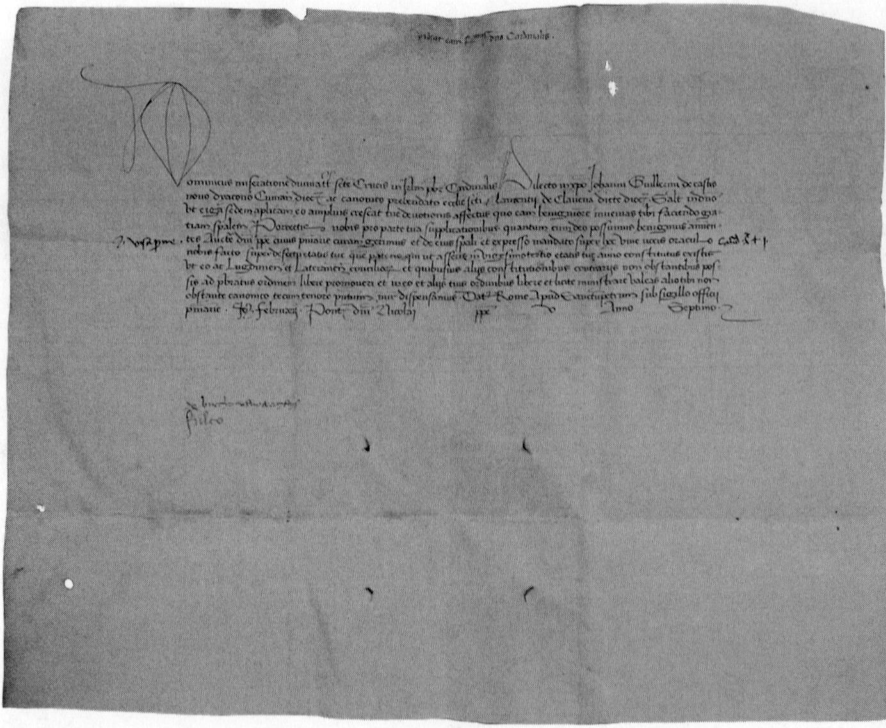

Illustration 16. Johannes de Castro Novo: Letter of Dispensation from the Penitentiary. Chiavenna, Archivio Capitolare Laurenziano, Pergamene 784.

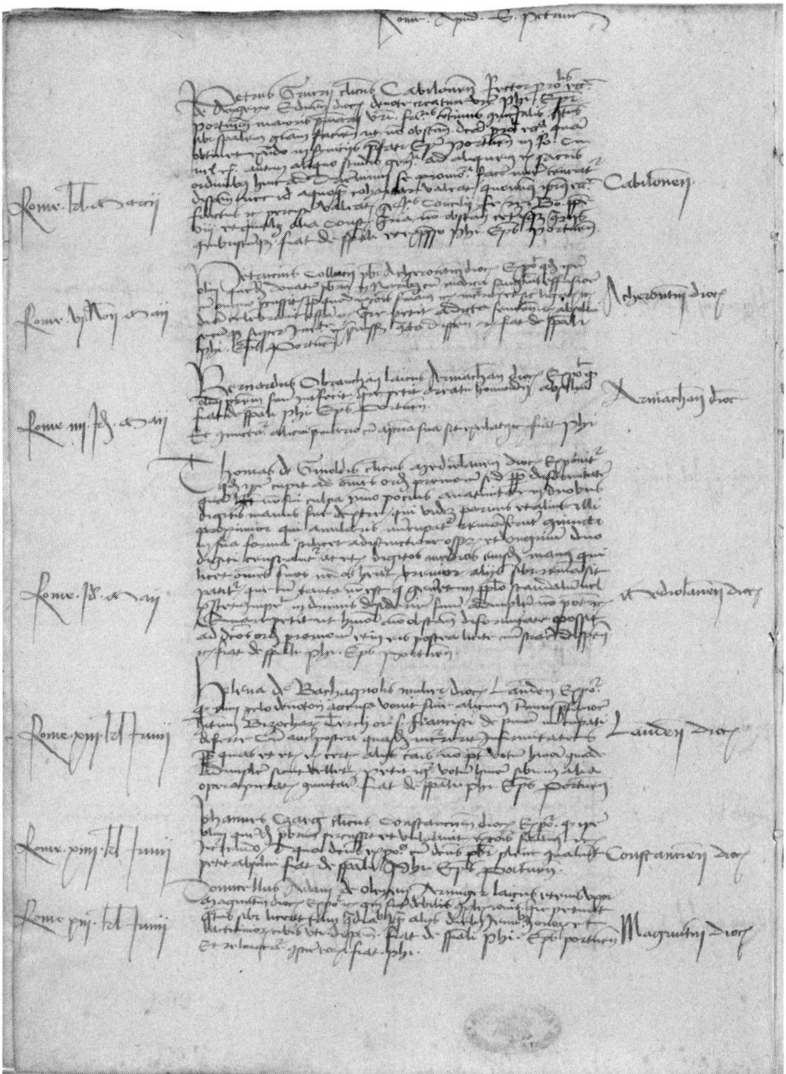

Illustration 17. Petrus Gruerii: Entry in the Penitentiary Registers. Archivio Segreto Vaticano, Registra matrimonialium et diversorum, vol. 20, fol. 204v.

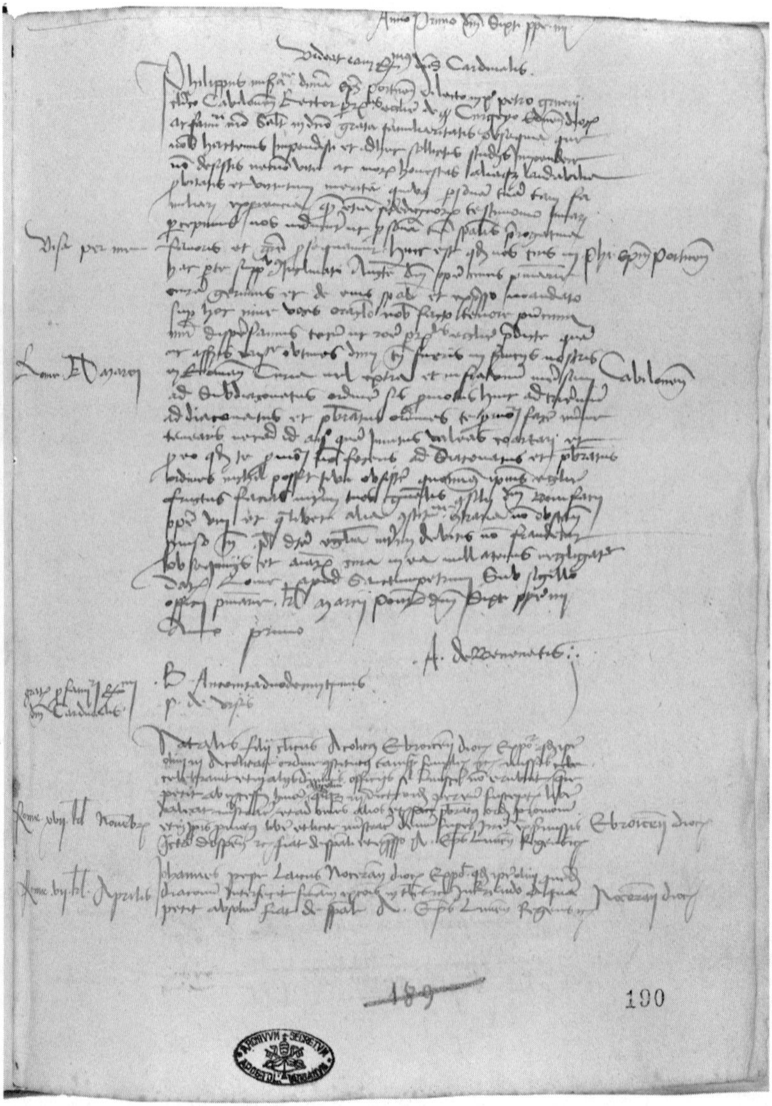

Illustration 18. Petrus Gruerii: Letter in the Penitentiary Registers. Archivio Segreto Vaticano, Registra matrimonialium et diversorum, vol. 20, fol. 190r.

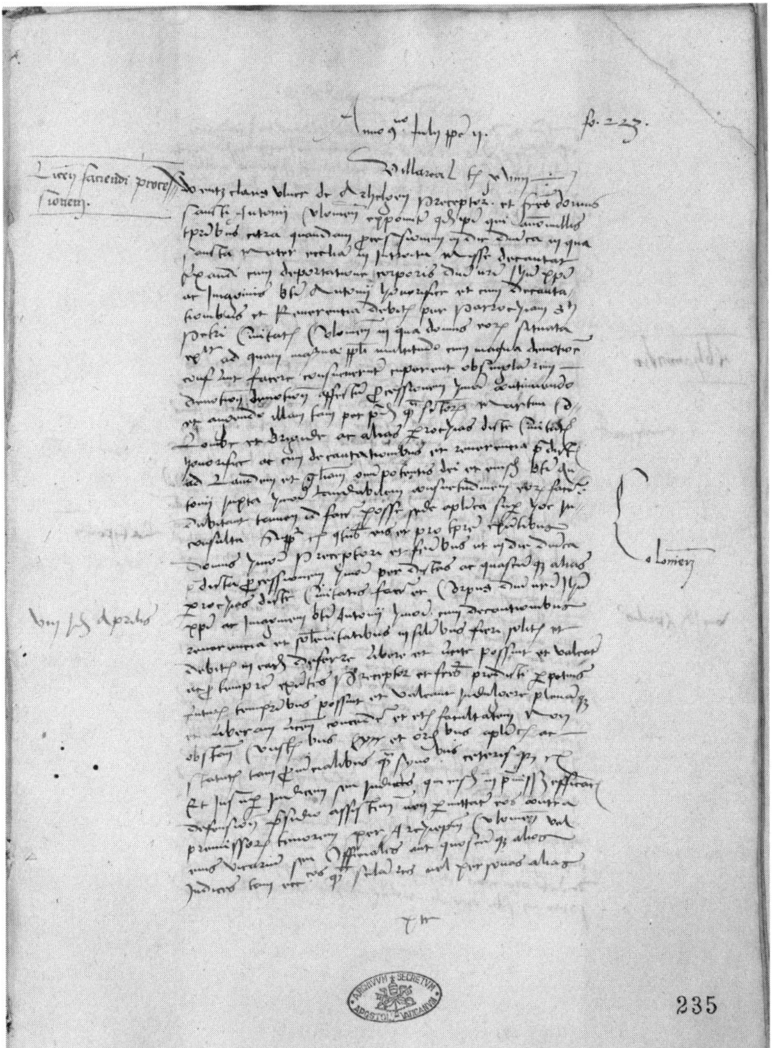

Illustration 19a. Friary of St. Anthony in Cologne: Privilege in the Penitentiary Register. Archivio Segreto Vaticano, Registra matrimonialium et diversorum, vol. 57, fol. 235r.

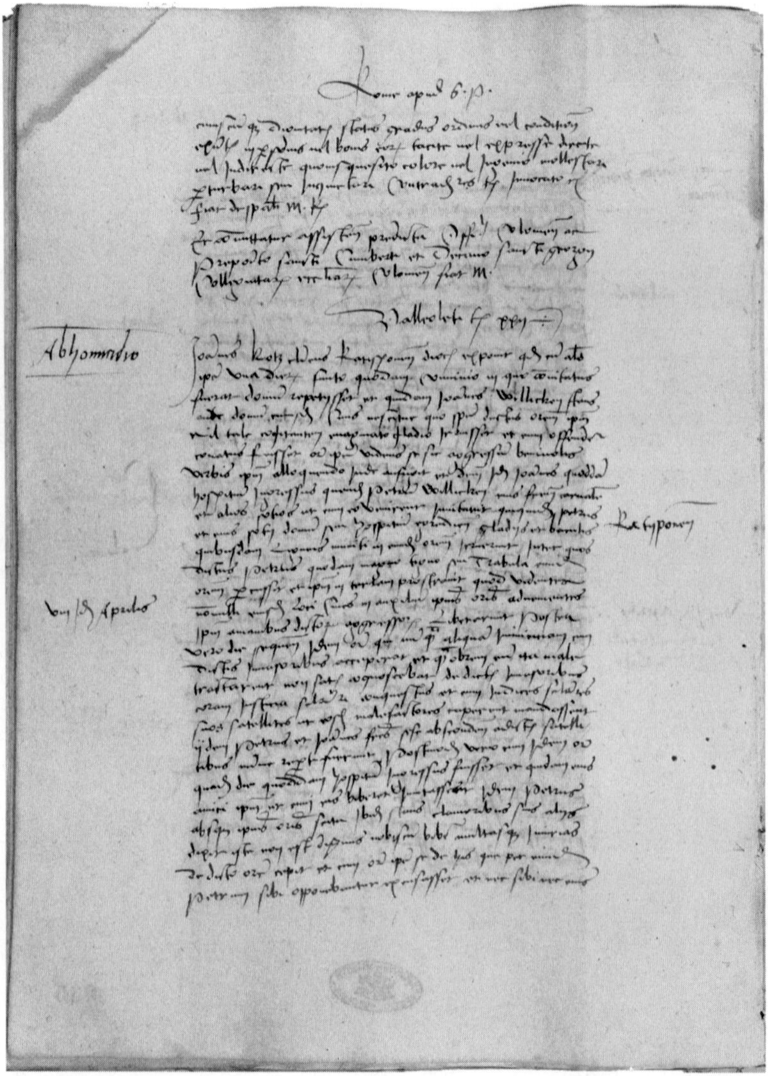

Illustration 19b. Friary of St. Anthony in Cologne: Privilege in the Penitentiary Register (cont.). Archivio Segreto Vaticano, Registra matrimonialium et diversorum, vol. 57, fol. 235v.

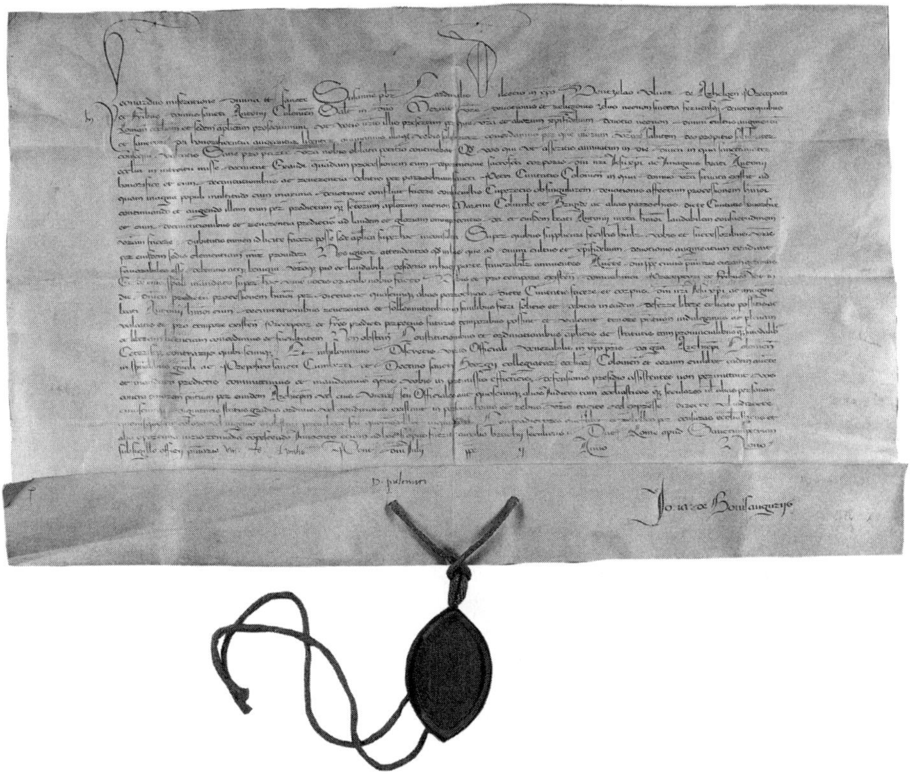

Illustration 20a. Friary of St. Anthony in Cologne: Original Privilege. Köln, Stadtarchiv, Haupturkundenarchiv 1, 3/15696 Recto.

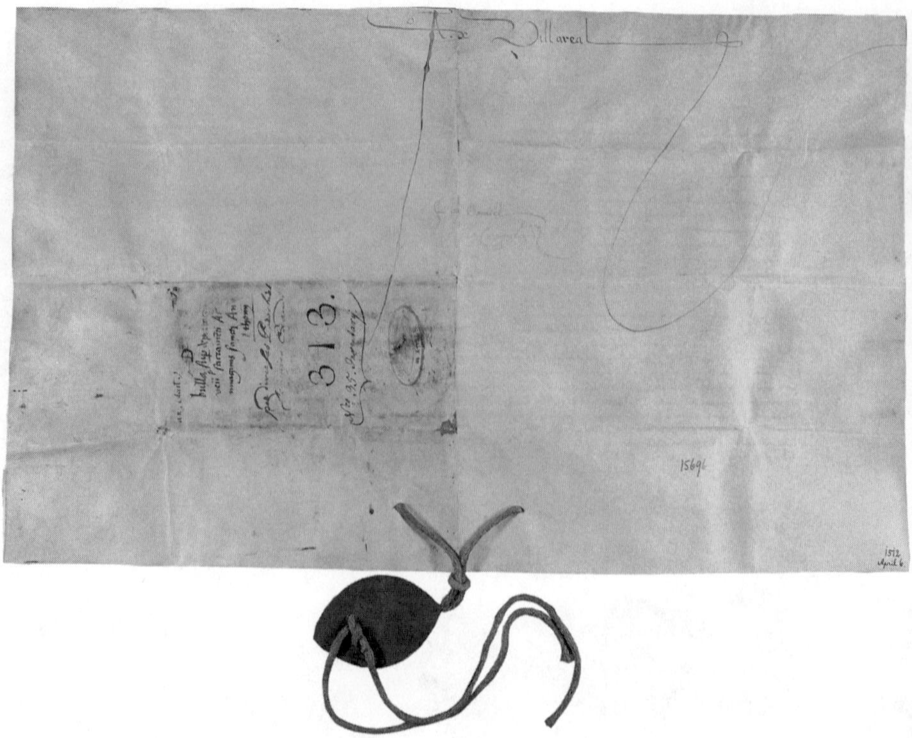

Illustration 20b. Friary of St. Anthony in Cologne: Original Privilege (cont.). Köln, Stadtarchiv, Haupturkundenarchiv 1, 3/15696 Verso.

Selected Bibliography

The following lists are presented in chronological order.

I. Classic Studies Concerning the Penitentiary

Vincentius de Petra. *De Sacra Poenitentieria Apostolica*. Rome 1712.

Heinrich Denifle. "Die älteste Taxrolle der apostolischen Pönitentiarie." *Archiv für Literatur- und Kirchengeschicte des Mittelalters* 4 (1888), 201–238.

Konrad Eubel. "Der Registerband des Kardinalgrosspönitentiars Bentevenga." *Archiv für katholisches Kirchenrecht* 64 (1890), 3–69.

Henry Charles Lea. *A Formulary of the Papal Penitentiary in the Thirteenth Century*. Philadelphia 1892.

Henry Charles Lea. "The Taxes of the Papal Penitentiary." *American Journal of Theology* 8 (1893), 424–438.

Charles Homer Haskins. "The Sources for the History of the Papal Penitentiary." *American Journal of Theology* 9 (1905), 421–450.

Alois Lang. "Beiträge zur Geschichte der apostolischen Pönitentiarie im 13. und 14. Jahrhundert." *Mitteilungen des Instituts für Österreichische Geschichtsforschung* 7 (1907), 20–43.

Pierre Chouët. *La Sacrée Pénitencierie apostolique: étude de droit et d'histoire*. Lyon 1908.

Emil Göller. *Die päpstliche Pönitentiarie von ihrem Ursprung bis zu ihrer Umgestaltung unter Pius V.* 2 vols. in 4 parts. Bibliothek des Königlich Preußischen Historischen Instituts in Rom 3, 4, 7, and 8. Rome 1907, 1911.

Emil Göller. "Das alte Archiv der päpstlichen Pönitentiarie." *Römische Quartalschrift,* Supplementband 20 (Festschrift A. de Waal), pp. 1–19. Rome–Freiburg i. Br., 1913.

Filippo Tamburini. *L'archivio della penitenzieria apostolica e il primo registro delle suppliche (1410–1411)*. Diss. MS. Rome 1969.

Matthaeus Meyer. *Die Pönitentiarie-Formularsammlung des Walter Murner von Strassburg*. Spicilegium Friburgense 25. Freiburg i. Ü. 1979.

Ludwig Schmugge. *Kirche, Kinder, Karrieren: Päpstliche Dispense von der unehelichen Geburt im Spätmittelalter.* Zurich 1995.

Filippo Tamburini. *Santi e peccatori: confessioni e suppliche dai Registri della Penitenzieria dell'Archivio Segreto Vaticano (1451–1586).* Milan 1995.

Ludwig Schmugge, Patrick Hersperger, and Béatrice Wiggenhauser, *Die Supplikenregister der päpstlichen Pönitentiarie aus der Zeit Pius' II. (1458–1464).* Bibliothek des Deutschen Historischen Instituts in Rom, Band 84. Tübingen 1996.

Filippo Tamburini. *Ebrei, Saraceni, Cristiani: Vita sociale e vita religiosa dai registri della Penitenzieria Apostolica (secoli XIV–XVI).* Milan 1996.

Filippo Tamburini and Ludwig Schmugge. *Häresie und Luthertum: Quellen aus dem Archiv der Pönitentiarie in Rom (15. und 16. Jahrhundert).* Quellen und Forschungen aus dem Gebiet der Geschichte. Neue Folge 19. Paderborn 2000.

Kirsi Salonen. *The Penitentiary as a Well of Grace in the Late Middle Ages: The Example of the Province of Uppsala 1448–1527.* Suomalaisen Tiedeakatemian Toimituksia—Annales Academiae Scientiarum Fennicae 313. Saarijärvi 2001.

II. Editions of Penitentiary Documents

This is not a complete list of all the publications in which Penitentiary documents have been edited, but a list of those source editions containing only Penitentiary documents. Therefore, such series as, for example, Bullarium Poloniae or Bullarium Franciscanum—which contain Penitentiary documents among other types of documents—are not included.

Repertorium Poenitentiariae Germanicum I (Eugen IV.), II (Nikolaus V.), III (Calixt III.), IV (Pius II.), V (Paul. II), VI (Sixtus IV.): Verzeichnis der in den Supplikenregistern der Pönitentiarie vorkommenden Personen, Kirchen und Orte des Deutschen Reiches. Bearbeitet von Ludwig Schmugge unter Mitarbeit von Paolo Ostinelli (vol I), Hans Braun (vol. II), Peter Clarke (vol. V), Alessandra Mosciatti (vol. II, V and VI), Wolfgang Müller (vol. III, V), Patrick Hersperger (vol. IV), Béatrice Wiggenhauser (vol. IV), Krystyna Bukowska (vol. II). Indices bearbeitet von Hildegard Schneider-Schmugge und Ludwig Schmugge. Tübingen 1996–2005.

Monique Maillard-Luypaert, *Les suppliques de la Pénitencerie Apostolique pour les diocèses de Cambrai, Liège, Thérouanne et Tournai (1410–1411) (ASV, Penitenzieria Ap., Reg. Matrim. et Div., 1).* Institut historique Belge de Rome, Analecta Vaticano-Belgica, Première Série, XXXIV. Brussels-Rome 2003.

Paolo Ostinelli. *Penitenzieria Apostolica: Le suppliche alla Sacra Penitenzieria Apostolica provenienti dalla diocesi di Como (1438–1484).* Materiali di storia ecclesiastica lombarda (secoli XIV–XVI), 5. Milan 2003.

Torstein Jørgensen and Gastone Saletnich. *Synder og Pavemakt: Botsbrev fra Den Norske Kirkeprovins og Suderøyene til Pavestolen 1438–1531.* Diplomatarium Poenitentiariae Norvegicum. Stavanger 2004.

III. A Selection of Articles and Collection of Articles about the Penitentiary

This is not a complete list of all books and articles published about the Penitentiary. We have decided to include only articles published in English that could be useful for the readers of this book. Good lists of further publications can be found, for example, in Ostinelli, *Penitenzieria Apostolica.* We have, also, not mentioned separately those articles that are published in the collections of articles, but have listed only the title of the book. The collections of articles are marked with an asterisk (*).

Ludwig Schmugge. "Cleansing on Consciences." *Viator* 29 (1998), 345–361.

Kirsi Salonen, "In Their Fathers' Footsteps: The Illegitimate Sons of Finnish Priests According to the Archives of the Sacred Penitentiary 1449–1523." In Jacqueline Hamesse, ed., *Roma magistra mundi: Itineraria culturae medievalis: Mélanges offerts au Père L.E. Boyle à l'occasion de son 75e anniversaire,* pp. 355–366. Fédération Internationale des Instituts d'Études Médiévales. Textes et Études du Moyen Âge, 10, 3. Louvain-la-Neuve 1998.

Kirsi Salonen, "Long Path to Forgiveness: The Relationship between Finland and the Holy See in the Late Middle Ages, Especially in the Light of the Cases in the Penitentiary Registers." *Quellen und Forschungen aus italienischen Archiven und Bibliotheken* 79 (1999), 283–318.

Kirsi Salonen. "Finnish Illegal Marriages 1449–1523." In Mia Korpiola, ed., *Nordic Perspectives on Medieval Canon Law,* pp. 151–167. Publications of Matthias Calonius Society II. Helsinki 1999.

Ludwig Schmugge. "Female Petitioners in the Papal Penitentiary." *Gender & History* 12/3 (November 2000), 685–703. Reprinted in Pauline Stafford & Anneke Mulder-Bakker, eds., *Gendering the Middle Ages,* pp. 155–173. Oxford 2001.

Kirsi Salonen. "Violence in Finland in the Middle Ages and the Sixteenth Century in the Light of Source Material from the Vatican Archives." In Anu Koskivirta and Sari Forsström, eds., *Manslaughter, Fornication and Sectarianism: Norm-breaking in Finland and the Baltic Area from Mediaeval to Modern Times,* pp. 100–120. Suomalaisen Tiedeakatemian Toimituksia—Annales Academiae Scientiarum Fennicae, Humaniora 319. Saarijärvi 2002.

Ludwig Schmugge. "Suppliche e diritto canonico." In *Suppliques et requêtes: Le gouvernement par la grâce en Occident (XIIe–XVe siècle),* under the direction of Hélène Millet, pp. 207–231. Collection de l'École française de Rome 310. Rome 2003.

* Kirsi Salonen and Christian Krötzl, eds. *The Roman Curia, the Apostolic Penitentiary and the Partes in the Later Middle Ages.* Acta Instituti Romani Finlandiae 28. Rome 2003.

* Gerhard Jaritz, Torstein Jørgensen, and Kirsi Salonen, eds. *The Long Arm of Papal Authority: Late Medieval Christian Peripheries and Their Communication with the Holy See.* Medium Aevum Quotidianum, Sonderband XIV. Bergen-Budapest-Krems 2004.

Peter D. Clarke. "The Records of the Papal Penitentiary as a Source for the Ecclesiastical Interdict." In Andreas Meyer, Constanze Rendtel, and Maria Wittmer-Butsch, eds., *Päpste, Pilger, Pönitentiarie: Festschrift für Ludwig Schmugge zum 65. Geburtstag,* pp. 411–433. Tübingen 2004.

Wolfgang P. Müller. "The Price of Papal Pardon—New Fifteenth-Century Evidence." In Andreas Meyer, Constanze Rendtel, and Maria Wittmer-Butsch, eds., *Päpste, Pilger, Pönitentiarie: Festschrift für Ludwig Schmugge zum 65. Geburtstag,* pp. 457–481. Tübingen 2004.

Kirsi Salonen, "The Decisions of Pope Pius II in the Penitentiary Registers." In Andreas Meyer, Constanze Rendtel, and Maria Wittmer-Butsch, eds., *Päpste, Pilger, Pönitentiarie: Festschrift für Ludwig Schmugge zum 65. Geburtstag,* pp. 515–530. Tübingen 2004.

Patrick Zutshi, "*Inextricabilis curie labyrinthus*—The Presentation of Petitions to the Pope in the Chancery and the Penitentiary during the Fourteenth and First Half of the Fifteenth Century." In Andreas Meyer, Constanze Rendtel, and Maria Wittmer-Butsch, eds., *Päpste, Pilger, Pönitentiarie: Festschrift für Ludwig Schmugge zum 65. Geburtstag,* pp. 393–410. Tübingen 2004.

Ludwig Schmugge. "Boyle and Boniface: *Cum ex eo*–Dispensations in the Fifteenth Century." In Ann Duggan, Joan Greatrex, Brenda Bolton, eds., *Omnia disce. Medieval Studies in Memory of Leonard Boyle, OP.* Aldershot 2004, pp. 61–69.

Peter D. Clarke. "English Royal Marriages and the Papal Penitentiary in the Fifteenth Century." *English Historical Review* 120, no. 488 (2005), 1014–1029.

Ludwig Schmugge. "Kanonistik in der Pönitentiarie." In Martin Bertram, ed., *Stagnation oder Fortbildung? Aspekte des allgemeinen Kirchenrechts im 14. und 15. Jahrhundert,* pp. 93–115. Bibliothek des Deutschen Historischen Instituts in Rom 108. Tübingen 2005.

Index of Names

Index of Places

A Sip from the "Well of Grace": Medieval Texts from the Apostolic Penitentiary was designed and typeset in Meridien by Kachergis Book Design of Pittsboro, North Carolina. It was printed on 60-pound EB Natural and bound by Edwards Brothers of Lillington, North Carolina.